real world
GLOBALIZATION

A Reader in Economics, Business and Politics from *Dollars & Sense*

EIGHTH EDITION

Edited by Amy Offner, Chris Sturr, Alejandro Reuss,
and the *Dollars & Sense* Collective

Real World Globalization

EIGHTH EDITION

Edited by Amy Offner, Alejandro Reuss, Chris Sturr, and the *Dollars & Sense* Collective.

ISBN: 1-878585-44-4

Published by:
Dollars & Sense
Economic Affairs Bureau, Inc.
740 Cambridge Street
Cambridge, MA 02141
617-876-2434
dollars@dollarsandsense.org

Real World Globalization is edited by the *Dollars & Sense* Collective, which also publishes *Dollars & Sense* magazine, along with *Real World Micro*, *Real World Macro*, *Real World Banking*, *Current Economic Issues*, *Introduction to Political Economy*, *The Environment in Crisis*, and *Unlevel Playing Fields*.

The *Dollars & Sense* Collective:
Marc Breslow, Beth Burgess, Chuck Collins, Ellen Frank, Amy Gluckman, Erkut Gomulu, Maryalice Guilford, John Miller, Amy Offner, Laura Orlando, Alejandro Reuss, Adria Scharf, Chris Sturr, Chris Tilly, Ramaa Vasudevan, Rodney Ward, Thad Williamson, Jeanne Winner, Jane Yager.

Cover design: Nick Thorkelson
Production: Sheila Walsh

Manufactured by Transcontinental Printing
Printed in Canada

Contents

CHAPTER 1

Critical Perspectives on Globalization

ARTICLE 1

A Short History of Neoliberalism

BY SUSAN GEORGE

November 2000

A few decades ago, if you had gotten up in front of an audience and seriously proposed the policies in today's standard neoliberal toolkit, you would have stood a good chance to get laughed off the stage. At least in Western Europe, at that time, the dominant points of view were Keynesian, social democratic, social Christian, or some shade of Marxist. Neoliberal ideas—that the market should be allowed to make major social and political decisions, that the state should voluntarily reduce its role in the economy, that corporations should be given total freedom, that trade unions should be curbed and citizens given much less rather than more social protection—were utterly foreign to the spirit of the time. Even if someone actually agreed with these ideas, he or she would have hesitated to take such a position In public, and would have had a hard time finding an audience if they had.

So what happened? Why have we reached this point half a century after the end of the Second World War? How did neoliberalism ever emerge from its ultra-minority status to become the dominant doctrine in the world today? Why can the International Monetary Fund and the World Bank intervene at will and force countries to participate in the world economy on basically unfavourable terms? Why is the welfare state under threat in all the countries where it was established? Why is the environment on the edge of collapse? Why are there so many poor

1

people in both the rich and the poor countries at a time when there has never existed such great wealth?

THE POWER OF IDEAS

Neoliberals have understood that ideas have consequences. Starting from a tiny embryo at the University of Chicago with the philosopher-economist Friedrich von Hayek and followers like economist Milton Friedman at its nucleus, the neoliberals and their funders have created a huge international network of foundations, institutes, research centers, publications, scholars, writers and public relations experts to develop, package, and push their doctrine.

They have built this highly efficient ideological cadre because they understand what the early-twentieth-century Italian Marxist thinker Antonio Gramsci called cultural hegemony. If you can occupy peoples' heads, their hearts and their hands will follow. The neoliberals' patrons have spent hundreds of millions of dollars, but the result has been worth every penny because they have made neoliberalism seem as if it were the natural and normal condition of humankind. No matter how many disasters the neoliberal system has created, no matter what financial crises it may engender, no matter how many losers and outcasts it may create, it is still made to seem inevitable, like an act of God, the only possible economic and social order available to us.

Let me stress how important it is to understand that neoliberalism has been deliberately created by particular people with a particular purpose. Once you grasp this, once you understand that neoliberalism is not a natural and inevitable force, you can also understand that it need not be our inevitable fate. What some people have created, other people can change. But they cannot change it without recognising the importance of ideas. I'm all for grassroots projects, but I also warn that these will collapse if the overall ideological climate is hostile to their goals.

IDEAS IN POWER

In 1979, Margaret Thatcher came to power and launched the neoliberal "revolution" in Britain. The Iron Lady was herself a disciple of Friedrich von Hayek. The central value of Thatcher's doctrine, like that of neoliberalism itself, is the notion of competition—competition between nations, regions, firms, and of course between individuals. Thatcher was an unapologetic social Darwinist. Competition was central to her program because it was supposed to separate the sheep from the goats, the men from the boys, the fit from the unfit. It was supposed to allocate all resources, whether physical, natural, human or financial with the greatest possible efficiency. As Thatcher once said, "It is our job to glory in inequality and see that talents and abilities are given vent and expression for the benefit of us all." In other words, don't worry about those who might be left behind in the competitive struggle. People are unequal by nature, but this is good because the contributions of the well-born, the best-educated, the toughest, will eventually benefit everyone.

Nothing in particular is owed to the weak. What happens to them is their own fault, never the fault of society. If the competitive system is let loose, society will be the better for it.

The history of the past 20 years teaches us that exactly the opposite is the case. During the 1980s, under Thatcher and her successor John Major, 1% of taxpayers received 29% of all the tax-reduction benefits, so that a single person earning half the average salary found his or her taxes had gone up by 7%, whereas a single person earning 10 times the average salary got a reduction of 21%. In pre-Thatcher Britain, about one person in ten was classed as living below the poverty line, not a brilliant result but honourable as nations go and a lot better than during the pre-War period. Now one person in four, and one child in three, is officially poor. This is the meaning of "survival of the fittest": some "survive" in luxury, while others cannot heat their houses in winter.

Since the public sector does not obey neoliberalism's basic law of competition, the neoliberals have also made privatization one of their prime aims. Prior to Thatcher's onslaught, a lot of the public sector in Britain was profitable. In 1984, public companies contributed over 7 billion pounds to the treasury. The neoliberals, however, defined anything public as necessarily "inefficient." What has happened since privatization? The government used taxpayer money to wipe out debts and recapitalise firms before putting them on the market—for example, the water authority got 5 billion pounds of debt relief plus 1.6 billion pounds called the "green dowry" to make the bride more attractive to prospective buyers. A lot of public relations fuss was made about how small stockholders would have a stake in these companies—and in fact 9 million people did buy shares—but half of them invested less than a thousand pounds and most of them sold their shares rather quickly, as soon as they could cash in on the instant profits.

The point of privatisation was neither economic efficiency nor improved services to the consumer, but simply to transfer wealth from the government—which could redistribute it to lessen social inequalities—into private hands. The managers of Britain's newly privatised enterprises, often exactly the same people as before, doubled or tripled their own salaries. The overwhelming majority of privatised company shares are now in the hands of financial institutions and very large investors. The employees of British Telecom bought only 1% of the shares; those of British Aerospace, 1.3%. All that money that public enterprises once contributed to the public purse is now going to private shareholders. Service in the privatised industries is now often disastrous. The *Financial Times* has reported, for example, an invasion of rats in the Yorkshire water system.

Thatcher got an added bonus from privatization. By destroying the public sector where labor unions were strongest, she was able to weaken them drastically. Between 1979 and 1994, the number of jobs in the public sector in Britain was reduced from over 7 million to 5 million, a drop of 29%. Virtually all the jobs eliminated were union jobs. Since private sector employment was stagnant during

those 15 years, the overall reduction in the number of British jobs came to 1.7 million, a drop of 7% compared to 1979. To the neoliberals, however, fewer workers
was always better than more because workers impinge on shareholder value.

Those in the top 20% of the income scale are likely to gain something from
neoliberalism. The higher up they are in the ladder, the more they gain. Conversely,
the bottom 80% all lose, and the lower they are to begin with, the more they lose
proportionally. Kevin Phillips, a Republican analyst and former aid to President
Nixon, charted in his 1990 book *The Politics of Rich and Poor* the way Reagan's
neoliberal policies had changed American income distribution. Over the decade
of the 1980s, the top 10% of American families increased their average family
income by 16%, the top 5% increased theirs by 23%, and the extremely lucky
top 1% could thank Reagan for a 50% increase. Their revenues went from an
affluent $270,000 to a heady $405,000. As for poorer Americans, the bottom
80% all lost something. The bottom 10% lost, proportionally, the most: 15% of
their already meagre incomes. From an already rock-bottom average of $4,113
annually, they dropped to $3,504. In 1977, the top 1% of American families had
average incomes 65 times as great as those of the bottom 10%. A decade later, the
top 1% was 115 times as well off as the bottom 10%.

America is one of the most unequal societies on earth, but virtually all countries have seen inequalities increase over the past twenty years because of neoliberal policies. There is nothing mysterious about this trend towards greater inequality. Policies are specifically designed to give the already rich more disposable
income, particularly through tax cuts and by pushing down wages. The theory
and ideological justification for such measures is that higher incomes for the rich
and higher profits will lead to more investment, better allocation of resources, and
therefore more jobs and welfare for everyone. In reality, moving money up the
economic ladder has led to untold paper wealth for the few, stock market bubbles,
and financial crises. If income were redistributed towards the bottom 80% of
society, it would be used for consumption and consequently benefit employment.
As wealth is redistributed towards the top, where people already have most of the
things they need, it does not go into the local or national economy but to international stockmarkets.

These mechanisms have been at work throughout the world. USAID and the
World Bank have pushed the privatization doctrine in the global South. By 1991,
the Bank had already made 114 loans to speed the process, and every year its
Global Development Finance report lists hundreds of privatizations carried out
in the Bank's borrowing countries. Over the past twenty years, the International
Monetary Fund (IMF) has been strengthened enormously. Thanks to the debt
crisis, it has moved from balance of payments support to being quasi-universal
dictator of so-called "sound" economic policies, meaning of course neoliberal
ones (including "free trade" in goods and services and uncontrolled international
circulation of capital). Thankfully, a major recent effort to make binding and

universal neoliberal rules, the Multilateral Agreement on Investment (MAI), failed due to popular opposition. It would have given all rights to corporations, all obligations to governments, and no rights at all to citizens. The World Trade Organisation (WTO) was put in place in January 1995 after long and laborious negotiations, often rammed through parliaments which had little idea what they were ratifying. Mass protest, however, has also prevented the full implementation of its neoliberal agenda.

THERE IS AN ALTERNATIVE

The common denominator of these institutions is their lack of transparency and democratic accountability. This is the essence of neoliberalism. It claims that the economy should dictate its rules to society, not the other way around. Democracy is an encumbrance, neo-liberalism is designed for winners, not for voters who necessarily encompass the categories of both winners and losers. It's time we set the agenda instead of letting the Masters of the Universe set it in Davos, Switzerland, where they meet annually. I hope funders may also understand that they should not be funding just projects but also ideas. We need to design workable and equitable international taxation systems, including a tax on all monetary and financial market transactions (known as the Tobin Tax) and taxes on transnational corporations' sales. The proceeds of an international tax system should go to closing the North-South gap and to redistribution to all the people who have been robbed over the past twenty years. Fortunately, there is plenty of money sloshing around out there—$1.5 trillion a day in international financial transactions. A tiny fraction of it would be enough to provide a decent life to every person on earth, to supply universal health and education, to clean up the environment and prevent further destruction to the planet—at least according to the United Nations Development Programme (UNDP), which calls for a paltry $40 billion a year to achieve these aims.

Neoliberalism is not the natural human condition. It can be challenged and replaced because its own failures will require this. We have to be ready with replacement policies which restore power to communities and democratic government while working to institute democracy, the rule of law and fair distribution at the international level. Business and the market have their place, but this place cannot occupy the entire sphere of human existence. Look at it this way. We have the numbers on our side, because there are far more losers than winners in the neoliberal game. We have the ideas, whereas theirs are finally coming into question because of the repeated crisis they have caused. What we lack, so far, is the organisation and the unity. Solidarity means finding the hidden synergies in each other's struggles so that our numerical force and the power of our ideas become overwhelming. The threat is clearly transnational, so our response must also be transnational.

Based on a lecture given at the Conference on Economic Sovereignty in a Globalising World, Bangkok, Thailand, March 24-26, 1999.

ARTICLE 2

Know-Nothings and Know-It-Alls

What's Wrong With the Hype About "Globalization"

BY JESSICA COLLINS AND JOHN MILLER

September/October 2000

Protesters against "globalization" have no idea what they are talking about. At least that is the verdict of the mainstream press. According to their coverage, the "protectionist" labor unions and the "privileged, cause-happy" college kids that took to the streets of Seattle and Washington, D.C., were content to accept as gospel "the vaguest snippets of knowledge" about the economics of "globalization", the World Trade Organization, the International Monetary Fund, and the World Bank.

"[The protesters'] tales rarely get fact-checked," complains Paul Krugman, the Princeton economics professor and *New York Times* columnist. "Nobody asks whether the moral of the story is really as clear-cut as it seems." Quick to dismiss the protesters' views as uninformed and illegitimate, Krugman would have done better to fact-check the mainstream media, which was itself guilty of recycling data uncritically and accepting as gospel the conclusions of the institutional powers themselves.

Take "Parsing the Protests," an article written by Thomas Friedman, the *Times'* star international reporter turned columnist, in anticipation of the April 16, 2000 Washington, D.C., protest. Friedman warned his readers that they would be hearing "much blarney" from the protesters. Under "facts you won't hear," Friedman provided his supposed antidote to the protesters' nonsense: the results from a recent study conducted by the A.T. Kearney Co., an economic consulting firm. The report proves, according to Friedman, that "globalization" promotes faster economic growth, higher standards of living, and greater political freedom. While he does note the downside reported by Kearney—greater inequality, corruption, and pollution—Friedman is quick to point out that, increased inequality notwithstanding, the economic growth he associates with "globalization" still results in decreased poverty.

Despite the appearance of evenhandedness and objectivity, the report contains, to borrow Thomas Friedman's phrase, "much blarney," including "snippets" that Friedman passes around uncritically. A.T. Kearney Co. itself is a for-profit research company with corporations for customers. It boasts a "distinguished 75-year history of helping business leaders gain and sustain competitive advantage."

But the Kearney Co.'s stake in promoting "globalization" is a fact Friedman never shared with his readers.

INSIDE THE KEARNEY REPORT

To make the pro-globalization case, Kearney's Global Business Policy Council ranked 34 developed and developing countries on a scale from "globalizing slow-ly" to "globalizing rapidly" based on their scores on ten different indices. The report uses this "globalization ledger" to engage in some crucial sleight of hand. It passes off "the greater integration of the economies around the world," measured by their "globalization" indices, as the equivalent of free trade. By misrepresenting isolation from the world economy as the only alternative to free trade, the study preordains its pro-globalization (really pro-free trade) conclusions. Opponents of free trade have not endorsed isolation from the world economy as a development strategy since the early days of dependency theory some three decades ago.

The "globalization" debate is not about economic isolation vs. integration into the world economy; but about what policies allow a developing economy to most successfully engage with the world economy. The Kearney Co., Friedman, and other "globalizers" presume that engagement requires complete submission to the neoliberal policy agenda promoted by international capital, economic pow-ers like the United States, and international agencies like the IMF. Opponents of "globalization" argue instead that a different form of engagement with the world economy—based on more democratic control of the economy, more pro-tections for workers and the environment, and greater limits on the movement of capital—is likely to produce a more widespread and equitable form of economic development.

The Kearney globalization ledger fails to distinguish between these two dif-ferent strategies for economic development in today's international economy. In one way or another, seven of the ten variables in its globalization index measure a country's *degree* of engagement with the world economy, but say little about the policies determining the *manner* of engagement.

TRADE, GROWTH, AND OPENNESS

One of Kearney's indices is a country's level of trade, the combined value of its exports and imports as a percentage of gross domestic product (GDP). This is an index used in many mainstream studies of "globalization". Finding a positive correlation between the levels of trade and economic growth (measured as GDP growth per capita), the report cites this data as support for free-trade policies. All the data really mean, however, is that international trade and economic growth tend to move in the same direction. It says nothing about whether trade *causes* faster economic growth. You might just as well conclude that economies enjoy high levels of trade because other economic policies promote rapid economic growth.

Even if international trade does promote economic growth, this does not mean that "free-trade" *policies* (lower tariffs and non-tariff barriers to trade) cause growth. Japan's export boom during the 1980s would have registered high marks on Kearney's trade index. But Japanese authorities oversaw their boom not with the free-trade policies endorsed by the Kearney study, but managed-trade policies, such as selective tariffs and export subsidies.

When economists address the current policy debate about "globalization" properly, the evidence fails to endorse the pro-globalization position touted in the Kearney study. In their exhaustive survey of the major studies on trade policy and economic growth, mainstream economists Francisco Rodríguez and Dani Rodrik find, "little evidence that open trade policies—in the sense of lower tariff and non-tariff barriers to trade—are significantly associated with economic growth." By weighing down their globalization index with trade *performance* variables that say little about trade *policies*, the Kearney study manages to obscure this anti-free trade finding.

The same criticisms apply to the Kearney report's claim that "globalization" alleviates absolute poverty (measured as the number of people living on less than US$1 per day). Apart from the problems presented by their use of the World Bank's measure of poverty, the correlation between the report's "globalization" index and reduced poverty tells us little more than that economic growth is associated with lower poverty rates. Over the last 50 years, the most dramatic reductions in poverty have actually occurred in East Asia, among countries such as South Korea, Taiwan, and China, all of which have implemented extensive trade restrictions and relied on government intervention into their economies.

Beyond all the problems with its method, the findings of the Kearney study are downright strange. Their globalization ledger is highly misleading. Look, for instance, at two Latin American countries. Chile, identified as an "aggressive globalizer," has surely embraced liberalization. But at the same time, Chilean authorities restrict the free movement of short-term international capital, requiring financial investors to make a one-year interest-free deposit, in their central banks, equaling 30% of their investments. Mexico, a "stalled globalizer," has during the last two decades adopted neoliberal policies. But when the Mexican economy sank into crisis, its trade performance deteriorated, causing several of its globalization indices to plummet. That hardly constitutes grounds for attributing Mexico's growth problems to a lack of openness.

The Kearney analysis of East Asia yields equally strange results. Part of the problem is that its globalization ledger ranks countries not by their absolute level of "globalization" but the change in their globalization index. For instance, China is classified as an "aggressive globalizer" because it has recently liberalized its trade policies. But Singapore, the most global economy on the Kearney list, is only a "strong globalizer." Despite its recent liberalization, China is no poster child for the neoliberal agenda. It does not have a convertible currency, it maintains state control of its banking system, and it allows little foreign ownership in equity markets.

Even Kearney's comparison of different countries' growth rates is problematic. The report looks at two different periods, 1978 to 1982 and 1993 to 1997, and finds that its "rapid globalizers" grew more quickly than the other countries, especially during the later period. Looking over the longer period from 1970 to 1998 eliminates much of the association between a high "globalization" score and rapid economic growth. For instance, five countries from the Kearney report made the IMF's list of fastest-growing developing economies over the last three decades (with per capita income growth over 3.75% a year). Just one, China, is classified a "rapid globalizer" (though inappropriately). The rest came from much further down on the Kearney globalization ledger. Thailand was but a "moderate globalizer"; South Korea, a "passive globalizer"; Indonesia and Malaysia, "stalled globalizers."

ACCEPTING THE CHALLENGE

In its period of most rapid economic development, the half century following the Civil War, the United States imposed import tariffs averaging around 40%, a level higher than those in almost all of today's developing economies. During the 19th and 20th centuries, German and Japanese economic development depended on managed trade, not free trade. Even the World Bank, in its 1993 report *The East Asian Miracle*, acknowledged as much for the Japanese postwar boom. South Korea and Taiwan, whose key growth periods came during the 1960s and 1970s, faced a world economy with far less capital mobility and engaged that world with managed-trade policies—export subsidies, domestic-content requirements, import-export linkages, and restrictions of capital flows, including foreign direct investment.

In his *New York Times* article, Thomas Friedman challenges the critics of "globalization" to name "a single country that has upgraded its living or worker standards, without free trade and integration." As the above list suggests, every single one of today's developed countries did exactly that. You can file that under "facts you won't hear" from the mainstream media.

ARTICLE 3

Learning From the Southeast Asian Crisis

BY JOHN MILLER

November/December 1998, revised November 2000

In summer 1997 bullishness on Asia's miracle economies disappeared. The Thai economy, the epicenter of the crisis, suffered a financial meltdown. The Thai currency, the baht, lost 40% of its value *vis-a-vis* the dollar. The Thai stock market crashed, off 70% from its peak in 1994.

The miracle economies of Southeast Asia fell into depression. Conditions varied from country to country but all were hurting. Recession prevailed in Malaysia and Thailand; a double-digit decline in real output cost over two million workers their jobs by the end of 1998. In Indonesia, crippling stagflation doubled the price of staple goods at the same time that it pushed nearly one half the population into poverty.

These once high-flying Southeast Asian economies fell into receivership. In Thailand and Indonesia, the International Monetary Fund (IMF) administered austerity measures in return for emergency loans to help repay foreign lenders. Meanwhile, Malaysia independently administered similar austerity measures. The $63 billion bailout crafted by the IMF and the U.S. Treasury exceeded the U.S.-financed bailout of Mexico in 1995. With South Korea added in, the East Asian bailout package was over $100 billion.

Economic growth returned to much of the region within two years, but the economic miracle seems to be a thing of the past. While Indonesia has yet to show signs of recovery, the Southeast Asian economies as a group registered 3.2% growth in real output in 1999. Still, that growth was less than half the 7.8% to 9.0% rates Thailand, Malaysia, and Indonesia posted in the three years before the crisis. And millions in the region continue to endure terrible hardships brought on by the crisis: aggravated poverty, lost jobs, reduced income, and diminished access to health and educational services.

The more pessimistic observers at the time of the crisis feared that the Southeast Asian financial debacle might trigger a deflationary spiral sucking all of East Asia, and perhaps the whole world, into a depression. The threat of economic collapse was in fact genuine (and might have become a reality if conditions had worsened in Japan, the region's most important economy and already the victim of a decade-long recession). During most of the 1990s, East Asia accounted for nearly one half of the expansion in the world economy. The region's financial crisis has rattled financial markets around the globe in a way the Mexican peso crisis of 1995 never did. Latin American, European, and Russian currencies all came under attack. Even the booming U.S. economy slowed in the summer of 1998 under the weight of a ballooning trade deficit caused by fewer exports to East Asia.

For those not blinded by free market faith, the Southeast Asian crisis is a shocking reminder of the failures of markets. Capitalism remains much as Marx and Engels described it one hundred and fifty years ago in the *Communist Manifesto*—dynamic but unstable and destructive. We need to look more closely at what lessons we can learn from the economic sufferings and financial miseries of Southeast Asia.

A STORY OF MARKET FAILURE

The financial crisis in Southeast Asia differs in important ways from previous crises in the developing world. Unlike the Latin American debt crisis of the 1980s, the roots of the current turmoil are in private sector, not public sector, borrowing. Most of the afflicted countries ran budget surpluses or minimal budget deficits in the years prior to the crisis. At the same time, private sector borrowing increased heavily, especially from abroad and especially on a short-term basis. For instance, loans to Thai corporations from international banks doubled from 1988 to 1994. By 1997, Thai foreign debt stood at $89 billion—four-fifths of which was owed by private corporations. But most disturbingly, one half of the debt was short-term, falling due inside a year.

The Southeast Asian miracle economies got into trouble when their export boom came to a halt as these short-term loans came due. For instance, stymied by a decline in First World demand, especially from recession-ridden Japan, Thai exports did not grow at all in 1996. Also, the opening of domestic markets to outside money (under an early round of pressure from the IMF) brought a deluge of short-term foreign investment and spurred heavy short-term borrowing from abroad, fueling a building boom. By the mid '90s, a speculative binge in everything from high-rise office towers to condos to golf courses accounted for nearly 40% of growth in Thailand. When the bubble burst, the region endured a horrendous drying-out process. Southeast Asian exports from autos to computer chips to steel to textiles glutted international markets, all made worse by intensified competition from Chinese exports. Foreign financial capital fled. Domestic spending collapsed. Banks failed at unprecedented rates. Unemployment mounted, and as more and more people across the region fell into poverty, the Southeast Asian financial crisis became a story of tremendous human suffering.

In the language of economists, the crisis is also a story of market failure. Southeast Asian capital markets failed in three critical ways. First, too much capital rushed in. Lured by the prospect of continued double-digit growth and searching for new places to invest its overflowing coffers, financial capital continued to flow into the real-estate sectors of these economies even when financial instability was widespread and obvious to all. Second, the capital markets and the banking system could not channel these funds into productive uses. Too much money went into real estate and too little went into productive investments likely to sustain the export boom. Third, too much capital rushed out, too quickly. The excessive inflow of capital reversed itself and fled with little regard for the actual strength of any particular economy.

In their more candid moments, leaders of the financial community owned up to these market failures. For instance, late in 1997, just a few months into the crisis, Stanley Fischer, economic director of the IMF, confessed at a regional meeting in Hong Kong, "Markets are not always right. Sometimes inflows are excessive and sometimes they may be sustained too long. Markets tend to react late; by then they tend to overreact."

WHERE THE RIGHT WENT WRONG

Despite the doubts of their high priests, most financial conservatives continue to believe that international markets are stable, if subject to periodic excesses, and that whatever their excesses in the East Asian crisis might be, they can be traced back to a misguided interference into those markets. The culprit varies—industrial policy, crony capitalism, fixed exchange rates, or some other shibboleth. But in each case, these conservatives would have it that the economies of Southeast Asia ran into trouble because nonmarket forces had a hand in allocating credit and economic resources better left entirely up to the financiers.

The conservative solution to the crisis? That is easy, if painful: Put an end to these nonmarket allocations of resources. Alan Greenspan, the chair of the U.S. Federal Reserve, argued that the East Asian crisis would root out "the last vestiges" of this sort of thing and ultimately would be regarded as a milestone in the triumph of market capitalism.

But none of the leading economies of the region relied on government-managed industrial policies to direct economic growth. One World Bank study placed Malaysian and Thai trade policies as among the most open in developing economies. Since the 1970s, another study reports, the Thai government tended to "allow free markets rather than to intervene with them."

Nor was the crony capitalism, which the right derides, the cause of the current crisis. This widespread practice—of political connections guiding private sector investment decisions—was a constant, not a new element in the Southeast Asian economic mix, just as present in the boom as in the crisis.

"Transparency" refers to the disclosure publicly traded companies are required to make about their operations to their investors. But signs galore of financial instability and overcapacity were there for anyone, even first-time visitors to the region, to see. Bangkok alone had over $20 billion of vacant residential and commercial units by 1997. Despite plunging returns, foreign investors pumped more loans into Thailand betting that double-digit growth would continue and make these risks pay off.

In addition, we should remember that this crisis hit first and hardest in Thailand and then Indonesia, the two Asian economies with private domestic banking systems that had been recently deregulated and opened to foreigners. The shortfall of Japanese investment in the early 1990s left Thailand desperate for foreign funds. Under pressure from the IMF and the WTO, Thai authorities moved to further open their economy to foreign investors, allowing foreigners to own stock, real estate and banking operations as well. On top of this, government policies lifted Thai interest rates above those in the West, making Thailand a place where Westerners could turn a quick buck.

Nor did tying the value of their currencies to the dollar cause these economies to fall into crisis. Having stable exchange rates was an important building block for the region's trade relations. It allowed manufacturers to import components from Japan and Korea for assembly in Thailand and elsewhere in Southeast Asia, before being sold in the United States and Europe. And pegging the value of their currency to that of the dollar allowed the Thais, for example, to lure capital into their country, fueling investments. But the Thai authorities did not take the next step of regulating the foreign capital that they attracted into the economy this way.

What seems clear now is that the cause of the economic crisis of Southeast Asia was not misaligned exchange rates, or mistaken domestic policy, or even a lack of transparency in the banking sector, although that surely didn't help. Rather, the root cause of the crisis that threatened the world with depression was the abrupt reversal of the excessively rapid rise of capital inflows and the falling global demand for the exports from the region. These arose from a global economy increasingly turned over to the rule of markets.

By the end of 1997, the Southeast Asian economies suffered "the equivalent of a massive bank run on the region without any lender of last resort," says economist Jan Kregel. In 1996, a net $78 billion flowed into the region from foreign bank loans and short-term portfolio investments like stocks. In 1997, that turned into a $38 billion outflow from the countries most hit by the crisis—Indonesia, Malaysia, South Korea, Thailand, and the Philippines. The biggest drop came in short-term portfolio investment, such as stocks, and bank lending.

The IMF, the prime candidate to act as lender of last resort, turned down the role—instead putting in place policies that imposed more austerity and yet tighter credit conditions. Steadfastly insisting that the cause of crisis was "home grown" as Stanley Fischer of the IMF put it, the IMF tightened credit for these countries already suffering from the disappearance of capital.

Even by the IMF's standards, these austerity measures were applied in an arbitrary and disproportionate manner. First World economies facing financial crises came in for far different treatment. The leading industrialized economies (and the IMF) urged Japan to increase government spending, cut taxes, and keep interest rates low to counteract its continued economic stagnation—just the opposite of the IMF prescription for the rest of East Asia.

In the Southeast Asian crisis, some reckless behavior was punished, while other reckless behavior was forgiven. Surely international investors are just as much or more responsible for the instability of the region as its local capitalists, bankers, governments, and workers. Yet foreign investors were being bailed out by the IMF, not punished. That is, foreign lenders had their loans repaid. The IMF did not deem the foreign shareholders ravaged by plummeting stock prices and collapsing currencies worthy of a bailout. Go figure.

LESSONS FOR THE LEFT

Left analyses of the crisis need to guard against two excesses: concluding with too much confidence that rapid growth is never to return to the Southeast Asian economies and that the severity of the crisis is proof that the growth that preceded it was artificial.

Depressions happen. Or depressions happen again, as Hyman Minsky, the left-leaning economic theorist of financial fragility, would have put it. Financial crises and economic downturns are the flipside of periods of unbridled capitalist growth. That these rapidly expanding, high debt, and now even less regulated Southeast Asian economies fell into crisis is hardly surprising.

But did the crisis bring the Asian miracle to an end or unleash the forces that would bring down the world economy? It seems not. Also, whether or not the current crisis was the death knell for rapid growth in the region, or the world economy for that matter, the growth preceding the crisis was dynamic and unstable—much like the capitalist growth that Marx and Engels observed transforming Europe in the middle of the last century. That the growth was based on brutal super-exploitation and relied more often on capital from the outside does not make it artificial or "ersatz," ready to disappear for that reason, as some claimed. After all, the region sustained growth over a long time, not just for the last decade, when Japanese investment was heaviest.

The enhanced mobility of capital—domestic and foreign—during the 1990s adds to the instability of these economies and reduces the bargaining power of labor. This is a very real concern, especially in economies such as Indonesia and Thailand where a numbing absence of social accountability has left the investors and corporations to operate unchecked. A profoundly flawed economic development has taken hold, both in the earlier period of rapid growth and since the crisis.

LIMITED CAPITAL MOBILITY, SOUND ECONOMIC DEVELOPMENT

A public policy that regulates capital, whatever its national origins, is called for in Southeast Asia. Only regulation demanding genuine accountability from both the cronies and the capitalists offers the prospect of genuine reform. The crunch of economic losses and slack labor markets makes reform more difficult. But to the extent that the crisis punctured the belief in infallible markets, strengthened the opposition to free markets, and spurred movements to organize, the potential for regulating capital has been enhanced, not diminished.

The proposal most favored in the region to limit capital mobility is a transaction tax on all cross-border flows of capital, designed by Nobel prize winning economist James Tobin. Although on its own it could not cool out a speculative fever or capital panic, the Tobin tax would discourage speculation. As a bonus, the tax revenues collected would more than adequately fund an IMF-style agency, freed from the dictates of the United States, that would bail out bankers and capital investors only when they invest long term, pay living wages, and respect international labor standards.

Malaysia took the more immediate action of imposing capital controls—banning the trading of the Malaysian currency, the ringgit, outside of the country. Malaysia's prime minister Mahathir called the plan "the only way to isolate the economy from the currency speculators and traders" whom he blamed for the country's economic crisis. Banning the trading of the ringgit in overseas markets in effect decoupled the Malaysian economy from the international currency markets. While Malaysian stock prices initially plummeted in response, the value of the ringgit remained steady, and Mahathir's move found support from some surprising sources. One maverick mainstream economist, Paul Krugman, endorsed the concept of capital controls, for they allowed Malaysian authorities to lower interest rates to counteract Malaysia's recession without causing the ringgit to collapse.

In addition to controlling international capital, whether internationally or domestically, public policy must also compel domestic capital and local elites to accept greater social accountability. Elites seldom pay taxes in these countries. Taxing elites would add to sources of domestic savings and at the same time make the distribution of income more equal. Also, giving these governments more money could add to domestic demand—providing a buffer against the shortfall in global demand that had a hand in this crisis. This social accountability must extend to conditions of work as well—notoriously dangerous in Southeast Asia—recognizing the rights of workers to organize, to work in safe conditions, and to earn a living wage.

These forms of social accountability would foster a more sustainable and equitable economic development, and perhaps lay the groundwork for a Southeast Asian economy that does more to relieve human suffering and less to add to it.

ARTICLE 4

Seven Lessons From Chile

Thirty Years After the Coup

BY ALEJANDRO REUSS

September 2003

The 1973 overthrow of Chile's Popular Unity government, led by the Chilean Socialist and Communist parties and headed by socialist President Salvador Allende, was what historians call a "world-historic" event. Chile's "democratic road to socialism" had held out hope to people around the world (as the Prague Spring had a few years earlier) that a democratic society could be truly socialist (unlike Scandinavian "social democracy") and a socialist society could be truly democratic (unlike Soviet "communism").

Not only was this hope crushed by violence, but the defeat was turned into a rout. The totalitarian regime that seized power in Chile on September 11, 1973, led by Gen. Augusto Pinochet, inflicted an extreme form of "free market" economic policy on the country's people. Chilean "neoliberalism" has since been held up, by both its perpetrators and their admirers, as a model to be emulated, from Latin America, to Russia, to the United States.

The arrest of Pinochet on human rights charges in England in 1998 revived worldwide consciousness of the dictatorship's crimes, and Chile's wrenching past more generally. People in the United States may know more about Chile than they do about other countries of similar size and distance, but much of what they "know" is wrong, or only half right. Here are seven lessons from Chile—seven corrections to the conventional wisdom—thirty years after the destruction of the "Chilean road."

MYTH 1: State intervention was successful in producing capitalist development in Chile prior to 1970.

Economists and politicians who have pushed the "free market" or neoliberal economic model across Latin America and the global South over the last three decades have claimed that "there is no alternative" to their economic prescriptions. In opposition, many progressive critics have pointed to examples of capitalist economic development in which the state played a leading role.

Tariff protection and other subsidies for infant industries, directed investment into key industries and infrastructure, and other forms of state intervention certainly spurred capitalist development in the United States, then in Germany and

Japan, and more recently in South Korea and other East Asian countries. In the half century or so between the Great Depression and the rise of neoliberalism, numerous Latin American governments also experimented with state-sponsored capitalist development. The dominant model, known as import substitution industrialization (ISI), involved state protection (tariffs, etc.) of manufacturing industries aimed at "substituting" domestic manufactured goods for those imported from abroad.

But the most important critiques of ISI were not made by neoliberals, but by theorists of dependency and underdevelopment. In the 1960s, like other countries pursuing ISI, Chile faced a number of bottlenecks to economic development that ISI seemed ill-equipped to break through. The new industrial capitalists exploited political connections to maintain virtual monopolies. They produced good jobs for only a minority of urban workers. The economic impact of the new industries was limited by the narrowness of the domestic market. This narrow market was the product of widespread poverty, especially in rural areas. This poverty was unlikely to be significantly reduced without a drastic redistribution of wealth (especially land) in rural areas, something these governments were not prepared to do. The low productivity of agriculture under the landed-estate system diverted resources from economic development to the import of food. Meanwhile, many of the most important and profitable industries, especially mining, were dominated by multinational corporations. These multinationals sent profits back to their base countries or invested them elsewhere, so the proceeds from these activities were not available for economic development. And the list of obstacles went on.

With the impasse of ISI as a development strategy, many workers and peasants turned their hopes toward more radical social and economic reforms.

MYTH 2: The "Chilean Road to Socialism" was only a radical reform from above.

For many of those familiar with Chile's recent history, the period 1970-1973 is synonymous with the "Popular Unity" government. They largely think of the story as beginning with the election of Allende, on his fourth try, to the presidency. They think of his government's attempts to improve the situation of ordinary Chileans—offering a free daily ration of milk to all children under fifteen, raising workers' wages, redistributing land. They think of Allende's attempt to break the domination of Chile's economy by multinational corporations—nationalizing Chile's copper, its banks, and its telecommunications system.

While all this is certainly an important part of that history, to make it synonymous with that history is incorrect, and denies the rightful place of Chile's workers, peasants, and poor in that history. The election of Allende removed the lid of state repression from the pressure cooker of Chilean society—and the ordinary people's pent-up demands let loose. Indigenous people retook lands that had been stolen from them or their ancestors. Peasants occupied landed estates rather than waiting for land reforms from above. Poor urban people took over unoccupied private and public lots and turned them overnight into ramshackle settlements. Workers in urban areas occupied their factories and declared them "territory free from exploitation."

New forms of grassroots government sprang up. Led by women, "Supply and Price Committees" monitored retail enterprises to prevent hoarding and price gouging. Workers at different companies created joint factory committees known as "Industrial Belts." And urban poor people and workers created new forms of grassroots government at the neighborhood level, known as "Communal Commands." Collectively known as the "People's Power," they were the beginnings of a new form of democracy in Chile.

MYTH 3: The economic failings of the Popular Unity government were primarily due to economic mismanagement.

The economic program of the Popular Unity government, in many ways, made a great deal of sense. In the late 1960s, Chile was spending about one-fifth of its foreign exchange earnings to import food from abroad, thanks to a system of agriculture dominated by big landlords with little interest in increasing productivity. Observing that smaller Chilean farms tended to be more productive than large estates, thanks to more intensive cultivation, the government concluded that it could increase agricultural production by redistributing land to the rural poor, either in the form of individual plots or cooperative farms. The savings from reduced food imports would provide additional resources for industrial development. The increased incomes of those who received land, and the general redistribution of income to workers and poor people, meanwhile, would create a broader domestic market for Chile's manufacturing industries.

The Popular Unity government also nationalized the most lucrative export industry, copper. In 1972, President Allende calculated that U.S. mining companies had exported $4 billion in profits since 1930. Political symbolism aside, the nationalization of copper was intended primarily as a way to harness resources from the export of Chilean raw materials for Chilean economic development. The Popular Unity government also nationalized many of Chile's main companies. The number of enterprises controlled by the Chilean government more than quadrupled between late 1970 and late 1972. The logic of expanding the state sector was that 1) state industries could engage in activities unlikely to be profitable, like supplying electric power to rural areas, 2) the state could develop industries that require a large initial investment and are likely to run deficits for some initial period, and 3) the state could take over profitable industries and use the proceeds for national economic development.

Nonetheless, it is true that the period from 1970-1973 saw a steadily deteriorating economic situation. This was due in no small measure to the United States government's efforts, in the words of Richard Nixon, to "make the [Chilean] economy scream." The United States government cut off aid to Chile, pressured U.S. banks to stop their lending, and used its influence with international lending institutions to increase the cost to Chile of borrowing from other sources. U.S. intelligence agencies also underwrote direct action to disrupt the Chilean economy. The CIA is widely believed to have bribed truck owners to take their rigs off the road during a costly trucking "strike" (really a lockout) in late 1972—this in a country completely dependent on trucking for transport. Domestic groups also engaged in economic sabotage, ranging from politically motivated hoarding of essential goods to right-wing newspapers announcing impending shortages (which then became self-fulfilling prophecies, as consumers rushed to buy whatever they could get their hands on).

The Popular Unity government did make critical errors. These were, however, largely political in nature. The government's economic team believed that their economic stimulus policies would make business profitable in the short run, and so would ensure steady investment as it implemented its structural reform program. It greatly underestimated capitalists' individual sensitivity to the political climate—including the danger that expropriation would extend to their businesses—and their ability to act in concert to undermine the government.

MYTH 4: The Popular Unity government fell due to a general loss of popular support.

The Popular Unity came into office as a minority government. In the 1970 election, left, center, and right each polled around 1/3 of the vote. Allende, who had gotten the most votes, won election in the Chilean Senate, as the Constitution specified in cases where no candidate gained an absolute majority. A year after assuming office, with the economy booming, wages increasing and inequality decreasing, and the government boasting major successes in agrarian reform and the nationalization of major industries (copper, banking, etc.), the Popular Unity polled just over 50% of the vote in the country-wide round of municipal elections in 1971. The long-sought electoral majority for socialism seemed at last at hand.

As the economic situation deteriorated, opposition groups went on the offensive, and right-wing groups within the armed forces attempted to overthrow the government, the Popular Unity probably lost some of its electoral support. With the government seemingly reeling, the right expected to win a two-thirds majority in the 1973 congressional elections and so to be able to depose Allende by impeachment. Instead, the Popular Unity polled over 43% of the vote, a decrease from the 1971 municipal elections, but an increase over its electoral support in the previous congressional elections (in 1969) and the presidential election (in 1970).

This election spelled the end of the "parliamentary" efforts to overthrow the government. The Chilean right realized that if mass support for the Popular Unity held even in conditions of economic crisis and political chaos, the government could consolidate its "revolution" if the situation were to stabilize. Not willing to risk another Popular Unity victory in 1976, the right turned to a coup as its only way out. Several coup attempts by rogue elements of the armed forces had failed; the September 11, 1973, coup succeeded, as "constitutionalist" military officers were neutralized politically and pro-coup elements gained control of the armed forces' high command. The military coup, in short, did not happen because the existing government had too little popular support, but because it has too much.

MYTH 5: The period of military dictatorship in Chile produced an economic "miracle."

In the course of the period of dictatorship, the regime's attempts to legitimate itself gradually shifted from its "rescue" of the country from communism to its "modernization" of the economy along neoliberal lines. Chilean economists trained in "free market" fanaticism at the University of Chicago (known as the "Chicago Boys") became key figures in the dictatorship—directing not only its macroeconomic and trade policies, but also directing the gutting of its social welfare system and the design of its new repressive labor laws. Far from producing an economic miracle, in actual fact the neoliberal model appeared an abject failure through the dictatorship's first decade. Chile suffered two severe recessions—in the mid 1970s and the early 1980s—exacerbated by the country being flung open to the forces of the world capitalist economy. During the latter crisis, the banking system went bankrupt and the dictatorship hastened to re-nationalize the banks (and their losses). Critics of neoliberalism sarcastically termed this the "Chicago road to socialism."

In the latter 1980s, increasing foreign investment resulted in faster economic growth. Overall, however, annual economic growth during the dictatorship years was no higher than it had been in the preceding decades, while it was more irregular (following a boom-and-bust pattern) and generated far more inequality of income and wealth. The dictatorship years saw a "boom" in poverty: 5 million people out of a total population of 13 million fell below the official poverty line at the end of the dictatorship. Along with the regime's human-rights violations—the "disappearance" (kidnapping and murder) of thousands and torture of tens of thousands—poverty was a key issue in the defeat of the dictatorship in the 1988 referendum that led to new civilian elections the following year.

MYTH 6: The aims and results of the dictatorship's neoliberal economic program were primarily economic.

Critics of the neoliberal policies imposed by the dictatorship have often focused their attention on its massive redistribution of income and wealth from poor to rich, from labor to capital. While absolutely true, this should not be seen as the main aim of the neoliberal economic regime. The neoliberal economists succeeded in "selling" their services to the dictatorship mainly on *political* grounds. While the generals knew little about economics (and to the extent they did were probably inclined toward a fascist-like state control of the economy), they harbored an extreme attachment to social "order" and an equally extreme hostility to the "politicization" of Chilean society, which they blamed for the conflicts of the Popular Unity years. The "Chicago Boys" (and other neoliberal economists) presented themselves as apolitical technocrats who would depoliticize economic life in Chile—dismantle the institutions of state intervention in the economy and any public obligation to provide for the well-being of Chile's people.

Far from embracing the "free market," privatization, and the rest of the neoliberal model for the sake of efficiency or growth, the dictatorship did so as a means of creating an atomized, apolitical society in which the political conflicts of the Popular Unity period would be impossible. Public schools, public pensions, and the like, they concluded, encouraged people to organize politically. If schools were underfunded or pension benefits inadequate, people could support political campaigns or join political movements to change public policies. Under the neoliberals' school privatization (and voucher) policies, people dissatisfied with their children's schools had not a political solution, but an individual one—change schools. Under privatized, stock-market based pension funds, people faced with an inadequate retirement income, likewise, had the solution of switching from one mutual fund to another. The neoliberals openly boasted of the political effects of these policies. The dictatorship's minister of labor, José Piñera, described the privatization of social security as "depoliticizing a huge sector of the economy," lessening "political conflict and election-time demagoguery," and "promot[ing] social and economic stability." Piñera now heads the right-wing Cato Institute's Social Security Privatization Project.

Lest any confusion remain that the neoliberals were motivated by a general hostility to the exercise of state power, Piñera himself was the principal architect of the dictatorship's 1983 labor law. This abolished Chilean workers' right to organize unions and bargain collectively, an abolition the dictatorship enforced by the "disappearance" of union activists when it deemed necessary. The neoliberal economists served willingly in a regime reviled worldwide for the most gruesome forms of torture and assassination. So much for their "libertarian" scruples.

MYTH 7: There is no alternative.

Margaret Thatcher, an admirer of the Chilean military dictatorship and personal friend of Gen. Pinochet, coined the now-famous mantra of neoliberalism: "There is no alternative." Nowhere has that seemed more true than in Latin America. Chile was the real birthplace of the "model," which proceeded to engulf the rest of Latin America more completely than any other part of the world. Not coincidentally, the crisis of neoliberalism is more severe there than anywhere else. So far, however, the alternatives are limited.

In Argentina, once the poster child of the IMF, economic crisis and mass protest brought down the neoliberal government in 2001, and brought back to power the populist wing of the party founded by former dictator Juan Peron. In Venezuela, a government led by former army officer Hugo Chavez has broken with neoliberalism and instituted redistributive economic policies, but does not aim to change the fundamental structure of the economy. Chavez's "Bolivarian revolution," moreover, is a modern version of strongman populism reminiscent of Peronism in many ways. In Brazil, the Workers Party, which originated with insurgent unions in the industrial area of Sao Paolo and played a major role in the transition from military dictatorship in the 1980s, now governs the country. President Luiz Inacio Lula da Silva, however, has brought representatives of business and orthodox economists into his administration. The party is clearly moving toward a social-democratic model—administering capitalism and attempting to ameliorate the condition of its victims.

The real alternatives are to be found in a heritage of mass struggle and social revolution handed down from the very recent history of Latin America. The Mexican revolution, recall, is less than a century old and still very much a part of contemporary Mexican politics (witness the rebirth and transfiguration of "Zapatismo" in southern Mexico). The Cuban revolution is less than a half century old. Though it has been tarnished by the undemocratic and repressive character of the Castro regime, people all over Latin America and the world still draw inspiration from its early idealism, exemplified by the life and martyrdom of Che Guevara.

Chile has its own contribution to make to this heritage. The triumph of neoliberalism has openly crowned money the supreme power. The best traditions of Chilean socialism offer the rejoinder of People's Power. Neoliberal capitalism has offered the country, its resources, and its people open to international exploitation. At the height of their struggles, Chile's workers proclaimed a "territory free of exploitation." Neither in Chile itself nor anywhere else in the world is this slogan a reality—or even an immediate possibility. But history has not come to an end yet. Not by a long shot.

ARTICLE 5

Free Markets, International Commerce, and Economic Development

BY ARTHUR MacEWAN

November 2000

NEO-LIBERAL THEORY

The essence of the neo-liberal position on international commerce is the proposition that economic growth will be most rapid when the movement of goods, services, and capital is unimpeded by government regulations... A simple logic lies at the basis of [this] free trade position. If, for whatever reasons, countries differ in their abilities to produce various goods, then they can all benefit if each specializes in the production of those items it produces most effectively (i.e., at least cost). They can then trade with one another to obtain the entire range of goods they need. In this manner, each country is using its resources to do what it can do best...

As an illustration of this logic, consider two countries, one with an abundance of good farm land and the other with a good supply of energy resources (hydro power, for example). It seems likely that each of these countries will gain from trade if the first specializes in the production of agricultural goods and the latter specializes in the production of manufactures. Moreover, if the governments impose no constraints on international trade, then this specialization is precisely what will occur. Without constraints on trade, people attempting to produce manufactured goods in the country with abundant good farm land will not be able to do so as cheaply as people in the country with a good supply of energy resources—and vice versa for people attempting to produce agricultural goods in the latter country...

The theory appears to run into trouble if one country produces everything more efficiently than the other. Yet the trouble is only apparent, not real. Under these circumstances, all will gain if each country specializes in the production of those goods where it has a *comparative advantage*. For example,... [l]et's assume that the country with abundant farm land produces agricultural goods at half what it costs to produce them in the other country. At the same time, this country with abundant farmland has a workforce with great capacity for industrial labor, and it therefore can produce manufactured goods at one-quarter of what it costs to produce them in the other country. Under these circumstances the country's skilled labor force gives it a greater advantage in the production of manufactures than the advantage that its abundant farmland gives it in the production of agricultural goods. Thus it has a *comparative* advantage in the production of manufactures. Similarly, the second country, even though it is less efficient in the production of both categories of goods, has a *comparative* advantage in the production of agricultural goods. To produce manufactures would cost four times as much in this country as in the other, whereas to produce agricultural goods would only cost twice as much. Consequently, both countries can gain if each specializes where it has a comparative advantage, and they then trade to obtain their full set of needs...

The theory of comparative advantage has played an important role in the history of economics, for it has provided an intellectual rationale for free trade policies. An intellectual rationale has been necessary because, whatever the larger efficacy of the policy, free trade is always costly to groups that have prospered under any prior trade restrictions...

Advocates of the neo-liberal position ... base their policy prescriptions as much on certain myths about history as on the internal coherence of their theory. They argue that their theory is validated by the history of successful economic growth, both in the longer experience of the relatively advanced economies and in the recent experience of successful growth in newly industrialized countries. They cite, in particular, the history of economic development in the United Kingdom, other countries of Western Europe, and the United States, and the more recent experiences of countries in East Asia.

An examination of these experiences, however, quickly demonstrates that the neo-liberal claims are but crude myths, having only a vague connection to reality...

HISTORICAL EXPERIENCE: A BRIEF SKETCH

Virtually all of our experience with economic development suggests that extensive regulation of foreign commerce by a country's government has been an essential foundation for successful economic growth. In the United Kingdom, perhaps the case most frequently cited to demonstrate the success of free trade, textile producers secured protection from import competition at the end of the 17th century, and high tariffs served British manufacturing well through the era of the country's rise to world economic preeminence. At the beginning of the 19th century, the average tariff rate on manufactures was 50 percent—high by almost any comparative standard. Later in the century, the United Kingdom did eliminate its tariffs on manufactures, but then it had passed the early stage of development and its industry was well established... Moreover, state support for industry in the United Kingdom came through the creation and maintenance of empire...

Tariff protection also played a large role in the emergence of U.S. industry. The textile industry, which was especially important in the country's economic development, got its start when the hostilities leading up to and through the War of 1812 provided implicit protection by limiting international shipping. After the war, the protection became explicit as a tariff was established. According to the World Bank, the average U.S. tariff on manufactures was 40 percent in 1820… [In] the last third of the 19th century, with tariff protection well established at an average of around 30 percent for most of the 1870 to 1910 period, the United States experienced a great industrial expansion. Only after World War II, when U.S. industry's dominant position in the world economy was secure, did a steady and lasting reduction of tariffs take place…

Countries that achieved their developmental advance at a later historical period were generally characterized by a significantly greater role for the state in the regulation of foreign commerce, both with regard to trade and investment. Japan's experience in joining the ranks of advanced capitalist countries provides the prime example… [and, insofar] as any country has broken out of underdevelopment in more recent decades, South Korea would provide the most important case study. In broad terms, the South Korean experience is very similar to that of Japan. From the early 1960s, the South Korean state followed policies of protecting domestic markets, heavily favoring Korean owned firms, and using state owned industries to develop national production in certain "strategic" sectors…

One of the important aspects of the South Korean experience is that in protecting and supporting the development of national industry the government did not by any means encourage Korean firms to abjure exports and follow an "inward looking" policy. On the contrary, the government used a firm's ability to compete in export markets as a measure of whether or not it was succeeding in becoming more efficient. The South Korean experience shows how economic policy can both regulate foreign commerce but at the same time make sure that national firms reap the many advantages associated with international commerce—including, especially, the transfer of knowledge and technology that come with foreign exposure…

RE-EXAMINING THE THEORY

So the neo-liberal theory of international commerce does not sit very well with historical experience, and this lack of congruence between theory and reality suggests that there are some problems with the theory. Indeed, there are several…

Technology in Economic Growth [T]he theory of free trade is fundamentally flawed because it fails to take account of the ways in which production itself affects technological change. "Learning-by-doing" is a particularly important form of the phenomenon. In a new activity, initial production may be very costly. Yet as time passes and experience accumulates, the people engaged in the activity learn. They change the way they do things, which is to say that they change the technology. Such an activity might never develop were it forced to compete with already established firms in other countries where the learning-by-doing had already taken place. Yet if the activity were protected from foreign competition during an initial phase in which experience could be accumulated, it could develop and become fully competitive...

Yet protection involves costs. Why should society in general bear the costs of protection in order to assure the development of any particular activity?... The answer to these questions lies in the concept of *location specific technological externalities*. Different kinds of production activities tend to bring about different kinds of changes in the overall economic environment. In the 18th and 19th century, for example, manufacturing tended to generate new methods of production and a development of skills that had far reaching technological impacts. In the current era, "high tech" production appears to have similar far reaching impacts. Because the gains from these sorts of changes are not confined to the industry or firm where they originate, they are not reflected in the profits of that industry or firm and will not be taken into account as a basis for investment decisions. These positive technological impacts of particular production activity that do not affect the profits and are outside of—or external to—the purview of the people making decisions about that production are "technological externalities." When positive technological externalities exist for a particular activity, then the value of that activity to society will be greater than the private value... [T]echnological externalities are often "location specific," having their greatest impact within relatively close geographic proximity to the site where they are originally generated—or at least having their principal impact within the same national unit....

The U.S. experience with the cotton textile industry, which I have cited above, provides a particularly good example of the generation of location specific technological externalities. The textile industry emerged in the early decades of the 19th century, prospering especially in the Northeastern part of the United States. Mill towns throughout southern New England became centers of growth. Not only did they create a demand for Southern cotton, but they also created a demand for new machinery, maintenance of old machinery, parts, dyes, *skills*, construction materials, construction machinery, *more skills*, equipment to move the raw materials and the products, parts and maintenance for that equipment, *and still more skills*. As centers of economic activity, innovation, and change, mill towns made a contribution to the economic growth of the United States that went far beyond the value of the textiles they produced...

Trade and Employment The theory of comparative advantage and arguments for free trade rest on the assumption that full employment exists, or at least that the level of employment is independent of the *pattern* of trade and production. In addition, the theory assumes that when patterns of trade and production change, labor will move from one activity to another instantaneously—or at least sufficiently rapidly so as to cause no great welfare loss or disruption of overall demand. In reality, most low income countries are characterized by very high levels of unemployment and underemployment, the pattern of trade and production does affect employment levels (at least in the short run), and labor markets adjust to change relatively slowly...

An illustration of the problems is provided by experience in many low income countries when trade restrictions on grain imports are lifted... In Mexico, where the internationalization of grain supply was proceeding apace in the 1980s, even before the establishment of the North American Free Trade Agreement (NAFTA), the replacement of peasant grain production by imports has not worked out so favorably. In fact, those parts of agriculture that have expanded in recent years—meat production and vegetable exports, for example—and export manu-facturing use relatively small amounts of labor. Peasants displaced by the import of inexpensive U.S. and Canadian grain, instead of finding employment in these sectors, swell the ranks of the unemployed or underemployed, often in cities. Consequently, instead of labor resources being used more efficiently under the pressure of import competition, labor resources are wasted...

Free Trade and Large Firms The neo-liberal argument for free trade is based on the assumption that if government did not intervene and regulate international commerce, then the economy would operate in a competitive manner with ad-vantageous results... International commerce, however, is often dominated by a relatively small number of very large firms that operate in a monopolistic manner. Competition among them exists, and in some cases is very intense. It is, however, monopolistic competition, not simply the price competition that is assumed in the argument for free trade. The patterns of trade and production engaged in by very large firms are determined as part of their complex global strategies—with results that do not necessarily coincide with either the price competition model of the free trade argument or the long run development interests of a particular country...

Large firms are sensitive to price considerations, and they are often quick to re-locate production to take advantage of low cost resources. Yet resource costs, the foundation of the theory of comparative advantage, are only one element in the strategies of large, internationally integrated firms. The Japanese automobile companies, for example, established their leading role in the industry through a strategy of developing linkages to suppliers in close physical proximity to the central plant. Resource costs were secondary to the issue of strategic control, which had important impacts on technological change and the management of inventory. In the international textile industry, flexibility is a paramount concern in the strategy of large firms, and issues of market proximity and control over product supply stand along side of resource costs as factors determining the loca-tion of production. Similarly, in the semi-conductor production of the electronics industry, many firms (particularly U.S. firms) have followed a strategy of vertical integration. When companies produce semi-conductors for use in their own final products, their location decisions tend to be dominated by concerns about control of the technology and production process; concerns about least-cost siting tend to be secondary. In all of these examples, selected from industries that are both highly international in their operations and in which very large companies play central roles, monopolistic firms employ strategies of control that enhance their own long run profits. There is no reason to expect the outcomes to conform to those envisioned in the theoretical arguments for free trade...

Primary Product Problems When the argument for free trade was developed in the 19th century, it was a rationalization for the particular character of the international division of labor that emerged so clearly at that time. That division of labor placed a few countries of Europe and North America in the position of specializing in the production and export of manufactured goods, while several other countries—many of which are today's low income countries—specialized in the production and export of primary products. Today, although the international division of labor has changed, there are still many low income countries characterized by primary product specialization.

Primary product specialization is problematic, first of all, because the prices of primary products are highly unstable. Primary products are, by definition, the raw materials that enter at an early stage into the production of other goods. Sugar, for example, is used largely in the manufacture of a great variety of sweets, and the cost of sugar plays a small role in affecting the final price of those sweets. Copper finds its demand as an input to houses, automobiles and other machinery. Like sugar, its cost plays a small role in determining the price of the final products of which it is a part. Grains, vanilla, cocoa, cotton, coffee and several other products fit this pattern. Consequently, the demand for such a product is very insensitive to its price (that is, the demand is very price inelastic). When the supply of a primary product increases—for example, because of good weather and a resulting good crop in some region of the world—prices will decline a great deal as producers compete with one another to unload their surpluses on the very limited market. Conversely, with a small decline in the supply—resulting, perhaps, from bad weather and a resulting crop failure—producers will be able to push up the price a great deal. Even when the average price of a primary product is in some sense "reasonable," price fluctuations create severe cyclical problems that, when the product is important, may disrupt the development of an entire national economy.

An additional problem of specialization in primary products... [is] that in general the average prices of primary products are not "reasonable," in the sense that the demand for the products is subject to long term downward pressure. Consider, for example, the case of foods—sugar, coffee, cocoa—exported from low income countries to the advanced economies of Europe and North America. As income rises in the advanced countries, the demand for food rises less rapidly... Under these circumstances, insofar as countries rely on primary product exports to the advanced countries for their national income, their national income must grow more slowly than income in those advanced countries...

INTERNATIONAL COMMERCE, INCOME DISTRIBUTION, AND POWER

The deregulation of international commerce that is envisioned in the neo-liberal model is largely, if not entirely, a deregulation of business. By removing constraints on the operation of business, it necessarily would give more power to the owners of capital. It would allow business to seek out profits with fewer constraints—on the location of production, on its sources of supply, on characteristics of production, and so on. Power is largely a question of options, and by providing more options to the owners of capital, neo-liberal globalization would give them more power. Most clearly, within a deregulated international environment, owners of capital can resist labor's demands by exercising, or threatening to exercise, their option of shifting production to regions of the world where labor costs are lower. This is not only an option of moving from high wage to low wage countries, from Britain to Sri Lanka, for example. Owners of businesses in Sri Lanka may move, or threaten to move, operations to Britain if productivity is sufficiently higher in the latter country. So the power that business gains vis-a-vis labor by the deregulation of international commerce can be important in low wage and high wage countries...

Power in economic life means primarily an ability to shift more and more of the value produced by society into one's own hands. In this way, neo-liberal globalization is a *de facto* formula for shifting income to the owners of capital, that is, for increasing inequality in the distribution of income...

Excerpted from Chapter 2 of the author's Neo-Liberalism or Democracy? Economic Strategy, Markets, and Alternatives for the 21st Century *(Zed Books, London, and St. Martin's Press, New York).*

CHAPTER 2

Corporate Power and the Global Economy

ARTICLE 6

U.S. Banks and the Dirty Money Empire

BY JAMES PETRAS

September/October 2001

Washington and the mass media have portrayed the United States as being in the forefront of the struggle against narcotics trafficking, drug-money laundering, and political corruption. The image is of clean white hands fighting dirty money from the Third World (or the ex-Communist countries). The truth is exactly the opposite. U.S. banks have developed an elaborate set of policies for transferring illicit funds to the U.S. and "laundering" those funds by investing them in legitimate businesses or U.S. government bonds. The U.S. Congress has held numerous hearings, provided detailed exposés of the illicit practices of the banks, passed several anti-laundering laws, and called for stiffer enforcement by public regulators and private bankers. Yet the biggest banks continue their practices and the sums of dirty money grow exponentially. The $500 billion of criminal and dirty money flowing annually into and through the major U.S. banks far exceeds the net revenues of all the information technology companies in the United States. These yearly inflows surpass the net profits repatriated from abroad by the major U.S. oil producers, military industries, and airplane manufacturers combined. Neither the banks nor the government has the will or the interest to put an end to practices that provide such high profits and help maintain U.S. economic supremacy internationally.

BIG U.S. BANKS AND DIRTY MONEY LAUNDERING

"Current estimates are that $500 billion to $1 trillion in illegal funds from orga-nized crime, narcotics trafficking and other criminal misconduct are laundered through banks worldwide each year," writes Senator Carl Levin (D-MI), "with about half going through U.S. banks." The senator's statement, however, only covers proceeds from activities that are crimes under U.S. law. It does not include financial transfers by corrupt political leaders or tax evasion by overseas busi-nesses, since in those cases any criminal activity takes place outside the United States. Raymond Baker, a leading U.S. expert on international finance and guest scholar in economic studies at the Brookings Institution, estimates the total "flow of corrupt money ... into Western coffers" from Third World or ex-Communist economies at $20 to $40 billion a year. He puts the "flow stemming from mis-priced trade" (the difference between the price quoted, for tax purposes, of goods sold abroad, and their real price) at a minimum of $80 billion a year. "My lowest estimate is $100 billion per year by these two means ... a trillion dollars in the decade, at least half to the United States," Baker concludes. "Including other ele-ments of illegal flight capital would produce much higher figures."

The money laundering business, whether "criminal" or "corrupt," is carried out by the United States' most important banks. The bank officials involved in money laundering have backing from the highest levels of the banking insti-tutions. These are not isolated offenses perpetrated by loose cannons. Take the case of Citibank's laundering of Raúl Salinas' $200 million account. The day after Salinas, the brother of Mexico's ex-President Carlos Salinas de Gortari, was ar-rested and his large-scale theft of government funds was exposed, his private bank manager at Citibank, Amy Elliott, said in a phone conversation with colleagues (the transcript of which was made available to Congressional investigators) that "this goes [on] in the very, very top of the corporation, this was known ... on the very top. We are little pawns in this whole thing."

Citibank is the United States' biggest bank, with 180,000 employees world-wide, operating in 100 countries, with $700 billion in known assets. It operates what are known as "private banking" offices in 30 countries, with over $100 billion in client assets. Private banking is the sector of a bank which caters to extremely wealthy clients, with deposits of $1 million or more. The big banks charge customers for managing their assets and for providing the specialized ser-vices of the private banks. These services go beyond routine banking services like check clearing and deposits, to include investment guidance, estate planning, tax assistance, off-shore accounts, and complicated schemes designed to secure the confidentiality of financial transactions. Private banks sell secrecy to their clients, making them ideal for money laundering. They routinely use code names for ac-counts. Their "concentration accounts" disguise the movement of client funds by co-mingling them with bank funds, cutting off paper trails for billions of dollars in wire transfers. And they locate offshore private investment corporations in countries such as the Cayman Islands and the Bahamas, which have strict banking secrecy laws. These laws allow offshore banks and corporations to hide a depositor's name, nationality, the amount of funds deposited, and when they were deposited. They do not require any declarations from bank officials about sources of funds.

Private investment corporations (PICs) are one particulary tricky way that big banks hold and hide a client's assets. The nominal officers, trustees, and shareholders of these shell corporations are themselves shell corporations controlled by the private bank. The PIC then becomes the official holder of the client's accounts, while the client's identity is buried in so-called "records of jurisdiction" in countries with strict secrecy laws. The big banks keep pre-packaged PICs on the shelf awaiting activation when a private bank client wants one. The system works like Russian matryoshka dolls, shells within shells within shells, which in the end can be impenetrable to legal process.

Hearings held in 1999 by the Senate's Permanent Subcommittee on Investigations (under the Governmental Affairs Committee) revealed that in the Salinas case, private banking personnel at Citibank—which has a larger global private banking operation than any other U.S. bank—helped Salinas transfer $90 to $100 million out of Mexico while disguising the funds' sources and destination. The bank set up a dummy offshore corporation, provided Salinas with a secret codename, provided an alias for a third party intermediary who deposited the money in a Citibank account in Mexico, transferred the money in a concentration account to New York, and finally moved it to Switzerland and London.

Instead of an account with the name "Raúl Salinas" attached, investigators found a Cayman Islands account held by a PIC called "Trocca, Ltd.," according to Minority Counsel Robert L. Roach of the Permanent Committee on Investigations. Three Panama shell companies formed Trocca, Ltd.'s board of directors and three Cayman shell companies were its officers and shareholders. "Citibank controls all six of these shell companies and routinely uses them to function as directors and officers of PICs that it makes available to private clients," says Roach. Salinas was only referred to in Citibank documents as "Confidential Client No. 2" or "CC-2."

Historically, big-bank money laundering has been investigated, audited, criticized, and subjected to legislation. The banks have written their own compliance procedures. But the big banks ignore the laws and procedures, and the government ignores their non-compliance. The Permanent Subcommittee on Investigations discovered that Citibank provided "services," moving a total of at least $360 million, for four major political swindlers, all of whom lost their protection when the political winds shifted in their home countries: Raúl Salinas, between $80 and $100 million; Asif Ali Zardari (husband of former Prime Minister of Pakistan), over $40 million; El Hadj Omar Bongo (dictator of Gabon since 1967), over $130 million; Mohammed, Ibrahim, and Abba Sani Abacha (sons of former

Nigerian dictator General Sani Abacha), over $110 million. In all cases Citibank violated all of its own procedures and government guidelines: there was no review of the client's background (known as the "client profile"), no determination of the source of the funds, and no inquiry into any violations of the laws of the country where the money originated. On the contrary, the bank facilitated the outflow in its prepackaged format: shell corporations were established, code names were provided, funds were moved through concentration accounts, and the funds were invested in legitimate businesses or in U.S. bonds. In none of these cases did the banks practice "due diligence," taking the steps required by law to ensure that it does not facilitate money laundering. Yet top banking officials have never been brought to court and tried. Even after the arrest of its clients, Citibank continued to provide them with its services, including moving funds to secret accounts.

Another route that the big banks use to launder dirty money is "correspondent banking." Correspondent banking is the provision of banking services by one bank to another. It enables overseas banks to conduct business and provide services for their customers in jurisdictions where the bank has no physical presence. A bank that is licensed in a foreign country and has no office in the United States can use correspondent banking to attract and retain wealthy criminal or corrupt clients interested in laundering money in the United States. Instead of exposing itself to U.S. controls and incurring the high costs of locating in the U.S., the bank will open a correspondent account with an existing U.S. bank. By establishing such a relationship, the foreign bank (called the "respondent") and its customers can receive many or all of the services offered by the U.S. bank (called the "correspondent"). Today, all the big U.S. banks have established multiple correspondent relationships throughout the world so they may engage in international financial transactions for themselves and their clients in places where they do not have a physical presence. The largest U.S. and European banks, located in financial centers like New York or London, serve as correspondents for thousands of other banks. Most of the offshore banks laundering billions for criminal clients have accounts in the United States. Through June 1999, the top five correspondent bank holding companies in the United States held correspondent account balances exceeding $17 billion; the total correspondent balances of the 75 largest U.S. correspondent banks was $34.9 billion. For billionaire criminals an important feature of correspondent relationships is that they provide access to international transfer systems. The biggest banks specializing in international fund transfers (called "money center banks") can process up to $1 trillion in wire transfers a day.

THE DAMAGE DONE

Hundreds of billions of dollars have been transferred, through the private-banking and correspondent-banking systems, from Africa, Asia, Latin America, and Eastern Europe to the biggest banks in the United States and Europe. In all these regions, liberalization and privatization of the economy have opened up lucrative opportunities for corruption and the easy movement of booty overseas. Authoritarian governments and close ties to Washington, meanwhile, have ensured impunity for most of the guilty parties. Russia alone has seen over $200 billion illegally transferred out of the country in the course of the 1990s. The massive flows of capital out of these regions—really the pillaging of these countries' wealth through the international banking system—is a major factor in their economic instability and mass impoverishment. The resulting economic crises, in turn, have made these countries more vulnerable to the prescriptions of the IMF and World Bank, including liberalized banking and financial systems that lead to further capital flight.

Even by an incomplete accounting (including both "criminal" and "corrupt" funds, but not other illicit capital transfers, such as illegal shifts of real estate or securities titles, wire fraud, etc.), the dirty money coming from abroad into U.S. banks amounted to $3.5 to $6.0 trillion during the 1990s. While this is not the whole picture, it gives us a basis for estimating the significance of the "dirty money factor" in the U.S. economy. The United States currently runs an annual trade deficit of over $400 billion. The gap has to be financed with inflows of funds from abroad—at least a third of which is "dirty money." Without the dirty money the U.S. economy's external accounts would be unsustainable. No wonder the biggest banks in the United States and Europe are actively involved, and the governments of these countries turn a blind eye. That is today's capitalism—built around pillage, criminality, corruption, and complicity.

RESOURCES "Private Banking and Money Laundering: A Case Study of Opportunities and Vulnerabilities," Permanent Subcommittee on Investigations of the Committee on Governmental Affairs, United States Senate, One Hundred Sixth Congress, November 9-10, 1000; "Report on Correspondent Banking: A Gateway to Money Laundering," Minority Staff of the U.S. Senate Permanent Subcommittee on Investigations, February 2001.

ARTICLE 7

The Business of War in the Democratic Republic of Congo

BY DENA MONTAGUE AND FRIDA BERRIGAN

July/August 2001

"This is all money," says a Western mining executive, his hand sweeping over a geological map toward the eastern Democratic Republic of Congo (DRC). He is explaining why, in 1997, he and planeloads of other businessmen were flocking to the impoverished country and vying for the attention of then-rebel leader Laurent Kabila. The executive could just as accurately have said, "This is all war."

The interplay among a seemingly endless supply of mineral resources, the greed of multinational corporations desperate to cash in on that wealth, and the provision of arms and military training to political tyrants has helped to produce the spiral of conflicts that have engulfed the continent—what many regard as "Africa's First World War."

When Westerners reach for their cell phones or pagers, turn on their computers, propose marriage with diamond rings, or board airplanes, few of them make the connection between their ability to use technology or buy luxury goods and a war raging in the DRC, half a world away. In what has been called the richest patch of earth on the planet, the DRC's wealth has also been its curse. The DRC holds millions of tons of diamonds, copper, cobalt, zinc, manganese, uranium (the atomic bombs dropped on Hiroshima and Nagasaki were built using Congolese uranium), niobium, and tantalum. Tantalum, also referred to as coltan, is a particularly valuable resource—used to make mobile phones, night vision goggles, fiber optics, and capacitors (the component that maintains the electrical charge in computer chips). In fact, a global shortage of coltan caused a wave of parental panic in the United States last Christmas when it resulted in the scarcity of the popular PlayStation 2. The DRC holds 80% of the world's coltan reserves, more than 60% of the world's cobalt, and the world's largest supply of high-grade copper.

These minerals are vital to maintaining U.S. military dominance, economic prosperity, and consumer satisfaction. Because the United States does not have a domestic supply of many essential minerals, the U.S. government identifies sources of strategic minerals, particularly in Third World countries, then encourages U.S. corporations to invest in and facilitate production of the needed materials.

Historically, the DRC (formerly Zaire) has been an important source of strategic minerals for the United States. In the mid-1960s, the U.S. government installed the dictatorship of Mobutu Sese Seko, which ensured U.S. access to those minerals for more than 30 years.

Today, the United States claims that it has no interest in the DRC other than a peaceful resolution to the current war. Yet U.S. businessmen and politicians are still going to extreme lengths to gain and preserve sole access to the DRC's mineral resources. And to protect these economic interests, the U.S. government continues to provide millions of dollars in arms and military training to known human-rights abusers and undemocratic regimes. Thus, the DRC's mineral wealth is both an impetus for war and an impediment to stopping it.

BACKGROUND TO THE WAR

Under colonialism, the Western countries perfected a system of divide-and-rule in Central Africa, callously dividing ancestral lands and orchestrating strife between ethnic groups. The current crisis represents a continuation of these insidious practices.

A flash point for the current war is the 1994 genocide in Rwanda, in which nearly one million people were killed. The U.S. government made every effort to block humanitarian intervention that could have stopped the slaughter of Rwandan Tutsis by the Hutu government, actively lobbying the United Nations to hold off on sending peacekeepers to the region. In the absence of UN forces, Paul Kagame, a U.S.-trained army commander, led the Rwandan Patriotic Front (RPF) in a military action that toppled the Hutu regime. After Kagame became Rwanda's vice president (a very powerful position) and defense minister, the United States sent $75 million in military aid to the new government. Additionally, U.S. Green Berets began to provide "humanitarian training" to Rwandan troops.

In October 1996, Kagame's RPF joined with members of Yoweri Museveni's Ugandan People's Defense Forces (UPDF) and Laurent Kabila, a Congolese rebel leader, in an invasion of Zaire. In 1997, they succeeded in toppling Mobutu. They also sought to dismantle camps controlled by the Hutu militia responsible for the Rwandan genocide. The coalition, known as the Democratic Forces for the Lib-

---

A SHORT CHRONOLOGY

October 1996 – AFDL movement begins

May 1997 – Mobutu flees Zaire; Laurent Kabila takes power in DRC

August 1998 – Rwandan and Ugandan troops invade DRC

July 1999 – Cease-fire agreement signed at Lusaka, Zambia

January 2001 – Laurent Kabila is killed; Joseph Kabila becomes President

eration of Congo-Zaire (AFDL), included U.S.-trained troops. Although Rwandan troops who participated in the AFDL invasion committed gross human-rights abuses that a UN report labeled "crimes against humanity," the U.S. government continued to provide military support to the Kagame regime.

During the conflict, U.S. corporations treated rebel-controlled Zaireian territory as open for business, even while Mobutu remained the internationally recognized leader of Zaire. Once the AFDL took control of Katanga (one of the DRC's richest mineral patches), Western friends and allies began negotiating with Kabila for access to mineral resources.

Under rebel leadership, the method of exploiting these resources fundamentally changed. During Mobutu's reign, locally based Congolese strongmen had controlled the distribution of resources on the government's behalf, effectively limiting the potential for massive mining deals. But after the AFDL invasion, well-connected Western businessmen were able to secure much larger mining interests than in previous years.

For example, in May 1997, American Mineral Fields (AMF)—whose chair is Mike McMurrough, a personal friend of President Clinton—cut a $1 billion mining deal with Kabila. According to Kabila advisors and news reports, the negotiations began immediately after Kabila captured Goma (a city right across the border with Rwanda) in February 1997, and were handled by Kabila's U.S.-trained finance commissioner. The deal allowed AMF to perform feasibility studies on reactivating the Kipushi mine, a high-grade zinc and copper deposit. The

WHO'S WHO IN THE DRC CONFLICT

THE LEADERS

Mobutu Sese Seko – President of Zaire, 1966-1997

Paul Kagame – Vice President and Minister of Defense of Rwanda, 1994-2000; President of Rwanda, 2000-present

Yoweri Musevini – President of Uganda, 1986-present

Laurent Kabila – President of the DRC, 1997-2001

Joseph Kabila (son of Laurent Kabila) – President of the DRC, 2001-present

THE ORGANIZATIONS

RPF – Rwandan Patriotic Front (led by Paul Kagame)

UPDF – Ugandan People's Defense Forces (led by Yoweri Museveni)

AFDL – Democratic Forces for the Liberation of Congo-Zaire (coalition of RPF, UPDF, and Kabila-led Congolese rebels)

RCD-Goma – Congolese Rally for Democracy (DRC rebels allied with Rwanda)

CLF – Congolese Liberation Front (DRC rebels allied with Uganda)

company also landed exclusive exploration rights to an estimated 1.4 million tons of copper and 270,000 tons of cobalt (about ten times the volume of current world cobalt production). While AMF admits that political problems have slowed the pace of its DRC operations, the company continues to develop plans for the Kipushi mine.

Also in 1997, Bechtel, the engineering and construction company, established a strong relationship with Kabila. Bechtel—whose history of collaboration with the CIA is well-documented in Laton McCartney's 1989 book, *Friends in High Places*—drew up a master development plan and inventory of the country's mineral resources free of charge. Bechtel also commissioned and paid for NASA satellite studies of the country for infrared maps of its mineral potential. Bechtel estimates that the DRC's mineral ores alone are worth $157 billion.

At the same time, Kabila enjoyed the support of Western military interests. Kabila was in frequent contact with Richard Orth, former deputy of the U.S. Defense Intelligence Agency for Africa. The agency, which operates as an arm of the Pentagon, supplies military intelligence to warfighters and weapons dealers around the world. During the Clinton administration, Orth was appointed U.S. military attaché to Kigali, the Rwandan capital, shortly before Kabila began his march across the DRC. Additionally, former Pentagon officials acted as military advisers to Kabila in Goma, producing a dangerous mix of business, politics, and military power.

RENEWED WAR IN THE EAST

After Kabila's rise to power, the desire for mineral wealth helped to escalate conflict between the DRC on the one hand and Rwanda and Uganda on the other. In August 1998, after falling out with Kabila, Kagame of Rwanda and Museveni of Uganda launched a new invasion of the DRC. Both leaders claimed that they entered the DRC to undermine Kabila's power and protect their borders from rebel groups that threatened to destabilize their countries.

In the name of pursuing peace, Kabila's former allies have been able to advance their own mineral interests. During the AFDL war, top Rwandan and Ugandan military officials learned first-hand about the lucrative business of mining. Since the 1998 war began, territories controlled by Rwandan- and Ugandan-supported rebel groups have become *de facto* states where mining companies have openly expressed interest in investing. Rwanda is allied with Congolese Rally for Democracy (RCD-Goma), while the Ugandan government has formed a close relationship with leaders of the Congolese Liberation Front (CLF), a Mobutuist rebel movement. The RCD and the CLF now control the entire eastern region of the DRC, the wealthiest in terms of natural resources.

Both Rwanda and Uganda provide arms and training to their respective rebel allies and have set up extensive links to facilitate the exploitation of mineral resources. Along with their rebel allies, the two countries seized raw materials stockpiled in DRC territory and looted money from DRC banks. Rwanda and Uganda also set up colonial-style systems of governance, appointing local authorities to oversee their territories in the DRC. Meanwhile, high-ranking members of the Rwandan and Uganda military (including relatives of Kagame and Museveni) retain significant control over illegal mineral exploitation. Local Congolese, including children, are forced to work in the mines for little or no pay, under guard of Rwandan and Ugandan troops. Rwanda prisoners also participate in mining. To transport weapons to the rebels in the DRC, and to fly resources out of the DRC to Rwanda and Uganda, the authorities rely on private companies owned or controlled by Kagame's and Museveni's friends and relatives. They also utilize international connections made during the AFDL war.

The illegal mining has been a huge windfall for Rwanda and Uganda. The two countries have very few mineral reserves of their own. But since they began extracting the DRC's resources, their mineral exports have increased dramatically. For example, between 1996 and 1997, the volume of Rwanda's coltan production doubled, bringing the Rwandans and their rebel allies up to $20 million a month in revenue. Also, the volume of Rwanda's diamond exports rose from about 166 carats in 1998 to some 30,500 in 2000—a 184-fold increase! From 1997 to 1998, the annual volume of Uganda's diamond exports jumped from approximately 1,500 carats to about 11,300, or nearly eight-fold; since 1996, Ugandan gold exports have increased tenfold. The final destination for many of these minerals is the United States.

Western corporations and financial institutions have encouraged the exploitation. For example, in 1999, RCD-Goma's financial arm—known as SONEX—received $5 million in loans from Citibank New York. Additionally, a member of the U.S. Ambassador to the DRC's honorary council in Bukavu has been promoting deals between U.S. companies and coltan dealers in the eastern region. He is also acting chair of a group of coltan-exporting companies based in Bukavu. (Bukavu is located in RCD-held territory.)

U.S. military aid has contributed significantly to the crisis. During the Cold War, the U.S. government shipped $400 million in arms and training to Mobutu. After Mobutu was overthrown, the Clinton administration transferred its military allegiance to Rwanda and Uganda, although even the U.S. State Department has accused both countries of widespread corruption and human-rights abuses. During his historic visit to Africa in 1998, President Clinton praised Presidents Kagame and Musevini as leaders of the "African Renaissance," just a few months before they launched their deadly invasion of the DRC with U.S. weapons and training. The United States is not the only culprit; many other countries, including France, Serbia, North Korea, China, and Belgium, share responsibility. But the U.S. presence has helped to open networks and supply lines, providing an increased number of arms to the region.

The International Monetary Fund (IMF) and World Bank have knowingly contributed to the war effort. The international lending institutions praised both Rwanda and Uganda for increasing their gross domestic product (GDP), which resulted from the illegal mining of DRC resources. Although the IMF and World Bank were aware that the rise in GDP coincided with the DRC war, and that it was derived from exports of natural resources that neither country normally produced, they nonetheless touted both nations as economic success stories. Although Uganda in particular has made significant strides in improving access to education and reducing the rate of new AIDS infections, debt relief has also allowed it the space to appropriate more money for its military ventures.

Although rebels control half of the DRC's territory, deals with the Congolese government itself are still attractive. In January 2000, Chevron—the corporation that named an oil tanker after National Security Advisor Condoleezza Rice—announced a three-year, $75 million spending program in the DRC, thus challenging the notion that war discourages foreign investment. In 1999, the company, which has been present in the Congo for 40 years, was producing 17,700 barrels of oil a day. It hopes that, by 2002, production will increase to 21,000 barrels per day. The gamble seems to be paying off. When Joseph Kabila, Laurent Kabila's son and successor, visited the United States in 2001, he reassured Chevron officials that stability under his leadership would ensure a safe environment for investment.

Of course, because of war and ongoing political unrest, these deals may not endure. But considering the potential for billions of dollars in profits, many mining corporations believe the investment is worth the risk. As one investor put it, "It is a good moment to come: it is in difficult times that you can get the most advantage."

PROSPECTS FOR PEACE

In August 1999, Uganda, Rwanda, and their rebel allies, among others, signed a cease-fire agreement with the DRC at Lusaka, Zambia. The agreement, which the U.S. government heavily supported, gave the Rwandan- and Ugandan-backed rebels significant power in developing a new Congolese government. It also allowed them to collaborate with the Congolese army in monitoring the withdrawal of foreign troops. If implemented, the Lusaka accord could bring the peace and stability that some Western corporations prefer.

But the demand for mineral resources continues to drive the DRC conflict. In April 2001, a scathing UN report argued that Presidents Kagame and Museveni are "on the verge of becoming the godfathers of the illegal exploitation of natural resources and the continuation of the conflict in the Democratic Republic of Congo." The two leaders, the report alleged, have turned their armies into "armies of business."

In light of these findings, the UN report calls for sweeping restrictions on Uganda, Rwanda, and their Congolese-based rebel allies. These would include:

embargoing the import or export of strategic minerals; embargoing the supply of weapons; freezing the financial assets of rebel movements and their leaders; and freezing the assets of companies or individuals who continue to illegally exploit the DRC's natural resources.

These proposals, however, would obstruct Western corporations' access to strategic minerals. Not surprisingly, the U.S. State Department has indicated that it is unlikely to recommend sanctions against its African allies. According to East African media reports, U.S. diplomats continue to view Rwanda and Uganda as "strategic allies in the Great Lakes region" and "would not want to upset relations with them at this time." Additionally, UN sources say that James Cunningham, the U.S. Ambassador to the UN, has simply asked Uganda to "address in a constructive way" the UN's findings. The IMF and World Bank have also indicated that their policies toward Rwanda and Uganda will remain unchanged.

Since 1994, close to four million people have perished in Rwanda and the eastern region of Congo. Many of the deaths are due to direct combat and torture by the belligerent parties, but most have been caused by starvation and malnutrition. Health services are practically nonexistent, and even where they do exist, many cannot reach them. Thousands of people hiding in the forest from soldiers have watched their villages burned to the ground and their families tortured. Soldiers have looted their possessions, their crops, and their life's savings. Foreign soldiers have manipulated ethnic tensions and encouraged neighbor killing neighbor. Oblivious to the suffering, many Westerners continue to reap the benefits of the rich Congolese soil.

Despite recent troop withdrawals, the illegal mining and trade continues unabated. The real party fueling the conflict is foreign capital investment by corporations, with the tacit support of their own governments. This war of genocidal proportions cannot end until U.S. and other Western corporations and governments are forced to change their priorities. Amnesty International, Human Rights Watch, and other organizations have helped to raise international awareness about the urgency of the situation in the DRC, through campaigns against "blood diamonds," economic exploitation, and the massive humanitarian crisis the country faces.

But the DRC's future is in the hands of its youth, the next generation, the students and grassroots organizers who are dedicated to establishing peace and stability in their country. It remains to be seen whether the United States will encourage this hopeful spirit of change and democracy, or continue to enable the exploitation and destruction of the most resource-rich country on the African continent.

ARTICLE 8

Enron in the Third World

BY THE INSTITUTE FOR POLICY STUDIES

July/August 2002, excerpted October 2003

The Institute for Policy Studies' (IPS) 2002 report, Enron's Pawns: How Public Institutions Bankrolled Enron's Globalization Game, *documents the extent to which Enron's ascendancy depended on public-sector financial assistance and governmental support for energy privatization policies worldwide. Since 1992, the U.S. government, the World Bank, and other government institutions have approved $7.2 billion in public financing for Enron's activities in 29 countries, with U.S. support totaling over $4 billion. These public actors also leveraged Enron's rise by actively promoting the deregulation of developing countries' energy sectors. The devastating consequences for these nations have included price hikes and blackouts more severe than California's and leading on numerous occasions to street rioting and state repression—and sometimes to protesters' deaths.*

The IPS report highlights Enron's misadventures in seven countries while detailing the role of public institutions in the company's activities in the United States and abroad. The excerpts below present the study's key findings and outline the efforts of the World Bank and Enron to forge a common agenda.

The full report can be found on IPS' Sustainable Energy and Economy Network website <www.seen.org>. —Aziza Agia

Many public officials have described Enron's demise as the product of corporate misbehavior. This perspective ignores a vital fact: Enron would not have scaled such grand global heights, nor fallen so dramatically, without its close financial relationships with government agencies.

Since 1992, at least 21 agencies, representing the U.S. government, multilateral development banks, and other national governments, helped leverage Enron's global reach by approving $7.219 billion in public financing toward 38 projects in 29 countries.

The now-fallen giant, until recently the country's seventh largest corporation, marched into risky projects abroad, backed by the "deep pockets" of government financing and with the firm, and at times forceful, assistance of U.S. officials and their counterparts in international organizations. Enron's overseas operations rewarded shareholders temporarily but often punished the people and governments of foreign countries with price hikes and blackouts worse than what California suffered in 2001, causing social unrest and riots that were sometimes brutally repressed. For example:

- In the Dominican Republic, eight people were killed when police were brought in to quell riots after blackouts lasting up to 20 hours followed a power price hike that Enron and other private firms initiated. The local population was further enraged by allegations that a local affiliate of Arthur Andersen had undervalued the newly privatized utility by almost $1 billion, reaping enormous profits for Enron.
- In India, police hired by the power consortium of which Enron was a part beat non-violent protesters who challenged the $30 billion agreement—the largest deal in Indian history—struck between local politicians and Enron.
- The president of Guatemala tried to dissolve the Congress and declare martial law after rioting ensued, following a price hike that the government deemed necessary after selling the power sector to Enron.
- In Panama, the man who negotiated the asking price for Enron's stake in power production was the brother-in-law of the head of the country's state-owned power company. Rioting followed suspicions of corruption, Enron's price hikes, and power outages.
- In Colombia, two politicians resigned amid accusations that one was trying to push a cut-rate deal for Enron on the state-owned power company.

While all this was occurring, the U.S. government and other public agencies continued to advocate on Enron's behalf, threatening poor countries like Mozambique with an end to aid if they did not accept Enron's bid on a natural gas field. So linked was Enron with the U.S. government in many people's minds that they assumed, as the late Croatian strongman Franjo Tjudman did, that pleasing Enron meant pleasing the White House. For Tjudman, he hoped that compliance with an overpriced Enron contract might parlay into an array of political favors, from softer treatment at The Hague's War Crimes Tribunal to the entry of his country into the World Trade Organization.

Only when Enron's scandals began to affect Americans did these same government officials and institutions hold the corporation at arm's length. And only when Enron leadership revealed their greed on home turf did it become the biggest corporate scandal in recent U.S. history.

THE WORLD BANK, INDIA, AND ENRON IN THE 1990S

The history of the United States' experiments with power and energy supplies over the past century has proven that public, regulated power utilities tend to provide both cheaper and more reliable service than their private counterparts. Unregulated utilities not only tend to impose higher prices on household consumers; they also strip away transparency, accountability, and citizen oversight from their operations. Deregulation has proven disastrous in the United States—with the California energy crisis costing the state billions of dollars...

Nevertheless, in 1991, India was willing to take desperate measures to attract foreign investors. Capital was fleeing the country, while foreign exchange reserves were low. The World Bank's largest client at the time, India was getting heavy pressure from the lender to change its policies and allow private capital into certain sectors, particularly its petroleum sector. Prime Minister Narasimha Rao decided to bow to World Bank pressure and allowed foreign direct investment into the country after decades of economic protectionism. Power sector privatization plans drawn up by the World Bank soon followed.

It was shortly thereafter that Enron came calling. Claiming to be one of the "world's leading power companies" (though the company was only six years old and its actual production of power amounted to several hundred megawatts globally), Enron proposed to set up a natural gas power plant in the town of Dabhol, in the western Indian state of Maharashtra... The size of the Dabhol power plant, 2,500 megawatts, would more than double Enron's power production globally.

In the fine print of the memorandum of understanding Enron and General Electric signed with the Maharashtra State Electricity Board (MSEB) on June 20, 1992, was buried the fact that the MSEB would owe Enron $35 billion over the life of the contract, regardless of how much power the state consumed. This deal would have been the single largest purchase in the history of India. After learning of the deal, India's other branches of government began to object, and the squabbles began.

Meanwhile, Enron's Ken Lay and former CEO Rebecca Mark began courting the World Bank, lobbying the Bank for support of their Dabhol project in India. Though the Bank refused to support the project, citing [its] "adverse financial impact" ... on the MSEB, Enron succeeded in gaining financial backers at the Overseas Private Investment Corporation (OPIC), the Export-Import Bank, and elsewhere.

Lay and Mark also succeeded in garnering other favors, including a formal exchange of staff through the World Bank's Staff Exchange Program and other relationship-building exercises. At the 1996 World Bank annual meetings, NGOs [nongovernmental organizations] observed, poverty and social development were not the focus of the meetings. Instead, they reported, "Special pleadings to the Annual Meeting [were] made by corporate presidents, such as Enron's Ken Lay, not by poor people or their representatives... Lay and other corporate representatives have also been pleading their case with the U.S. Congress through a task force on multilateral development banks chaired by Senator Bill Bradley and Representative John Kasich."

Though Lay gained access to top officials at the World Bank, he complained that World Bank officials were blocking guarantees for their projects. His efforts paid off here, too—with three Multilateral Investment Guarantee Agency (MIGA) guarantees in 1996, 1997 and 2001, totalling $80 million, for its power projects in Hainan Island, China; East Java, Indonesia; and Bahia las Minas, Panama.

However, the East Java project, joined at the hip with Suharto, shared the ruler's demise. Enron then filed the first-ever claim to MIGA. In 2000, MIGA paid Enron $15 million for its political risk insurance claim on the cancelled East Java 500-megawatt power plant in Indonesia. MIGA demanded—and received last year—reimbursement from the new Indonesian government, citing the dictates of "international law."...

While the World Bank Group—the International Bank for Reconstruction and Development, the IDA, the International Finance Corporation, and MIGA—ultimately provided less financing for Enron-related projects—$761 million for 12 projects over the last decade—than OPIC [which provided $2.62 billion], they played a key role in Enron's global reach in other ways.

DEREGULATION, THE WORLD BANK, AND ENRON

Deregulation proved to be a more indirect, but extremely helpful, way in which the World Bank advanced Enron's global agenda. Here is how it worked: The World Bank would issue loans for privatization of the energy or the power sector in a developing country or make this a condition of further loans, and Enron would be amongst the first, and often the most successful, bidders to enter the country's newly privatized or deregulated energy markets.

... Enron's activities in Argentina, Bolivia, Colombia, Dominican Republic, Guatemala, Mozambique, and Panama reveal ways in which the World Bank acted as a pawn for Enron, allowing the corporation entrée into some of the poorest countries in the world. As in Dabhol, India, the changes the two institutions introduced made things worse for the poor; protests and riots—even deaths—ensued as a result. But in almost all cases, Enron came out unscathed, paying no price in the form of restricted access to future capital, despite a growing list of dubious, and controversial practices.

ARTICLE 9

"We Can't Just Up and Move"

Camden Residents Take Polluters to Court

BY HEIDI VOGT

March/April 2003

Camden, New Jersey, was always a factory town—the city hosted more than 125 manufacturers at the end of the 19th century. But most of those factories are gone now, and Camden has been left with one particular type of industry: the polluting plants that only the most desperate cities would accept.

Camden depends on its 30 recycling plants, a trash incinerator, and a sewage treatment facility for jobs and tax revenue. But many of Camden's citizens are experiencing health problems as a result, and they say that's too high a price to pay for low-road economic growth.

"It's not that we're against anybody having a business or a job," said Bonnie Sanders, president of South Camden Citizens for Action. But as a result of the air pollution, "people are suffering, especially the children." According to one neighborhood survey, 60% of people living near the factories in South Camden report respiratory problems—twice the rate of people living in North Camden, away from the plants.

And so residents of Camden have made this city of 80,000 a testing ground for the environmental justice movement. Three large environmental lawsuits are currently in the courts accusing businessmen and city officials of taking advantage of low-income residents. Such a concentration of environmental justice cases in one area is unprecedented in the United States.

Sanders' group is one of the plaintiffs in a lawsuit to close down the St. Lawrence Cement factory that opened in 2000 in South Camden. She argues that the plant is poisoning residents who can't afford to live elsewhere.

"People here worked most of their lives to buy their homes," says Sanders. "We can't just up and move."

Camden is one of the poorest cities in the country and has the highest infant mortality rate in the state of New Jersey. About 90% of the residents of the Waterfront South neighborhood of South Camden—located beside the cement factory—are African-American or Latino. The median household income in the neighborhood is $15,000, less than one-fourth of the $67,000 statewide median.

A second suit claims that St. Lawrence is lowering property values and creating a nuisance in the neighborhood by sending diesel trucks loaded with slag, a metal waste, through city streets. The third lawsuit charges the city of Camden with knowingly selling contaminated water to residents.

In April 2001, it looked like local activists had succeeded in their fight to shut down the St. Lawrence Cement factory: a federal judge demanded that the company stop construction on the $50 million facility. But the decision was overturned on appeal on the grounds that the plaintiffs could not sue under the statute they used. The suit has been returned to a lower court. The other suits have yet to be decided.

Big industry and activists alike are watching Camden to see what precedents these suits will set for protecting poor neighborhoods from toxic waste and polluting industry.

ARTICLE 10

The Real Winners
A Rogue's Gallery of War Profiteers

BY TODD TAVARES

July/August 2003

Even as bombs were raining down on Baghdad in spring 2003, a short list of private beneficiaries was being drawn up behind closed doors. As the invasion entered its final phase, the United States Agency for International Development (USAID) and the Army Corps of Engineers (funded through the Pentagon) began doling out contracts. Citing security concerns and time constraints, they hand picked the companies that would be allowed to bid for the contracts (American firms only, thank you), and in some cases they awarded colossal sums with no bidding at all.

USAID, whose mission is to further "America's foreign policy interests in expanding democracy and free markets while improving the lives of the citizens of the developing world," invited 21 firms to bid on eight contracts worth $1.7 billion. Many of the contract details have not been revealed to American taxpayers or the Iraqi people. A look at the past records of the companies that received contracts reveals that most have long histories of project work with USAID, specialize in privatization, and maintain strong political connections. These are the firms that benefited most from the reconstruction largesse. In fact, they may be the war's real winners.

Where two figures are given for award amount, the low number is money allocated to begin work and the high number is the estimated final cost.

STEVEDORING SERVICES OF AMERICA (SSA)

Seattle-based private operator of port facilities.
Awarded: $4.8 million (initially)
For: Seaport Administration (to assess Umm Qasr port facilities; develop improvement plan; hire port pilots; facilitate cargo-handling services; coordinate transport shipments from Umm Qasr)

Stevedoring Services of America is the largest marine and rail-cargo handler in the United States and the largest terminal operator in the world, with annual revenue of $1 billion. A notorious union-buster, SSA is the dominant member of the Pacific Maritime Association (PMA), the stevedoring trade association responsible for paying longshore workers. Joseph Miniace, the PMA president alleged to have been installed by SSA, worked for years to break union power by outsourcing and automating the ports. It was the International Longshore and Warehouse Union's (ILWU) effort to resist his changes and maintain full unionization that prompted the PMA to lock out port workers in September 2002.

After USAID gave SSA the Iraq contract, its security office discovered that the firm did not have the necessary security clearance. Instead of revoking the contract and awarding it to a company with the correct clearance credentials, USAID waived the requirement.

INTERNATIONAL RESOURCES GROUP (IRG)

Washington, D.C.-based private consulting firm.
Awarded: $7.1 million minimum (90 day initial contract, renewable for two additional 1-year terms)
For: Personnel Support (to provide technical expertise for reconstruction)

USAID contacted International Resources Group to discuss the post-war reconstruction contract in January 2003, well before the U.S. and allied invasion began, according to the *Washington Post*. Granted, the agency and the consulting conglomerate have a longstanding relationship—since 1978, USAID has awarded IRG over 200 contracts amounting to hundreds of millions of dollars. About one-third of the company's total business is done for USAID. Its other projects are funded by government agencies, foreign states, the World Bank, and the Asian Development Bank. IRG also does extensive energy-related consulting work in the private sector, notably for large oil firms. Its contract to provide personnel services for the reconstruction of Iraq was "sole sourced," meaning the job was simply handed to IRG. No other bids were solicited.

ABT ASSOCIATES, INC.

Cambridge, Massachusetts-based government and business consulting firm; employee owned and for-profit.

Awarded: $10 million to $43.8 million (12 month contract)

For: Public Health (supporting the Iraqi Ministry of Health; delivering health services; providing medical equipment and supplies; training and recruiting health staff; providing health education and information; and determining the specific needs of the health sector and vulnerable populations such as women and children)

One of the largest for-profit research and consulting firms in the world, ABT's clients include governments, international organizations, business and industry, foundations, and nonprofit associations. One of its specialty areas is privatization. The firm offers client states "technical assistance to facilitate policy reforms in countries moving from command economies to market-oriented economies." The firm helped privatize government-owned pharmaceutical industries in Kazakhstan and worked on other privatization efforts in the former Soviet Union involving health, financing, and service delivery activities. ABT has also undertaken privatization projects in Central America, the Caribbean, African and Asia. USAID has a history of funding these "market-based reforms."

CREATIVE ASSOCIATES INTERNATIONAL, INC. (CAII)

Washington, D.C.-based private for-profit international consulting firm.

Awarded: $1 million to $62.6 million (12-month contract)

For: Primary and Secondary Education (to increase enrollment and quality; provide necessary supplies; retain students and increase baseline indicators)

Since 1977, Creative Associates International has assisted "the stabilization of post-conflict environments" in many countries—including such casualties of U.S.-sponsored conflict as Angola, El Salvador, Guatemala, and Nicaragua, according to its website. Ninety percent of its business is funded by USAID. In March, CAII snagged an agency grant of $6 million to produce textbooks for students in Afghanistan. It won the bid over the previous bid-holder, the University of Nebraska at Omaha (UNO). UNO had insisted the textbooks be produced by Afghans themselves in order to employ residents of Kabul and provide a small measure of self-sufficiency to the Afghan people. CAII promptly transferred the printing to Indonesia, resulting in job losses in Kabul.

RESEARCH TRIANGLE INSTITUTE (RTI)

Research Triangle Park, North Carolina-based nonprofit research and development organization.

Awarded: $7.9 million to $167.9 million (12 month contract)

For: Local Governance (strengthening of management skills and capacity of local administrations and civic institutions; training programs in communications, conflict resolution, leadership skills and political analysis)

Research Triangle Institute does a strange mix of business through its 12 offices. The 2,100-person firm helps transfer NASA research to the private sector, "commercializing" NASA's technologies and "bringing them to markets." It also receives Defense Department funding. RTI was recently awarded a USAID grant for $60 million to implement Pakistan's "Education Sector Reform Action," a plan for reforming Pakistan's education system, increasing literacy, and increasing public-private partnerships in the education sector. In Iraq the firm will provide local governance support through a project dubbed the "Iraq Sub-National Governance and Civic Institution Support Program." Little detailed information about the program has been made public.

BECHTEL GROUP

San Francisco-based, private for-profit engineering and construction firm; one of the largest in the world.
Awarded: $34.6 million to $680 million (18 month contract)
For: Capital Construction (to repair and rehabilitate water, power, and sewage infrastructure; repair and upgrade Umm Qasr seaport; repair hospitals, schools, ministry buildings, irrigation and transportation links)

The construction giant now in control of repairing the water and irrigation systems of Iraq is a renowned water privatizer. A Bechtel subsidiary privatized the water of Cochabamba, Bolivia in the late 1990s, making it unaffordable to the poor. Massive protests ensued, in which at least six people were killed and hundreds injured by the police. When the Bolivian government canceled the company's contract, the firm sued for loss of potential profit.

The $13.3 billion family-owned conglomerate has strong connections to the current and previous Republican administrations. In fact, a revolving door between Bechtel and Washington has been spinning around for decades. Caspar Weinberger was a Bechtel executive before he became Secretary of Defense under Reagan. Former CIA Director William Casey also rose from the Bechtel ranks.

Current Bechtel board member George Shultz was president and director of the company from 1974 until he became Secretary of State under Reagan in 1982. Earlier this year, the good Mr. Schultz cheered loudly for the Iraq war, not only in op-ed pieces, but also as a member of the Committee for the Liberation of Iraq (CLI), an eclectic mix of warmongers—Democrat and Republican—lobbying for combat. The CLI included former Senator Bob Kerrey, former House speaker Newt Gingrich, and Senators John McCain (R-Ariz.) and Joseph Lieberman (D-Conn.).

In February 2003, President Bush appointed company CEO (and Republican

Party loyalist) Riley Bechtel to the Export Council, a group dedicated to expanding the U.S. export market. Other senior executives of Bechtel who double as government advisors include Senior Vice President Jack Sheehan, who advises the Pentagon through the Defense Policy Board, and Senior Vice President Daniel Chao, who serves on the advisory committee of the U.S. Export-Import Bank.

Bechtel is also a major campaign contributor—its employees gave $1.3 million to federal candidates and party committees between 1999 and 2002 (59% to Republicans, 41% to Democrats).

Another interesting plotline in the story of Bechtel's contract coup is the company's relationship with the current head of USAID, Andrew Natsios. As chairman of the Massachusetts Turnpike Authority in 2000-2001, Natsios worked closely with Bechtel on Boston's "Big Dig" construction project—Bechtel was and is the project's principal contractor. In the 1980s, Bechtel estimated the Big Dig's price tag would be $2.5 billion. Since then the cost has ballooned by more than 560% to over $14 billion due in large part to Bechtel mismanagement and the lack of state oversight of its work. When Natsios took over the Turnpike Authority, he promised to rein in the overruns. He worked with Bechtel to renegotiate its Big Dig contract, and succeeded in reducing their management fees. But Natsios permitted the Bechtel team to continue to review and evaluate their own work, basically changing little. During Natsios' tenure, the cost estimate of the Big Dig continued to rise. A few months after he left for his post at USAID, $300 million more in cost overruns were announced. Natsios denies allegations that he gave preferential treatment to Bechtel for the Iraq reconstruction contract.

KELLOGG BROWN AND ROOT (KBR) (A HALLIBURTON SUBSIDIARY)

KBR is the engineering and construction wing of the Houston, Texas-based petroleum and gas service firm; Halliburton is publicly traded on NYSE (HAL).
Amount: Unlimited
For: Repair of Petroleum Infrastructure (putting out oil fires, contingency planning)

The contract to extinguish and repair the oil infrastructure of Iraq is the true gem of the reconstruction spoils. For starters it is a "cost plus" contract in which the government pays the total cost of work done, plus a profit. The Army Corps of Engineers predicts the total value will amount to $7 billion over two years with KBR taking 7% (about $490 million) as profit. The contract also gives KBR the right to produce and sell oil inside the country of Iraq. Remarkably, this was a closed-door handout granted to KBR without bidding.

It seems odd that the Halliburton subsidiary would be chosen for the plum contract, given that a recent KBR contract in the Balkans resulted in $2 million in fines to resolve claims that the firm committed fraud. And KBR recently admitted to the SEC that it had bribed Nigerian officials to avoid paying its fair share of taxes. This is not exactly the type of organization you'd think the administration would want heading the "we're here to help you" parade in a newly occupied country.

But Halliburton is not only a darling of Republican fundraisers—95% of its $700,000 donations between 1999 and 2002 went to Republican candidates—the company also has an intimate relationship with vice president Dick Cheney, a relationship that helps explain the firm's good fortune. As Secretary of Defense under George H. W. Bush, Cheney hired then-Brown and Root to consult the army about privatizing army jobs. Brown and Root would later win a contract to provide worldwide logistics for the Army Corps of Engineers. When Cheney became Halliburton CEO (1995-2000), the company became the 18th largest Pentagon contractor, up from 73rd. Cheney also helped change tax payments of $302,000,000 in 1998 to tax refunds of $85,000,000 in 1999 in part by quintupling its offshore subsidiaries. Since he left Halliburton to run for vice president, Cheney has continued to receive deferred compensation from his former company of between $100,000 and $1,000,000 per year.

QUALCOMM, INC.

San Diego-based, publicly traded wireless communications technology firm.
Awarded: Nothing

Although it has not yet been decided who will build the cell-phone network in post-war Iraq, it seems likely that it will be built to the specifications of GSM technology—the Middle East and European standard. For Qualcomm, which produces and collects royalties from chip sales of a rival system (CDMA), Iraq's adoption of GSM would represent a tremendous loss. Upon learning of the GSM plans, a Qualcomm lobbyist went to Rep. Darrel E. Issa (R-Calif.), the recipient of $5,500 in Qualcomm campaign contributions. Together the wireless technology firm and the congressman drafted a letter advocating use of CDMA technology in Iraq, had it signed by 41 lawmakers, and sent it to USAID and Defense Secretary Donald Rumsfeld.

The letter argued that CDMA is technologically superior and that the money spent on reconstruction should benefit American firms, not the European firms that developed GSM. Unfortunately for Qualcomm, the use of GSM would isolate Iraq from neighboring countries. And in terms of American benefits, many firms make GSM handsets and at least one owns royalty-gaining GSM patents. The only real beneficiary of a CDMA system in Iraq would be Qualcomm itself.

Rep. Issa introduced a bill that would mandate the use of Qualcomm's technology to the House of Representatives at the end of March. It is not expected to pass.

SOURCES *Financial Times* May 6, 2003; *New York Times* April 9, 2003, April 11, 2003; <www. citizenworks.org>; <www.corpwatch.org>. Campaign contribution information is from Open Secrets <www.opensecrets. org>. USAID contracts and updates can be found at <www.usaid.gov/iraq/ activities.html>.

CHAPTER 3

Trade, Investment, and Debt

ARTICLE 11

The Gospel of Free Trade

The New Evangelists

BY ARTHUR MACEWAN

November 1991, updated September 2003

Free trade! It's the cure-all for the world's economic problems. With all the zeal of Christian missionaries, the U.S. government has been preaching, advocating, pushing, and coercing around the globe for "free trade."

In the 1990s, the United States signed onto NAFTA, and today, a Free Trade Area of the Americas, the FTAA, is the immediate focus of the U.S. government efforts. But George W. Bush and Bill Clinton before him have also pushed hard for a *global* free trade agenda. After the demise of the Soviet Union, U.S. advisers prescribed unfettered capitalism for Eastern and Central Europe, and ridiculed as unworkable any move toward a "third way." In low-income countries from Mexico the Malaysia, the prescription is the same: open markets, deregulate business, privatize, and let the free market flourish.

In the push for world-wide free trade, the World Trade Organization (WTO) has been the principal vehicle of change, establishing rules of commerce that assure markets are open and resources are available to those who can pay. And the International Monetary Fund (IMF) and World Bank, which provide international loans, use their financial power to pressure governments around the world to accept the gospel and open their markets.

Of course, as with any gospel, the preachers often ignore their own sermons—

55

the U.S. government, for instance, protects textiles and provides large agricultural subsidies. But publicly at least, free trade boosters insist that the path to true salvation—or economic expansion, which, in this day and age, seems to be the same thing—lies in opening our markets to foreign goods. Get rid of trade barriers at home and abroad, allow business to go where it wants and do what it wants. We will all get rich.

Yet the history of the United States and other advanced capitalist countries does not fit well with the free trade gospel. Virtually all advanced capitalist countries found economic success through heavy government regulation of their international commerce, not in free trade. Likewise, a large role for government intervention has characterized those cases of rapid and sustained economic growth in low-income countries.

Free trade, does, however, have its uses. Highly developed nations can use free trade to extend their power and their control of the world's wealth, and business can use it as a weapon against labor. Most important, free trade can limit efforts to redistribute income more equally, undermine progressive social programs, and keep people from democratically controlling their economic lives.

A DAY IN THE PARK

At the beginning of the 19th century, Lowell, Massachusetts, became the premier site of the U.S. textile industry. Today, thanks to the Lowell National Historical Park, you can tour the huge mills, ride through the canals that redirected the Merrimack River's power to those mills, and learn the story of the textile workers, from the Yankee "mill girls" of the 1820s through the various waves of immigrant laborers who poured into the city over the next century.

During a day in the park, visitors get a graphic picture of the importance of 19th-century industry to the economic growth and prosperity of the United States. Lowell and the other mill towns of the era were centers of growth. They not only created a demand for Southern cotton, they also created a demand for new machinery, maintenance of old machinery, parts, dyes, *skills*, construction materials, construction machinery, *more skills*, equipment to move the raw materials and products, parts maintenance for that equipment, *and still more skills*. The mill towns also created markets—concentrated groups of wage earners who needed to buy products to sustain themselves. As centers of economic activity, Lowell and similar mill towns contributed to U.S. economic growth far beyond the value of the textiles they produced.

The U.S. textile industry emerged decades after the industrial revolution had spawned Britain's powerful textile industry. Nonetheless, it survived and prospered. British linens inundated markets throughout the world in the early 19th century, as the British navy nurtured free trade and kept ports open for commerce. In the United States, however, hostilities leading up to the War of 1812 and then a substantial tariff made British textiles relatively expensive. These limitations on trade allowed the Lowell mills to prosper, acting as a catalyst for other industries and helping to create the skilled work force at the center of U.S. economic expansion.

Beyond textiles, however, tariffs did not play a great role in the United States during the early 19th century. Southern planters had considerable power, and while they were willing to make some compromises, they opposed protecting manufacturing in general because that protection forced up the prices of the goods they purchased with their cotton revenues. The Civil War wiped out the planters' power to oppose protectionism, and from the 1860s through World War I, U.S. industry prospered behind considerable tariff barriers.

DIFFERENT COUNTRIES, SIMILAR STORIES

The story of the importance of protectionism in bringing economic growth has been repeated, with local variations, in other advanced capitalist countries. During the late 19th century, Germany entered the major league of international economic powers with substantial protection and government support for its industries. Likewise, in 19th-century France and Italy, national consolidation behind protectionist barriers was a key to economic development.

Britain—which entered the industrial era first—is often touted as the prime example of successful development without tariff protection. Yet, Britain embraced free trade only after its industrial base was well established; as in the U.S., the early and important textile industry was erected on a foundation of protectionism. In addition, Britain built its industry through the British navy and the expansion of empire, hardly prime ingredients in any recipe for free trade.

Japan provides an especially important case of successful government protection and support for industrial development. In the post-World War II era, when the Japanese established the foundations for their economic "miracle," the government rejected free trade and extensive foreign investment and instead promoted its national firms.

In the 1950s, for example, the government protected the country's fledgling auto firms from foreign competition. At first, quotas limited imports to $500,000 (in current dollars) each year; in the 1960s, prohibitively high tariffs replaced the quotas. Furthermore, the Japanese allowed foreign investment only insofar as it contributed to developing domestic industry. The government encouraged Japanese companies to import foreign technology, but required them to produce 90% of parts domestically within five years.

The Japanese also protected their computer industry. In the early 1970s, as the industry was developing, companies and individuals could only purchase a foreign machine if a suitable Japanese model was not available. IBM was allowed to produce within the country, but only when it licensed basic patents to Japanese firms. And IBM computers produced in Japan were treated as foreign-made machines.

In the 20th century, no other country matched Japan's economic success, as it moved in a few decades from a relative low-income country, through the devastation of war, to emerge as one of the world's economic leaders. Yet one looks back in vain to find a role for free trade in this success. The Japanese government provided an effective framework, support, and protection for the country's capitalist development.

Likewise, in the Third World, capitalism has generated high rates of economic growth where government involvement, and not free trade, played the central role. South Korea is the most striking case. "Korea is an example of a country that grew very fast and yet violated the canons of conventional economic wisdom," writes Alice Amsden in *Asia's Next Giant: South Korea and Late Industrialization,* widely acclaimed as perhaps the most important analysis of the South Korean economic success. "In Korea, instead of the market mechanism allocating resources and guiding private entrepreneurship, the government made most of the pivotal investment decisions. Instead of firms operating in a competitive market structure, they each operated with an extraordinary degree of market control, protected from foreign competition."

Free trade, however, has had its impact in South Korea. In the late 1990s, South Korea and other East Asian governments came under pressure from the U.S. government and the IMF to open their markets, including their financial markets. When they did so, the results were a veritable disaster. The East Asian financial crisis that began in 1997 was a major set back for the whole region, a major disruption of economic growth. After extremely rapid economic growth for three decades, with output expanding at 7% to 10% a year, South Korea's economy plummeted by 6.3% between 1997 and 1998.

MEXICO AND THE NAFTA EXPERIENCE

In the case of Mexico, after the country's debt debacle of the 1980s, the government proclaimed free trade the solution to its woes, opened its markets to foreign commerce, and entered into the North American Free Trade Agreement (NAFTA) with the United States and Canada. Along with NAFTA in 1994 came the first free-trade-related disruption of the Mexican economy, a severe financial crisis that sent the economy into a tailspin.

Still, during the 1990s, before and after the financial crisis, free traders extolled short periods of moderate economic growth—3% to 4% per year—as evidence of success. Yet, compared to earlier years, Mexico's growth under free trade has been poor. From 1940 to 1990 (including the no-growth decade of the 1980s), when Mexico's market was highly protected and the state actively regulated economic affairs, output grew at an average annual rate of 5%.

Most important, Mexico's experience puts to rest any notion that free-market policies will improve living conditions for the masses of people in low-income countries. The Mexican government paved the way for free trade policies by reducing or eliminating social welfare programs, and Mexican wages have declined sharply during the free trade era; the real minimum wage is down 60% since 1982 and down 23% since the advent of NAFTA in 1994. The number of households living in poverty has grown 80% since 1984, and some 75% of Mexico's population was below the poverty line at the beginning of the 21st century.

THE USES OF FREE TRADE

While free trade is not the best economic growth or development policy, the largest and most powerful firms in many countries find it highly profitable. As Britain preached the loudest sermons for free trade in the early 19th century, when its own industry was already firmly established, so the United States—or at least many firms based in the United States—finds it a profitable policy at the beginning of the 21st century.

For U.S. firms, access to foreign markets is a high priority. Mexico, for example, may be relatively poor, but with a population of 105 million it provides a substantial market. Furthermore, Mexican labor is cheap relative to U.S. labor; using modern production techniques, Mexican workers can be as productive as workers in the United States. For U.S. firms to obtain full access to the Mexican market, the United States has to open its borders to Mexican goods. Also, if U.S. firms are to take full advantage of cheap foreign labor and sell the goods produced abroad to U.S. consumers, the United States has to be open to imports.

On the other side of the border, wealthy Mexicans face a choice between advancing their interests through national development or advancing their interests through ties to U.S. firms and access to U.S. markets. For many years, they chose the former route. This led to some development of the Mexican economy but also—due to corruption and the massive power of the ruling party, the PRI—huge concentrations of wealth in the hands of a few small groups of firms and individuals. Eventually, these groups came into conflict with their own government over regulation and taxation. Having benefited from government largesse, they came to see their fortunes in greater freedom from government control and, particularly, in greater access to foreign markets and partnerships with large foreign companies. National development was a secondary concern when more involvement with international commerce would produce greater riches more quickly.

In addition, the old program of state-led development in Mexico ran into severe problems. These problems came to the surface in the 1980s with the international debt crisis. Owing huge amounts of money to foreign banks, the Mexican government was forced to respond to pressure from the IMF, the U.S. government, and large international banks which sought to deregulate Mexico's trade and investment. That pressure meshed with the pressure from Mexico's own richest elites, and the result was the move toward free trade and a greater opening of the Mexican economy to foreign investment.

Since the early 1990s, these changes for Mexico and the United States (as well as Canada) have been institutionalized in NAFTA. The U.S. government's agenda ten years later is to spread free trade policies to all of the Americas through the FTAA. On a broader scale, the U.S. government works through the WTO, the IMF, and the World Bank to open markets and access to resources beyond the Western Hemisphere. In fact, while markets remain important everywhere, low-wage manufacturing is increasingly concentrated in Asia—especially China—instead of Mexico or Latin America.

WHO GAINS, WHO LOSES?

Of course, in the United States, Mexico, and elsewhere, advocates of free trade claim that their policies are in everyone's interest. Free trade, they point out, will mean cheaper products for all. Consumers in the United States, who are mostly workers, will be richer because their wages will buy more. In both Mexico and the United States, they argue, rising trade will create more jobs. If some workers lose their jobs because cheaper imported goods are available, export industries will produce new ones.

Such arguments obscure many of the most important issues in the free trade debate. Stated, as they usually are, as universal truths, these arguments are plain silly. No one, for example, touring the Lowell National Historical Park could seriously argue that people in the United States would have been better off had there been no tariff on textiles. Yes, in 1820, they could have purchased textile goods more cheaply, but in the long run the result would have been less industrial advancement and a less wealthy nation. One could make the same point with the Japanese auto and computer industries, or indeed with numerous other examples from the last two centuries of capitalist development.

In the modern era, even though the United States already has a relatively developed economy with highly skilled workers, a freely open international economy does not serve the interests of most U.S. workers, though it will benefit large firms. U.S. workers today are in competition with workers around the globe. Many different workers in many different places can produce the same goods and services. Thus, an international economy governed by the free trade agenda will tend to bring down wages for U.S. workers.

The problem is not simply that of workers in a few industries—such as auto and steel—where import competition is the most obvious and immediate problem. A country's openness to the international economy affects the entire structure of earnings in that country. Free trade forces down the general level of wages across the board, even of those workers not directly affected by imports. The simple fact is that when companies can produce the same products in several different places, it is owners who gain because they can move their factories and funds around much more easily than workers can move themselves around. Capital is mobile; labor is much less mobile. Businesses, more than workers, gain from having a larger territory in which to roam.

CONTROL OVER OUR ECONOMIC LIVES

But the difficulties with free trade do not end with wages. In both low-income and high-income parts of the world, free trade is a weapon in the hands of business when it opposes any progressive social programs. Efforts to place environmental restrictions on firms are met with the threat of moving production abroad. Higher taxes to improve the schools? Business threatens to go elsewhere. Better health and safety regulations? The same response.

Some might argue that the losses from free trade for people in the United States will be balanced by gains for most people in poor countries—lower wages in the United States, but higher wages in Mexico. Free trade, then, would bring about international equality. Not likely. In fact, as pointed out above, free trade reforms in Mexico have helped force down wages and reduce social welfare programs, processes rationalized by efforts to make Mexican goods competitive on international markets.

Gains for Mexican workers, like those for U.S. workers, depend on their power in relation to business. Free trade and the imperative of international "competitiveness" are just as much weapons in the hands of firms operating in Mexico as they are for firms operating in the United States. The great mobility of capital is business's best trump card in dealing with labor and popular demands for social change—in the United States, Mexico, and elsewhere.

None of this means that people should demand that their economies operate as fortresses, protected from all foreign economic incursions. There are great gains that can be obtained from international economic relations—when a nation manages those relations in the interests of the great majority of the people. Protectionism often simply supports narrow vested interests, corrupt officials, and wealthy industrialists. In rejecting free trade, we should move beyond traditional protectionism.

Yet, at this time, rejecting free trade is an essential first step. Free trade places the cards in the hands of business. More than ever, free trade would subject us to the "bottom line," or at least the bottom line as calculated by those who own and run large companies.

RESOURCES Arthur MacEwan, *Neo-Liberalism or Democracy? Economic Strategy, Markets and Alternatives for the 21st Century* (Zed Books, 1999); Timothy A. Wise and Kevin P. Gallagher, "NAFTA: A Cautionary Tale," <http://www.fpip.org/americas/commentary/2002/0210nafta_body.html>; World Bank, World Development Report, various years.

ARTICLE 12

What Causes Exchange-Rate Fluctuations?

BY ARTHUR MAcEWAN

March/April 2001

Dear Dr. Dollar:
  What are the primary forces that cause foreign exchange rates to fluctuate, and what are the remedies to these forces?
                                            —*Mario Anthony, West Palm Beach, Florida*

A foreign exchange rate is the price, in terms of one currency, that is paid for another currency. For example, at the end of December 2000, in terms of the U.S. dollar, the price of a British pound was $1.50, the price of a Japanese yen was 0.9 cents, and the price of a Canadian dollar was 67 cents. Like any other prices, currency prices fluctuate due to a variety of forces that we loosely categorize as "supply and demand." And as with other prices, the forces of "supply and demand" can have severe economic impacts and nasty human consequences.

Two factors, however, make exchange rates especially problematic. One is that they are subject to a high degree of speculation. This is seldom a significant problem for countries with stable economies—the "developed" countries. But for low-income countries, where instability is endemic, small changes in economic conditions can lead speculators to move billions of dollars in the time it takes to press a button, resulting in very large changes in the prices of currencies. This can quickly and greatly magnify small changes in economic conditions. In 1997 in East Asia, this sort of speculation greatly worsened the economic crisis that arose first in Thailand and then in several other countries. The speculators who drive such crises include bankers and the treasurers of multinational firms, as well as individuals and the operatives of investment companies that specialize in profiting off of the international movement of funds.

The second factor making exchange rates especially problematic is that they affect the prices of many other commodities. For a country that imports a great deal, a drop in the price of its currency relative to the currencies of the countries from which it imports means that a host of imported goods—everything from food to machinery—become more costly. When speculators moved funds out of East Asian countries in 1997, the price of foreign exchange (e.g., the price of the dollar in terms of local currencies) rose, imports became extremely expensive (in local currencies), and both living standards and investment fell dramatically. (Strong speculative movement of funds into a country can also create problems—driving up the price of the local currency, thereby hurting demand for the country's exports, and limiting economic growth.)

In the "normal" course of international trade, short-term exchange-rate fluctuations are seldom large. Consider, for example, trade between the United States and Canada. If people in the United States increasingly buy things from Canada—lumber, vacations in the Canadian Rockies, fish, minerals, auto parts—they will need Canadian dollars to do so. Thus these increased purchases of Canadian goods by people in the United States will mean an increased demand for Canadian dollars and a corresponding increased supply of U.S. dollars. If nothing else changes, the price of the Canadian dollar in terms of the U.S. dollar will tend to rise.

A great deal of the demand and supply of international currencies, however, is not for trade but for investment, often speculative investment. (Regarding the difference between real and speculative investment, see "Ask Dr. Dollar," *Dollars & Sense*, May/June 2000.) With the strong U.S. stock market in the late 1990s, investors in other countries bought a large amount of assets in the United States. To do so, they demanded U.S. dollars and supplied their own currencies. As a result, the price of the dollar in terms of the currencies of other countries rose substantially, by about 25% on average between the middle of 1995 and the end of 2000. One of the results has been to make imports to the U.S. relatively cheap, and this has been a factor holding down inflation in the United States. Also, as the cost of foreign currency dropped, the cost (in terms of dollars) of hiring foreign workers to supply goods also dropped. The result was more severe competition for many U.S. workers (including, for example, people employed in the production of auto parts, glass goods, textiles, and apparel) and, no surprise, their wages suffered.

There is little point in attempts by governments to constrain the "normal" fluctuations in foreign exchange rates that are associated with trade adjustments (as in the U.S.-Canada example above) or those associated with long-run investment movements (as in the case of the United States during the late 1990s). Although these fluctuations can create large problems—like their impact on U.S. wages—it would be very costly and very difficult, if not impossible, to eliminate them. There are other ways to deal with declining wages (see "Ask Dr. Dollar," *Dollars & Sense*, March/April 1999).

The experience of the East Asian countries in 1997 is another matter. Speculative investment drove huge exchange-rate changes and (along with other factors) severely disrupted these countries' economies. Between mid-1997 and early 1998, for example, the value of the Thai baht lost close to 60% of its value in terms of the U.S. dollar, and the Malaysian ringgit lost close to 50%. Governments can control such speculative swings by a variety of limits on the quick movement of capital into and out of countries. One mechanism would be a tax on short-term investments. Another would be direct limits on movements of funds. These sorts of controls are not easy to implement, but they have worked effectively in many cases—notably in Malaysia following the 1997 crisis.

It has become increasingly clear in recent years that effective development policies in low-income countries cannot be pursued in the absence of some sort of controls on the movement of funds in and out of those countries. Otherwise, any successful program—whatever its particular aims—can be disrupted and destroyed by the actions of international speculators.

ARTICLE 13

Disarming the Debt Trap

BY ELLEN FRANK

November 2000

QUESTION: What if the IMF, World Bank and G-7 governments canceled the debts of the poorer countries right now, fully and with no strings attached?

ANSWER: Within five years, most would be up to their necks in debt again. While a Jubilee 2000 debt cancellation would provide short-term relief for heavily indebted countries, the bitter reality of the current global financing system is that poor countries are virtually doomed to be debtors.

When residents of Zambia or Zaire buy maize or medicine in America, they are required to pay in dollars. If they can't earn enough dollars through their own exports, they must borrow them—from the IMF, the World Bank, a Western government agency, or from a commercial lender. But foreign currency loans are problematic for poor countries. If CitiCorp loans funds to a U.S. business, it fully expects that the business will realize a stream of earnings from which the loan can be repaid. When the IMF or World Bank makes foreign currency loans to poor countries—to finance deficits or development projects—no such foreign currency revenue stream is generated and the debt becomes a burdensome obligation that can be met only by abandoning internal development goals in favor of export promotion.

Few poor countries can avoid the occasional trade deficit—of 93 low- and moderate-income countries, only 11 currently have trade surpluses—and most are heavily dependent on imports of food, oil, and manufactured goods. Even the most tightly managed economy is only an earthquake or crop failure away from a foreign currency debt. Once incurred, interest payments and other debt-servicing charges mount quickly. Because few countries can manage payments surpluses large enough to service the debt regularly, servicing charges are rolled over into new loans and the debt balloons. This is why, despite heroic efforts by many indebted less-developed countries (LDCs) to pump up exports and cut imports, the outstanding foreign currency debt of developing countries has more than tripled during the past two decades.

Many poorer nations, hoping to avoid borrowing, have attempted recently to attract foreign investor dollars with the bait of high interest rates or casino-style stock exchanges. But the global debt trap is not so easily eluded. An American financial firm that purchases shares on the Thai stock exchange with baht (the Thai currency) wants, eventually, to distribute gains to shareholders in dollars. Big banks and mutual funds are wary, therefore, of becoming ensnared in minor currencies and, to compensate against potential losses when local currencies are converted back into dollars, they demand sky-high interest rates on LDC bonds. Thailand, Brazil, Indonesia and many other countries recently discovered that speculative financial investors are quick to turn heel and flee, driving interest rates up and exchange rates down, and leaving debtor countries even deeper in the hole.

If plans to revamp the international "financial architecture" are to help anyone but the already rich, they must address these issues. Developing countries need many things from the rest of the world—manufactured goods, skilled advisors, technical know-how—but loans are not among them. A global payments system based on the borrowing and lending of foreign currencies is, for small and poor nations, a life sentence to debtor's prison.

There are alternatives. Rather than scrambling endlessly for the foreign currency they cannot print, do not control, and cannot earn in sufficient amounts through exporting, developing countries could be permitted to pay for foreign goods and services in their own currencies. Americans do this routinely, issuing dollars to cover a trade deficit that will exceed $300 billion this year. Europe, too, finances external deficits with issues of euro-denominated bonds and bank deposits. But private financial firms will generally not hold assets denominated in LDC currencies; when they do hold them, they frequently demand interest rates several times higher than those paid by rich countries. But the governments of the world could jointly agree to hold these minor currencies, even if private investors will not.

The world needs an international central bank, democratically structured and publicly controlled, that would allow countries to settle payments imbalances politically, without relying on loans of foreign currencies. The idea is not new. John Maynard Keynes had something similar in mind in the 1940s, when the International Monetary Fund was established. Cambridge economist Nicholas Kaldor toyed with the idea in the 1960s. Recently, Jane D'Arista of the Financial Markets Center and a number of other international financial specialists have revived this notion, calling for a global settlements bank that could act not as a lender of last resort to international banks (as the IMF does), but as a lender of first resort for payments imbalances between sovereign nations. Such a system would take the problems of debts, deficits, and development out of the marketplace and place them in the international political arena, where questions of fairness and equity could be squarely and openly addressed.

The idea is beguilingly simple, eminently practicable, and easy to implement. It would benefit poor and rich countries alike, since the advanced nations could export far more to developing countries if those countries were able to settle international payments on more advantageous terms. A global settlements bank, however, would dramatically shift the balance of power in the world economy and will be fiercely opposed by those who profit from the international debt trap. If developing countries were not so desperate for dollars, multinational corporations would find them less eager to sell their resources and citizens for a fistful of greenbacks. That nations rich in people and resources, like South Africa, can be deemed bankrupt and forced into debt peonage for lack of foreign exchange is not merely a shame. It is absurd, an unacceptable artifact of a global finance system that enriches the already rich.

ARTICLE 14

The Decline of the Dollar System

BY JAMES K. GALBRAITH

May/June 2003

Today, the U.S. dollar is the world's reserve currency. Nations around the world invest most of their foreign exchange reserves in dollar assets. The international economic position of the United States depends on this.

So long as foreign central banks and international investors are willing to take and hold U.S. assets (including stocks, bonds, and cash) this system works—and shamefully to the interest of Americans. Their demand keeps the value of the dollar high. This means that we have been able to consume comfortably, and in exchange for very little effort, the products of hard labor by poor people. (As the supplier of liquidity to the world system, our situation is akin to that of, say, Australia in the late 19th century when gold fields were discovered, except that, in our case, no actual effort is required to extract the gold.) And meanwhile (thanks to ample cheap imports), we are not obliged to invest unduly in maintaining our own industrial base, which has substantially eroded since the 1970s. We could afford to splurge on new technologies and telecommunications systems whose benefits were, to a very great extent, figments of the imagination. And even when the bubble burst in those sectors, life went on, for most Americans, substantially undisturbed—at least for now.

But for how long can this system endure? There can be no definitive answer; the few economists who have worried about this issue are far from being in agreement. On one side, it is argued that the dominant currency holds a "lock-in advantage"; that is, there are economies (reduced transaction costs and reduced risk) associated with keeping all reserves in one basket. The United States in particular is in a strong position to pressure foreign central banks—notably Japan's—to absorb the dollars that private parties may not wish to hold, at least within limits.

Furthermore, oil is bought and sold in dollars. As a result, oil importers must buy dollars in order to buy oil, and oil exporters accumulate dollars as they sell oil. To some extent this arrangement further strengthens the dollar—though it is not obvious why it requires anyone to hold dollars for very long, once they start falling in value.

Against this, the question remains: As the U.S. trade position continues to erode, will foreigners be willing to add to their holdings of dollar assets by enough to allow the United States to return to full employment? The amount to be absorbed at present—the trade deficit at full employment—is in the range of half a trillion dollars per year. This was easily handled when dollar asset prices were rising. But now that these prices are falling, they are not as attractive as they once were. If foreigners are not willing to absorb all the dollars we need to place, and if asset prices do not quickly fall to the point where U.S. stocks appear cheap to investors, dollar dumping is, sooner or later, inevitable.

To keep the dollar's fall from getting out of hand, the United States will be strongly tempted to slow the rate at which new U.S. assets reach the world system, by restricting its imports. Having renounced the traditional tools of trade protectionism, it can only do this by raising interest rates, holding down economic growth, and keeping incomes, and therefore imports, well below the full-employment level. In that situation—which may actually already have arrived—the United States joins Brazil and other developing nations as a country effectively constrained by its debts. Indeed, the world prognosis from that point forward becomes grim, since high levels of American demand have been just about the only motor of growth and development (outside, perhaps, of China and India) in recent years.

THE UNITED STATES AS A DEBTOR NATION

There are economists who advocate dollar devaluation, believing that the richer countries of the world would quickly rally to purchase increasing quantities of made-in-America exports, thus reversing the manufacturing decline of the past 20 years. But this is very unlikely. Exports to the rich regions may not be very price-sensitive.

And exports to the developing regions are very sensitive to income and credit conditions, which would get worse. At least in the short and medium term, there is no foolproof adjustment process to be had by these means. Where a high dollar provides U.S. consumers with cheap imports and capital inflows to finance domestic activity, a falling dollar would have opposite effects. A falling dollar would raise the price of imports into the United States, especially from the richer countries. Meanwhile, a declining dollar would hit at the value of developing countries' reserves and their access to credit, and so it would diminish their demand for our exports. (It would help, in some cases, on their debts.) The most likely outcome from dollar devaluation is a general deepening of the world slump, combined with pressure on American banks and markets as global investors seek safer havens in Europe.

This specter of financial vulnerability means that for the United States, the combination of falling internal demand, falling asset prices, and a falling dollar represents a threat that can best be described as millennial. (My colleague Randall Wray has called it the "perfect fiscal storm.") The consequences at home would include deepening unemployment. There would be little recovery of privately financed investment, amid a continued unraveling of plans—both corporate and personal—that had been based on the delirious stock market valuations of the late 1990s. The center of the world banking industry would move, presumably to continental Europe. Over time, the United States could lose both its position as the principal beneficiary of the world financial order and its margin of maneuver on the domestic scene. This would be not unlike what happened to the United Kingdom from 1914 to 1950.

It is not obvious that senior financial policymakers in the United States have yet grasped this threat, or that there is any serious planning under way to cope with it—apart from a simpleminded view among certain strategic thinkers about the financial advantages of the control of oil. Instead it appears that the responsible officials are confining themselves to a very narrow range of Third-World debt management proposals, whose premises minimize the gravity of the issue and whose purpose is to keep the existing bonds of debt peonage in place as long as possible.

The alternative? It would involve rebuilding a multilateral monetary system, demolished for the benefit of the private commercial banks in 1973. The way forward would probably entail new regional systems of financial stabilization and capital control, such as the Asian Monetary Fund proposed by Japan in 1997. Such a course would be unpalatable to current American leadership. But we may find, down the road, that for the sake of our own prosperity, let alone that of the rest of the world, there is no other way.

Adapted from "The Brazilian Swindle and The Larger International Monetary Problem," published by the Levy Economics Institute in 2002. The full article is available at <www.levy.org>.

ARTICLE 15

How Has NAFTA Affected Trade and Employment?

BY ELLEN FRANK

January/February 2003

Dear Dr. Dollar:

Free-traders claim that free trade will increase U.S. exports, providing more jobs for Americans. So I would expect that NAFTA increased U.S. exports and reduced our trade deficit. I would also expect to see employment increase both in our country and in our trading partners. Has that in fact happened?

—*Lane Smith, Ronkonkoma, New York*

Since the North American Free Trade Agreement (NAFTA) between the United States, Mexico, and Canada went into effect, trade within North America has increased dramatically. Exports from the United States to Mexico have risen 150% and exports to Canada are up 66%. This much is beyond dispute.

NAFTA's effects on employment, on the other hand, are hotly debated. Clinton administration officials estimated in the late 1990s that expanded trade in North America had created over 300,000 new U.S. jobs. Economic Policy Institute (EPI) economists Robert Scott and Jesse Rothstein contend, however, that such claims amount to "trying to balance a checkbook by counting the deposits and not the withdrawals."

This is because NAFTA and other trade agreements have also increased U.S. imports from Canada and Mexico—and by quite a lot more than exports. Since 1993, America's trade deficit with its North American trading partners (exports minus imports) has ballooned from $16 billion to $82 billion annually. As Scott points out, "increases in U.S. exports create jobs in this country, but increases in imports destroy jobs because the imports displace goods that otherwise would have been made in the U.S. by domestic workers."

Employment in virtually all U.S. manufacturing industries has declined since NAFTA went into effect. Counting jobs that actually left the United States plus those that would have been created if not for rising imports, EPI estimates that NAFTA caused a net loss of 440,000 U.S. jobs. In fact, during the 1990s, the overall U.S. trade deficit quadrupled, resulting in a net loss of 3 million jobs, according to EPI president Jeff Faux.

Of course, in a large and complex economy, trade is only one of many factors that affect job creation, and its influence is difficult to isolate. As trade expanded during the 1990s, for example, the United States also experienced an investment boom that created jobs faster than rising imports destroyed them; overall, the number of jobs in the United States has risen by 28 million since 1994.

Any free-trade booster worth her lobbying fees would argue that the boom itself resulted from liberalized trade. Lower trade and investment barriers, the story goes, unleash entrepreneurial talents, spurring innovation and productivity gains. Old jobs lost are offset by new jobs gained, and falling wages by cheaper prices on imported goods. Moreover, free-traders contend, any reckoning of NAFTA's impact should tote up new jobs and factories in Mexico against shuttered plants in the United States.

So what about NAFTA's effect on Mexico? In a study for the Interhemispheric Resource Center, analysts Timothy Wise and Kevin Gallagher conclude that NAFTA has given Mexico "trade without development." Since NAFTA weakened barriers to U.S. investment in Mexico, foreign investment into the country tripled and exports grew rapidly. But the development promised by free-trade advocates never materialized. Mexican employment did grow during the early years of NAFTA, but in recent years, it has declined as mobile manufacturers have sought even cheaper labor in Asia. Mexican manufacturing wages fell 21% during the 1990s and poverty worsened.

Wise's and Gallagher's findings echo the conclusions of Harvard development specialist Dani Rodrik. Poor countries that turn to trade as a cure for poverty find themselves ensnared in the "mercantilist fallacy": they can't all export their way to riches, since one country's exports are another's imports. Someone has to buy all this stuff. The United States, with its annual trade deficit approaching $500 billion, is the world's buyer and its manufacturing industries suffer as a result. But poor countries don't fare much better. They face increasing competition from low-wage manufacturers in other poor countries, and world markets are now saturated with cheap apparel and electronics, driving prices and wages down.

The result is one thing that almost everybody who studies trade now agrees upon. Whatever else they have wrought—more jobs, fewer jobs, more or less poverty—globalized trade and production coincide with greater inequality both within and between countries. The reasons for this are complex—globalization weakens unions, strengthens multinationals, and increases competition and insecurity all around—but the data are clear. Markets do not distribute wealth equitably.

RESOURCES Robert Scott and Jesse Rothstein, "NAFTA and the States: Job Destruction is Widespread," <www.epinet.org>; Jeff Faux, "Why U.S. Manufacturing Needs a 'Strategic Pause in Trade Policy,'" Testimony before the Senate Committee on Commerce, Sciences and Transportation, June 21, 2001; Timothy Wise and Kevin Gallagher, "NAFTA: A Cautionary Tale," *FPIF Global Affairs Commentary*, 2002; Dani Rodrik, *The New Global Economy and Developing Countries: Making Openness Work* (Overseas Development Council, 1999).

CHAPTER 4

International Institutions

ARTICLE 16

The ABCs of the Global Economy

BY THE *DOLLARS & SENSE* COLLECTIVE

March/April 2000

In the 1960s, U.S. corporations changed the way they went after profits in the international economy. Instead of producing goods in the U.S. to export, they moved more and more toward producing goods overseas to sell to consumers in those countries and at home. They had done some of this in the 1950s, but really sped up the process in the '60s.

Before the mid-1960s, free trade probably helped workers and consumers in the United States while hurting workers in poorer countries. Exporters invested their profits at home in the United States, creating new jobs and boosting incomes. The AFL-CIO thought this was a good deal and backed free trade.

But when corporations changed strategies, they changed the alliances. By the late 1960s, the AFL-CIO began opposing free trade as they watched jobs go overseas. But unionists did not see that they had to start building alliances internationally. The union federation continued to take money secretly from the U.S. government to help break up red unions abroad, not a good tactic for producing solidarity. It took until the 1990s for the AFL-CIO to reduce (though not eliminate) its alliance with the U.S. State Department. In the 1990s, unions also forged their alliance with the environmental movement to oppose free trade.

But corporations were not standing still; in the 1980s and 1990s they were working to shift the architecture of international institutions created after World War II to work more effectively in the new global economy they were creating.

More and more of their profits were coming from overseas—by the 1990s, 30% of U.S. corporate profits came from their direct investments overseas, up from 13% in the 1960s. This includes money made from the operations of their subsidiaries abroad. But the share of corporate profits earned overseas is even higher than that because the 30% figure doesn't include the interest companies earn on money they loan abroad. And the financial sector is an increasingly important player in the global economy.

Financial institutions and other global corporations without national ties now use governments to dissolve any national restraints on their activities. They are global, so they want their government to be global too. And while trade used to be taken care of through its own organization (GATT) and money vaguely managed through another organization (the International Monetary Fund), the new World Trade Organization erases the divide between trade and investment in its efforts to deregulate investment worldwide.

In helping design some of the global institutions after World War II, John Maynard Keynes assumed companies and economies would operate within national bounds, with the IMF and others regulating exchanges across those borders. The instability created by ruptured borders is made worse by the deregulation sought by corporations, and especially, the financial sector. The most powerful governments of the world seem oblivious to this threat in giving them what they want.

This is a world-historical moment in which it is possible to stop the corporate offensive, a moment when the ruling partnership composed of the United States, Europe and to a lesser extent Japan is fracturing, as the European Union reaches its limit on the amount of deregulation it will take and Japan's economy is in turmoil. This may allow those opposing the ruling bloc—Third World governments (which may be conservative), labor, and environmentalists worldwide—to build alliances of convenience with sympathetic elements within the EU to guide the reshaping of the global institutions in a liberatory manner.

What follows is a primer on the most important of those institutions.

—Abby Scher

The World Bank and the International Monetary Fund (IMF)

The basic institutions of the postwar international capitalist economy were framed in 1944, at an international conference in Bretton Woods, New Hampshire, dominated by the United States and the United Kingdom. Among the institutions coming out of this conference were the World Bank and the International Monetary Fund (IMF).

At both the World Bank and the IMF, the number of votes a country receives is based on how much capital it contributes to the institution, so rich countries like the United States enjoy disproportionate voting power. At both, five powerful countries—the United States, the United Kingdom, France, Germany, and Japan—get to appoint their own representatives to the institution's executive board, with 19 other directors elected by the rest of the 150-odd member countries. The president of the World Bank is elected by the Board of Executive Directors, and traditionally nominated by the U.S. representative. The managing director of the IMF is traditionally a European.

Just after World War II, the World Bank mostly loaned money to Western European governments to help rebuild their countries. But during the long presidency (1968-1981) of former U.S. Defense Secretary Robert S. McNamara, the bank turned toward "development" loans to Third World countries. McNamara brought the same philosophy to development that he had used in the war against Vietnam: more is better. Ever since, the Bank has favored large, expensive projects regardless of their appropriateness to local conditions. Critics argue that the Bank pays little heed to the social and environmental impact of the projects it finances, that it creates dependence on imports and capital from rich countries, and that it often works through dictatorial elites that channel benefits to themselves rather than to those who need help. The poor are left to foot the bill later.

The most important function of the IMF is as a "lender of last resort" to member countries that cannot borrow money from other sources, usually when they are in danger of defaulting on previous loans from private banks. The IMF lends money on the condition that the country implement policy changes that are formally known as a "structural adjustment program" (SAP), but more often referred to as an "austerity plan." Typically, a government is told to devalue its currency, eliminate price controls and subsidies, and eliminate labor regulations like minimum wage laws—all changes that hurt the working class and the poor by cutting their real incomes.

The IMF and the World Bank wield power disproportionate to the size of the loans they give out because private lenders follow their lead in deciding which countries are credit-worthy. Both institutions have taken advantage of this leverage—and of debt crises in Latin America, Africa, and Asia—to impose a cookie-cutter model of "development" based on "free market" principles, against varying levels of resistance, on the people and governments of poor countries around the world.   —*Alejandro Reuss*

The Multilateral Agreement on Investment (MAI) and Trade Related Investment Measures (TRIMs)

WHERE DID THEY COME FROM?

You're probably not the sort of person who would own a chemical plant or luxury hotel, but imagine you were. Imagine you built a chemical plant or luxury hotel in a foreign country, only to see a labor-friendly government take power and threaten your profits. This is the scenario which makes the CEOs of footloose global corporations wake up in the middle of the night in a cold sweat. To avert such threats, ministers of the richest countries met secretly at the Organization for Economic Cooperation and Development (OECD) in Paris in 1997 and tried to hammer out a bill of rights for international investors, the Multilateral Agreement on Investment (MAI).

When protests against the MAI broke out in the streets and the halls of government alike in 1998 and 1999, scuttling the agreement in that form, the corporations turned to the World Trade Organization to achieve their goal. (See Chantell Taylor, "Rage Against the MAchIne," *Dollars & Sense*, September/October 1998.)

WHAT ARE THEY UP TO?

Both the MAI and Trade Related Investment Measures (or TRIMs, the name of the WTO version) would force governments to compensate companies for any losses (or reductions in profits) they might suffer because of changes in public policy. Governments would be compelled to tax, regulate, and subsidize foreign businesses exactly as they do local businesses. Policies designed to protect fledgling national industries (a staple of industrial development strategies from the United States and Germany in the 19th century to Japan and Korea in the 20th) would be ruled out.

TRIMs would also be a crowning blow to the control of governments over the movement of capital into or out of their countries. Until fairly recently, most governments imposed controls on the buying and selling of their currencies for purposes other than trade. Known as capital controls, these curbs significantly impeded the mobility of capital. By simply outlawing conversion, governments could trap investors into keeping their holdings in the local currency. But since the 1980s, the IMF and the U.S. Treasury have pressured governments to lift these controls so that international companies can more easily move money around the globe. Corporations and wealthy individuals can now credibly threaten to pull liquid capital out of any country whose policies displease them.

Malaysia successfully imposed controls during the Asian crisis of 1997 and 1998, spurring broad interest among developing countries. The United States wants to establish a new international discussion group—the Group of 20 (G-20), consisting of ministers from 20 developing countries handpicked by the U.S.—to consider reforms. Meanwhile, it continues to push for the MAI-style liberation of capital from any control whatsoever.

WHY SHOULD YOU CARE?

It is sometimes said that the widening chasm between the rich and poor is due to the fact that capital is so easily shifted around the globe while labor, bound to family and place, is not. But there is nothing natural in this. Human beings, after all, have wandered the earth for millennia—traversing oceans and continents, in search of food, land, and adventure—whereas a factory, shipyard, or office building, once built, is almost impossible to move in a cost effective way. Even liquid capital (money) is less mobile than it seems. To be sure, a Mexican can fill a suitcase with pesos, hop a plane and fly to California, but once she disembarks, who's to say what the pesos will be worth, or whether they'll be worth anything at all? For most of this century, however, capitalist governments have curbed labor's natural mobility through passports, migration laws, border checkpoints, and armed border patrols, while capital has been rendered movable by treaties and laws that harmonize the treatment of wealth around the world. The past two decades especially have seen a vast expansion in the legal rights of capital across borders. In other words, labor fights with the cuffs on, while capital takes the gloves off.

—Ellen Frank

World Intellectual Property Organization (WIPO) and Trade-Related Aspects of Intellectual Property Rights (TRIPs)

One of the less familiar members of the "alphabet soup" of international economic institutions, the World Intellectual Property Organization (WIPO) has governed "intellectual property" issues since its founding in 1970. In the old days, "intellectual property" only covered property rights over inventions, industrial designs, trademarks, and artistic and literary works. But WIPO has been busy staking out a brave new world of property rights, especially in the electronic domain. Now "intellectual property" includes computer programs, electronic images, and digital recordings, as well as pharmaceuticals and even biological processes and genetic codes.

A 1996 WIPO treaty would outlaw the "circumvention" of electronic security measures. It would be illegal, for example, to sidestep the security measures on a website (such as those requiring that users register or send payment in exchange for access). The treaty would also prevent programmers from cracking open commercial software to view the underlying code. Similar restrictions have already gone into effect in the United States, thanks to the Digital Millennium Copyright Act (DMCA). These laws prevent programmers from crafting their own programs so that they are compatible with existing software, and prevent innovation in the form of "reengineering"—drawing on one design as the basis of another. Reengineering has been at the heart of many countries' economic development, including the United States'. In the 19th century, for example, Lowell, Massachusetts, textile manufacturers built their looms based on English designs.

In recent years, WIPO has faced a turf war over the intellectual property issue with none other than the World Trade Organization (WTO). Wealthy countries are attempting an end run around WIPO because it lacks enforcement power and because some poor countries have resisted its agenda. But the mass media, information technology, drug, and biotechnology industries in wealthy countries stand to lose a great deal from "piracy" and to gain a fortune in fees and royalties if given more extensive property rights. So they have introduced, under the name "Trade-Related Aspects of Intellectual Property Rights" (TRIPs), extensive provisions on intellectual property into recent WTO negotiations.

TRIPs would put the muscle of trade sanctions behind intellectual property rights. It would also stake out new intellectual property rights over plant, animal, and even human genetic codes. The governments of some developing countries have objected, warning that private companies based in rich countries will declare ownership over the genetic codes of plants long used for healing or crops within their countries—what activists have called "biopiracy." By manipulating just one gene of a living organism, a company can be declared the sole owner of an entire plant variety.

These proposals may seem like a new frontier of property rights, but except for the issue of ownership of life forms, TRIPs actually defend the old regime of property rights. It is because current electronic, chemical, and biological technology make virtually unlimited production and free distribution possible that the fight for private property has become so extreme.   —*Alejandro Reuss*

The World Trade Organization (WTO)

WHERE DID IT COME FROM?

Since the 1950s, government officials from around the world have met irregularly to hammer out the rules of a global trading system. Known as the General Agreements on Trade and Tariffs (GATT), these negotiations covered, in excruciating detail, such matters as what level of taxation Japan would impose on foreign rice, how many American automobiles Brazil would allow into its market, and how large a subsidy France could give its vineyards. Every clause was carefully crafted, with constant input from business representatives who hoped to profit from expanded international trade.

The GATT process however, was slow, cumbersome and difficult to monitor. As corporations expanded more rapidly into global markets they pushed governments to create a more powerful and permanent international body that could speed up trade negotiations as well as oversee and enforce provisions of the GATT. The result is the World Trade Organization, formed out of the ashes of GATT in 1994.

WHAT IS IT UP TO?

The WTO functions as a sort of international court for adjudicating trade disputes. Each of its 135 member countries has one representative, who participates in negotiations over trade rules. The heart of the WTO, however, is not its delegates, but its dispute resolution system. With the establishment of the WTO, corporations now have a place to complain to when they want trade barriers—or domestic regulations that limit their freedom to buy and sell—overturned.

Though corporations have no standing in the WTO—the organization is, officially, open only to its member countries—the numerous advisory bodies that provide technical expertise to delegates are overflowing with corporate representation. The delegates themselves are drawn from trade ministries and confer regularly with the corporate lobbyists and advisors who swarm the streets and offices of Geneva, where the organization is headquartered. As a result, the WTO has become, as an anonymous delegate told the *Financial Times,* "a place where governments can collude against their citizens."

Lori Wallach and Michelle Sforza, in their book *The WTO: Five Years of Reasons to Resist Corporate Globalization*, point out that large corporations are essentially "renting" governments to bring cases before the WTO, and in this way, to win in the WTO battles they have lost in the political arena at home. Large shrimping corporations, for example, got India to dispute the U.S. ban on shrimp catches that were not sea-turtle safe. Once such a case is raised, the resolution process violates most democratic notions of due process and openness. Cases are heard before a tribunal of "trade experts," generally lawyers, who, under WTO rules, are required to make their ruling with a presumption in favor of free trade. The WTO puts the burden squarely on governments to justify any restriction of what it considers the natural order of things. There are no amicus briefs (statements of legal opinion filed with a court by outside parties), no observers, and no public record of the deliberations.

The WTO's rule is not restricted to such matters as tariff barriers. When the organization was formed, environmental and labor groups warned that the WTO would soon be rendering decisions on essential matters of public policy. This has proven absolutely correct. Currently, the WTO is considering whether "selective purchasing" laws are a violation of "free trade." The organization has already ruled against Europe for banning hormone-treated beef and against Japan for prohibiting pesticide-laden apples.

WHY SHOULD YOU CARE?

At stake is a fundamental issue of popular sovereignty—the rights of the people to regulate economic life, whether at the level of the city, state, or nation. The U.S. does not allow businesses operating within its borders to produce goods with child labor, so why should we allow those same businesses—Disney, Gap, or Walmart—to produce their goods with child labor in Haiti and sell the goods here?   *—Ellen Frank*

The International Labor Organization (ILO)

WHERE DID IT COME FROM?

The ILO was established in 1919 in the wake of World War I, the Bolshevik revolution in Russia, and the founding of the Third (Communist) International, a world federation of revolutionary socialist political parties. Idealistic motives mingled with the goal of business and political elites to offer workers an alternative to revolution, and the result was an international treaty organization (established by agreement between governments) whose main job was to promulgate codes of practice in work and employment.

After World War II the ILO was grafted onto the UN structure, and it now serves a wide range of purposes: drafting conventions on labor standards (182 so far), monitoring their implementation, publishing analyses of labor conditions around the world, and providing technical assistance to national governments.

WHY SHOULD YOU CARE?

The ILO's conventions set high standards in such areas as health and safety, freedom to organize unions, social insurance, and ending abuses like workplace discrimination and child labor. It convenes panels to investigate whether countries are upholding their legal commitment to enforce these standards, and by general agreement their reports are accurate and fair. ILO publications, like its flagship journal, *The International Labour Review,* its *World Labor and Employment Reports*, and its special studies, are of very high quality. Its staff, which is headquartered in Geneva and numbers 1,900, has many talented and idealistic members. The ILO's technical assistance program is minuscule in comparison to the need, but it has changed the lives of many workers. (You can find out more about the ILO at its website: www.ilo.org.)

As a rule, international organizations are reflections of the policies of their member governments, particularly the ones with the most clout, such as the United States. Since governments are almost always biased toward business and against labor, we shouldn't expect to see much pro-labor activism in official circles. The ILO provides a partial exception to this rule, and it is worth considering why. There are probably four main reasons:

- The ILO's mission explicitly calls for improvements in the conditions of work, and the organization attracts people who believe in this cause. Compare this to the mission of the IMF (to promote the ability of countries to repay their international debts) or the WTO (to expand trade), for instance.
- Governments send their labor ministers (in the U.S., the Secretary of Labor) to represent them at the ILO. Labor ministers usually specialize in social protection issues and often serve as liaisons to labor unions. A roomful of labor ministers

will generally be more progressive than a similar gaggle of finance (IMF) or trade (WTO) ministers.

- The ILO's governing body is based on tripartite principles: representatives from unions, employers, and government all have a seat at the table. By institutionalizing a role for nongovernmental organizations, the ILO achieves a greater degree of openness and accountability.
- Cynics would add that the ILO can afford to be progressive because it is largely powerless. It has no enforcement mechanism for its conventions, and some of the countries that are quickest to ratify have the worst records of living up to them.

The ILO has significant shortcomings as an organization. Perhaps the most important is its cumbersome, bureaucratic nature: it can take forever for the apparatus to make a decision and carry it out. (Of course, that beats the IMF's approach: decisive, reactionary, and authoritarian.) The experience of the ILO tells us that creating a force capable of governing the global economy will be extremely difficult, and that there are hard tradeoffs between democracy, power, and administrative effectiveness. But it also demonstrates that reforming international organizations—changing their missions and governance systems—is worth the effort, especially if it brings nongovernmental activists into the picture.

Peter Dorman

RESOURCES Arthur MacEwan, "Markets Unbound: The Heavy Price of Globalization," *Real World International* (*Dollars and Sense*, 1999); David Mermelstein, ed., *The Economic Crisis Reader* (Vintage, 1975); Susan George and Fabrizio Sabelli, *Faith and Credit: The World Bank's Secular Empire* (Penguin Books, 1994); Hans-Albrecht Schraepler, *Directory of International Economic Organizations* (Georgetown University Press, 1997); Jayati Ghosh, Lectures on the history of the world economy, Tufts University, 1995; S.W. Black, "International Monetary Institutions," *The New Palgrave: A Dictionary of Economics*, John Eatwell, Murray Milgate, and Peter Newman, eds. (The Macmillan Press Limited, 1987).

ARTICLE 17

The ABCs of Free-Trade Agreements

BY THE *DOLLARS & SENSE* COLLECTIVE

January/February 2001

In the United States, the corporate media have framed the debate over "global-ization" largely as a struggle between cosmopolitan advocates and their pro-vincial opponents. The pro-globalization types are celebrated as champions not only of a "global marketplace," but also of a worldwide community of peoples brought together by communications, transportation, and commerce, a "global village." Meanwhile, "anti-globalization" protesters face not only tear gas and truncheons, but also accusations of protectionism, isolationism, and disregard for those outside the United States.

International institutions—like the World Trade Organization (WTO), Inter-national Monetary Fund (IMF), and World Bank—as well as regional associa-tions—such as the North American Free Trade Agreement (NAFTA), the European Union (EU), the Association of Southeast Asian Nations (ASEAN), and, perhaps soon, the Free Trade Area of the Americas (FTAA)—are primarily concerned with granting capital the freedom to move from country to country. It is true that many opponents of globalization have invoked national sovereignty as a first line of defense against this new wave of aggressive capitalist expansion. In some cases, this reaction has been accompanied by ugly nativist impulses, which join hostility towards international institutions and multinational corporations with hostility towards "foreign" workers. To its credit, however, much of the "global economic justice" movement has deftly avoided the nativist pitfall—avowing a solidarity that crosses all lines of nation and national origin, that stands up "for humanity and against neoliberalism."

Already, part of the movement is grappling with the problematic defense of national sovereignty, advocating instead a brand of grassroots democracy that does not exist very often in either international institutions or national states. Many activists even reject the "anti-globalization" label that has been hung on them, posing their own vision of "globalization from below" against a "glo-balization dominated by capital." Today, goods and capital pass freely across national frontiers while people run a gauntlet of border patrols and barbed wire. "Globalization from below" turns this status quo, which combines the worst of both worlds, on its head. Instead of the free movement of capital across national borders, "globalization from below" champions the free movement of people. Instead of equal treatment for all investors, no matter where they are investing, it demands equal human and civil rights for all people, no matter where they are living. Instead of greater worldwide integration of multinational corporations, it raises the banner of greater international solidarity among popular movements and organizations. Instead of the "race to the bottom," it calls for an "upward harmonization." Instead of the rule of capital, the rule of the people. Instead of more inequality, less. Instead of less democracy, more.

That is an appealing vision for the future. At this point, however, "globalization dominated by capital" is still on the march—operating through both global institutions and regional associations. The recent protests against the WTO and IMF (not only in the United States, but across the world) have shown that resistance is not futile. The immediate effect, however, may be to channel the globalization agenda back into regional "free-trade" agreements. Ultimately, the forces of resistance will need to be far greater to turn the tide. In the meantime, here's what we're up against.   —*Alejandro Reuss*

The North American Free Trade Agreement (NAFTA)

The North American Free Trade Agreement (NAFTA) came into effect on January 1, 1994. The agreement eliminated most barriers to trade and investment among the United States, Canada and Mexico. For some categories of goods—certain agricultural goods, for example—NAFTA promised to phase out restrictions on trade over a few years, but most goods and services were to be freely bought and sold across the three countries' borders from the start. Likewise, virtually all investments—financial investments as well as investments in fixed assets such as factories, mines, or farms (foreign direct investment)—were freed from cross-border restrictions.

NAFTA, however, made no changes in the restrictions on the movement of labor. Mexican—and, for that matter, Canadian—workers who wish to come to the United States must enter under the limited immigration quotas or illegally. Thus NAFTA gave new options and direct benefits to those who obtain their income from selling goods and making investments, but the agreement included no parallel provision for those who make their incomes by working.

Supporters of NAFTA have argued that both firm owners and workers in all three countries can gain from the removal of trade and investment barriers. For example, the argument goes, U.S. firms that produce more efficiently than their Mexican counterparts will have larger markets, gain more profits, generate more jobs, and pay higher wages. The prime examples would include information technology firms, bio-tech firms, larger retailers, and other U.S. corporations that have an advantage because of skilled U.S. labor or because of experience in organization and marketing. On the other hand, Mexican firms that can produce at low cost because of low Mexican wages will be able to expand into the U.S. market. The main example would be assembly plants or *maquiladoras*.

Critics of the agreement have focused on problems resulting from extreme differences among the member countries in living standards, wages, unionization, environmental laws, and social legislation. The options that NAFTA creates for business firms put them at a great advantage in their dealings with workers and communities. For example, U.S. unions are weakened because firms can more easily shut down domestic operations and substitute operations in Mexico. With the government suppressing independent unions in Mexico, organization of workers in all three countries is undermined. (Actually, the formal Mexican labor laws are probably as good or better than those in the United States but they are usually not enforced.) While NAFTA may mean more jobs and better pay for computer software engineers in the United States, auto-assembly and parts workers in the United States, for example, see their wages stagnate or fall. Similarly, the greater freedom of international movement that NAFTA affords to firms gives them greater bargaining power over communities when it comes to environmental regulations. One highly visible result has been severe pollution problems in Mexican *maquiladora* zones along the U.S. border.

An additional and important aspect of NAFTA is that it creates legal mechanisms for firms based in one country to contest legislation in the other countries when it might interfere with their "right" to carry out their business. Thus, U.S. firms operating in Mexico have challenged stricter environmental regulations won by the Mexican environmental movement. In Canada, the government rescinded a public-health law restricting trade in toxic PCBs as the result of a challenge by a U.S. firm; Canada also paid $10 million to the complaining firm, in compensation for "losses" it suffered under the law. These examples illustrate the way in which NAFTA, by giving priority to the "rights" of business, has undermined the ability of governments to regulate the operation of their economies in an independent, democratic manner.

Finally, one of NAFTA's greatest gifts to business has been the removal of restrictions on the movement of financial capital. The immediate result for Mexico was the severe financial debacle of 1994. Investment funds moved rapidly into Mexico during the early 1990s, and especially after NAFTA went into effect. Without regulation, these investments were able to abandon Mexico just as rapidly when the speculative "bubble" burst, leading to severe drops in production and employment.   — *Arthur MacEwan*

The Free Trade Area of the Americas (FTAA) and "Dollarization"

After the implementation of NAFTA, it looked like the Americas were on a fast track to a hemisphere-wide free-trade zone. In 1994, Clinton proposed to have the world's largest trading block in place by 2005. Instead, the Free Trade Area of the Americas (FTAA) stalled in its tracks when, in 1997, Congress denied Clinton "fast-track" negotiating authority. Bush revived the fast-track push in 2001 and succeeded in getting fast-track legislation through both the House of Representatives and the U.S. Senate in 2002.

What would a realized FTAA look like? There are two near-certainties. First, labor and environmental standards are unlikely to be on the agenda unless popular movements force the issue. Canadian Trade Minister Pierre Pettigrew, for example, told Parliament that labor and environmental side agreements like those in NAFTA would only impede negotiations (Canada chaired the FTAA negotiations process until late 1999 and remains an important booster of the pact). Second, the United States, which accounts for 70% of the hemispheric economy, would dominate any hemisphere-wide economic bloc. As a Brazilian businessman succinctly put it at a July 2000 meeting of the Common Market of the South (Mercado Comun del Sur, or Mercosur), Latin America's largest trading bloc, "Who rules in FTAA is the U.S."

The economic integration of Western Europe has included a unified currency, and the same may result from the integration of the Americas. But a unified currency under the FTAA is unlikely to be a new invention like the "Euro." Panama, Ecuador, and El Salvador already use the U.S. dollar as their official currency, the last two having adopted it in 2000. Proponents of "dollarization" view it as a way of inflation-proofing Latin America's economies. Fighting inflation (rather than reducing unemployment, fighting poverty, etc.) has been the principal goal of the region's governments since the 1980s, as it has been in the United States, Great Britain, and elsewhere. The IMF and the U.S. government both praised the Salvadoran government for taking the "dollarization" plunge, which then-Treasury Secretary Lawrence H. Summers said would "help contribute to financial stability … in El Salvador and its further integration into the global economy." This suggests that, unpopular though it may be now, "dollarization" is not just going to drop off the agenda.

"Dollarization" would threaten sovereignty over economic policy for the countries that embrace it. One key tool for economic policymakers is "monetary policy"—the control of the money supply and interest rates. Central banks lower interest rates and increase the money supply to stimulate growth (and combat unemployment). They raise interest rates and tighten the money supply it to combat inflation. The government of a "dollarized" country would no longer be able to stimulate growth if the U.S. Federal Reserve were trying to combat inflation, and vice-versa. Granted, U.S. policymakers already exert a great deal of control over Latin American economies, and the people of Latin America have historically not enjoyed much popular sovereignty over economic affairs. But openly ceding authority over regional economic policy to the U.S. Federal Reserve would hardly help matters.   *—Alejandro Reuss*

The European Union (EU)

The European Union (EU) forms the world's largest single market. From its beginnings in 1951 as the six-member European Coal and Steel Community, the association has grown both geographically (now including 15 countries in Central and Western Europe, with plans to expand into Eastern Europe) and especially in its degree of unity. Eleven of the EU's members now share a common currency (the Euro), and all national border controls on goods, capital, and people were abolished between member countries in 1993.

Open trade within the EU poses less of a threat for wages and labor standards than NAFTA or the WTO. Even the poorer member countries, such as Spain, Portugal, and Greece, are fairly wealthy and have strong unions and decent labor protections. Moreover, most EU countries, including top economic powers like France, Germany, Italy, and the United Kingdom, are ruled by parties (whether "socialist," social democratic, or labor) with roots in the working-class movement. This relationship has grown increasingly distant in recent years; still, from the perspective of labor, the EU represents a kind of best-case scenario for freeing trade. The results are, nonetheless, cautionary.

The main thrust of the EU, like other trade organizations, has been trade. Labor standards were never fully integrated into the core agenda of the EU. In 1989, 11 of the then-12 EU countries signed the "Charter of the Fundamental Social Rights of Workers," more widely known as the "Social Charter." (Only the United Kingdom refused to sign.) Though the "Social Charter" did not have any binding mechanism—it is described in public communications as "a political instrument containing 'moral obligations'"—many hoped it would provide the basis for "upward harmonization," that is, pressure on European countries with weaker labor protections to lift their standards to match those of member nations with stronger regulations. The 11 years since the adoption of the "Social Charter" have seen countless meetings, official studies, and exhortations but few appreciable results.

Since trade openness was never directly linked to social and labor standards and the "Social Charter" never mandated concrete actions from corporations, European business leaders have kept "Social Europe" from gaining any momentum simply by ignoring it. Although European anti-discrimination rules have forced countries like Britain to adopt the same retirement age for men and women, and regional funds are dispersed each year to bring up the general living standards of the poorest nations, the social dimension of the EU has never been more than an appendage for buying off opposition. As a result, business moved production, investment, and employment in Europe toward countries with low standards, such as Ireland and Portugal.

The EU also exemplifies how regional trading blocs indirectly break down trade regulations with countries outside the bloc. Many Europeans may have hoped that the EU would insulate Europe from competition with countries that lacked social, labor, and environmental standards. While the EU has a common external tariff, each member can maintain its own non-tariff trade barriers. EU rules requiring openness between member countries, however, made it easy to circumvent any EU country's national trade restrictions. Up until 1993, member states used to be able to block indirect imports through health and safety codes or border controls, but with the harmonization of these rules across the EU, governments can no longer do so. Since then, companies have simply imported non-EU goods into the EU countries with the most lax trade rules, and then freely transported the goods into the countries with higher standards. (NAFTA similarly makes it possible to circumvent U.S. barriers against the importation of steel from China by sending it indirectly through Mexico.) EU members that wished to uphold trade barriers against countries with inadequate social, labor, and environmental protections ended up becoming less important trading hubs in the world economy. This has led EU countries to unilaterally abolish restrictions and trade monitoring against non-EU nations. The logic of trade openness seems to be against labor and the environment even when the governments of a trading bloc individually wish to be more protective. *—Phineas Baxandall*

RESOURCES Brian Hanson, "What Happened to Fortress Europe?: External Trade Policy Liberalization in the European Union," *International Organization*, 52, no. 1 (Winter 1998), 55-86

The Association of South East Asian Nations (ASEAN) and Asia-Pacific Economic Cooperation (APEC)

Founded in 1967 at the height of the Vietnam War, the Association of South East Asian Nations (ASEAN) sought to promote "regional security" for its five original members (Indonesia, Malaysia, Philippines, Singapore, and Thailand). After 1975, it focused on counteracting the spread of communism following the defeat of the U.S. military in Vietnam. Beginning in the 1980s, and especially since the collapse of the Soviet Union, the ASEAN agenda turned from fighting communism to "accelerating economic growth" through cooperation and trade liberalization. At the same time, the organization added the remaining countries of Southeast Asia (Brunei Darussalam, Cambodia, Laos, Myanmar, and even Vietnam) to its member list. Today ASEAN oversees a cohesive geographical region with a population of nearly 500 million (about twice that of the United States) and combined output of nearly $750 billion (about one-tenth that of the United States).

ASEAN has pushed for member countries to open up to international trade and capital. While Singapore grew rapidly beginning in the 1960s, and Indonesia, Malaysia, and Thailand grew quickly beginning in the 1970s, high levels of Japanese foreign direct investment pushed the growth rates of these Southeast Asian economies to near double-digit levels in the late 1980s. Still, in the 1990s, increased competition from other developing countries and regional trading partnerships (such as NAFTA and the EU) threatened the stability of these export economies. In 1992, ASEAN adopted its own "free trade" agreement. AFTA, the ASEAN Free Trade Area, lowered tariffs among member nations, and promoted intra-regional trade which now stands at about 25% of the exports of these nations, about twice the level in the early 1970s. In response to the Asian economic crisis, ASEAN member nations agreed at their 1998 summit to further open up their economies, especially their manufacturing sectors, to foreign investment. Ignoring the calls of grassroots movements for controls or taxes on international capital movements, the summit implemented plans allowing 100% foreign ownership of enterprises in member countries, duty-free imports of capital goods, and a minimum for corporate tax breaks of three years.

The ASEAN tradition of "non-intervention" in the internal political affairs of its member states meant that the organization turned a blind eye to the repression of pro-democracy movements in Myanmar, Indonesia, Cambodia, and other countries in the region. Nor has ASEAN insisted that member nations meet International Labor Organization (ILO) core labor conventions. Member states have failed to sign and even denounced conventions recognizing the freedom of workers to organize trade unions, abolishing child and forced labor, and outlawing discrimination in employment. At times, they have brutally attacked trade union movements. ASEAN has also failed to intervene in regional environmental problems, witnessed by its inability in 1999 to fashion an effective regional response to Indonesia's uncontrolled forest fires. ASEAN reaction to the December 1999 WTO conference was no different. Leaders of ASEAN nations objected to U.S. calls to include core labor standards as part of trade agreements, insisting that they were an attempt to protect U.S. jobs. And Rodolfo Severino, secretary-general of ASEAN, complained that the United States and other rich countries had not lived up to the new WTO textile agreement that would allow ASEAN garment exporters greater access to First World markets.

It is China's entry into the WTO, however, that most threatens ASEAN interests. China has already replaced Southeast Asia as the favorite location of Japanese foreign direct investment, and Chinese exporters of toys, textiles, and other low-wage manufactured products have put ASEAN exporters under pressure. Unfortunately, the most likely ASEAN response to Chinese competition will be to further liberalize its own rules on foreign direct investment.

Long before this year's WTO conference, ASEAN member states recognized that their economic interests went well beyond the boundaries of Southeast Asia. In late 1980s, Prime Minister Mahathir Mohammed of Malaysia called for the formation of a pan-Asian regional economic bloc to include, along with the ASEAN countries, Japan, China, Korea, Taiwan, and Hong Kong, the largest investors in Southeast Asia. Mahathir's proposal was met with stiff opposition from the West. At the United States' insistence, the Asia-Pacific Economic Cooperation forum (including the United States, Canada, Australia, New Zealand, and Korea, along with ASEAN members Brunei Darussalam, Indonesia, Malaysia, and the Philippines) was formed instead.

Asia-Pacific Economic Cooperation (APEC) today consists of 21 members, having added Chile, China, Hong Kong, Taiwan, Mexico, Papua New Guinea, Peru, Russia, and Vietnam to its 12 founding members. Unlike ASEAN, APEC members do not form a cohesive region other than bordering on the Pacific. APEC has no formal criteria for membership, but actual or promised trade liberalization is a de facto condition for entry. While commitments made by APEC members are formally voluntary and non-binding, APEC pressures governments to remove trade and investment restrictions faster than they would following their own agenda. APEC is heavily influenced by large corporations, going so far as to adopt as its official slogan for 1996, "APEC means business." While not an official trading bloc, APEC's push for lower tariffs has proceeded further and faster than the WTO's free-trade agenda. APEC is calling for free trade among APEC nations by 2010 for "developed nations" and 2020 for "developing nations." In addition, APEC pushes labor market policies guaranteed to impose hardships on workers. For instance, in response to the Asian economic crisis, APEC counseled member countries to "maintain flexibility in domestic labor markets," advice sure to mean lower wages and more layoffs for workers already suffering from the effects of the Asian economic crisis. And while pledging to promote "environmentally sustainable development," APEC has done little to combat the depletion of national resources and deforestation, especially in developing nations. APEC has also insisted that member economies harmonize food and product safety standards, which means high standards are likely to be replaced by the lowest common denominator.   —*John Miller*

RESOURCES Linda Lim, "ASEAN: New Modes of Economic Cooperation," in *Southeast Asia in the New World Order*, Wurfel and Burton; ASEAN Web <www.asean.or.id>; APEC Secretariat <www.apecsec. org.sg>; SAY NO TO APEC <www.apec.gen.nz>.

The IMF and World Bank's Cosmetic Makeover

BY SARAH ANDERSON

January/February 2001

Medieval doctors always prescribed the same "cure"; no matter what the ailment, they applied leeches to the patient and bled them. For the past decade and a half, critics have likened the World Bank and the International Monetary Fund (IMF) to medieval doctors. The two institutions have thrown millions of people deeper into poverty by promoting the same harsh economic reforms—including privatization, budget cuts, and labor "flexibility"—regardless of local culture, resources, or economic context. Strapped with heavy debts, most developing countries have reluctantly accepted these reforms, known as structural adjustment programs (SAPs), as a condition for receiving IMF or World Bank loans.

In recent years, the doctors' harsh medicine has been exposed in dozens of studies and in increasingly vocal street protests. In response, the World Bank and the IMF have been attempting to revamp their public image into that of anti-poverty crusaders. While the World Bank has long claimed a commitment to helping the poor, this is a real departure for the IMF, which has unrepentantly elevated the financial and monetary stability above any other concern. Considering the two institutions' records, it is not surprising that the sudden conversion from crude medieval doctors to institutional Mother Theresas has provoked considerable skepticism.

MAIN ELEMENTS OF THE SAP FORMULA

Reducing the size of the state: The IMF requires that countries privatize public companies and services and fire public sector workers. While this may free up more funds to pay off loans, domestic capacity is crippled as a result. In Haiti, for example, the IMF admits that privatization of schools has seen extreme deterioration in school quality and attendance that will likely hamper the country's human capacity for many years to come. For example, only 8% of teachers in private schools (now 89% of all schools) have professional qualifications, compared to 47% in public schools. Secondary school enrollment dropped from 28% to 15% between 1985 and 1997. Nevertheless, the IMF recommends further privatization in Haiti.

Balancing the government budget: Even though rich country governments commonly engage in deficit spending, the IMF and World Bank believe this is a big no-no for poor countries. Faced with tough choices, governments often must cut spending on health, education, and environmental protection, since these don't generate income for the federal budget. According to Friends of the Earth, Brazil was pressured to slash funding for environmental enforcement by over 50% after accepting an IMF bailout agreement in 1999.

Deregulating the economy: The World Bank and IMF continue to push for the elimination of trade and investment barriers, and for the export-orientation of poor countries' economies. Again, if poor countries increase their foreign currency earnings by boosting exports, they may be more able to repay international creditors. The people, however, will not necessarily benefit. The World Bank's own statistics show that, in many regions of the world, increased exports are not associated with increased personal consumption. For example, while export volume increased by 4.3% in Sub-Saharan Africa between 1989 and 1998, per capita consumption declined by 0.5%.

Weakening labor: The institutions have also ardently promoted so-called "labor market flexibility" through measures that make it easier to fire workers or undermine the ability of unions to represent their members. In the spring of 2000, Argentine legislators passed the harsher of two labor law reform proposals after IMF officials spoke out strongly in support of it. The IMF, backed up by the might of the global financial community, appears to have carried more weight than the tens of thousands of Argentines who carried out general strikes against the reform. Even though a recently released World Bank study shows a correlation between high rates of unionization and lower levels of inequality, the Bank and Fund maintain that they cannot engage in promoting labor rights because this would constitute interference in domestic politics.

Although the Bank and Fund have promoted SAPs as a virtual religion for nearly 20 years, they cannot even claim that they have achieved a reduction in the developing world's debt burden. Between 1980 and 1997, the debt of low-income countries grew by 544% and that of middle-income countries by 481%.

THE IMF GETS A FACELIFT

In 1999, in response to increasing opposition, the IMF gave its Enhanced Structural Adjustment Facility (through which it made SAP loans) the new moniker of Poverty Reduction and Growth Facility. Both the IMF and World Bank announced that under their new approach, they would require governments seeking concessional lending and debt relief to consult with civil society to develop strategies for poverty reduction. In addition, the institutions vowed increased commitment to debt relief for the poorest countries. World Bank President James Wolfensohn expressed his pride in these efforts by commenting that he comes in to work every day "thinking I'm doing God's work."

Although most of the new poverty reduction initiatives are in an early stage, the World Bank and IMF have given plenty of evidence to support the skeptics:

Anti-poverty PR stunts: NGOs have raised strong criticism of the civil society consultation processes that are supposed to take place as governments develop the required Poverty Reduction Strategy Papers. Sara Grusky of the Washington-based Globalization Challenge Initiative (GCI) doubts the value of "consultation" if countries will still have to accept the standard policies to get the IMF's "seal of approval." Carlos Pacheco Alizaga of Nicaragua's Center for International Studies says that civil society consultation is restricted to narrow discussions of social policy. He argues that the process "tries to dilute the central discussion which is the lack of a new model of development for the impoverished countries and the creation of a new world trade system that should not be controlled by the rich countries of the north and the transnational companies." As of October 2000, only two countries (Uganda and Burkina Faso) had completed a Poverty Reduction Strategy Paper. Another 13 had completed interim drafts, but in several cases civil society groups have reported either a complete lack of public consultation or mere public relations stunts that excluded groups more critical of Bank and Fund policies.

Debt rhetoric: A year ago, the World Bank and IMF initiated a joint plan, called the "Heavily Indebted Poor Country" (HIPC) initiative to provide a measure of debt relief to certain countries that agree to structural adjustment conditions. The World Bank touts HIPC as an example of their "leadership to relieve the unsustainable debt burdens that stand in the way of development and poverty reduction." The IMF may be more candid about HIPC's true goals. A statement on its web site identifies the main objective not as poverty reduction but rather the reduction of poor countries' debt burdens to levels that will "comfortably enable them to service their debt" and "broaden domestic support for policy reforms." As Soren Ambrose of the Alliance for Global Justice puts it, "HIPC is just a cruel hoax designed to trick developing countries into accepting more structural adjustment."

The World Bank and IMF have tried to tout the HIPC initiative as a permanent solution to the debt crisis by concocting wildly unrealistic predictions of the eligible countries' future economic performance. (As of October 2000, only 10 of the 41 countries had met the rigid HIPC criteria.) They estimate that export, GDP, and government revenue growth will average 7 to 12 percent in nominal dollar terms for the next 20 years—optimism that is completely unjustified by the countries' past performance.

Ecuador eruption: There is perhaps no stronger evidence of the continued havoc wreaked by IMF/World Bank orthodoxy than Ecuador. During the past year, indigenous groups, trade unions, and others have organized mass protests against a harsh IMF reform program that shifts the country's economic crisis onto the backs of the poor. In the midst of a general strike against the program in June

2000, a delegation of Ecuadoran human rights, women's, and trade union groups came to Washington, D.C., to ask the World Bank to postpone consideration of a new loan agreement conditioned on further implementation of IMF reforms. The NGOs argued that there had been a total lack of public consultation on the deal, which required low levels of social spending and removal of subsidies for basic goods, while ignoring the country's need for debt relief. Despite their pleas, the World Bank approved the loan package the following week.

Censorship: The dramatic resignations in the spring of 2000 of two high-level World Bank employees raised further doubts about the institutions' commitment to poverty reduction and civil-society participation. Former Chief Economist Joseph Stiglitz claims that U.S. Treasury Secretary Lawrence Summers and IMF bigwigs succeeded in pushing him out of the Bank in retaliation for his charges that the Fund's policies helped precipitate and worsen the global financial crises that erupted in mid-1997. Stiglitz pointed out that while reckless international investors, domestic banks, and fickle investors caused the crises, the costs were borne by the workers.

Then in June, the editor of the World Bank's *World Development Report*, Ravi Kanbur, broke his contract, reportedly in protest over demands that he water down content that had been developed through extensive civil society participation. Once again, Summers and other supporters of "free market" orthodoxy had allegedly intervened to quash the report's calls for economic redistribution, claiming that economic growth was the ultimate solution for poverty.

Although the final report released in September 2000 contains some strong language about the need to empower the poor, there is no indication that the institutions are willing to consider a substantial reform of their policies. One chapter, "Making Markets Work Better for Poor People," attributes all problems of economic collapse and poverty growth to deficiencies in "market access." The report implies that those former Communist countries that have been mired in economic collapse and stagnation should have followed the examples of the countries that implemented reforms "forcefully and early." This contrasts sharply with the findings of many researchers that the most successful former Communist countries were those that adopted a more gradual and cautious approach.

OLD LEECHES, NEW JARS

So far there is little evidence of a genuine conversion on the part of the IMF and World Bank. They have not fundamentally rethought their formula of "structural adjustment," nor their overall commitment to the "free market" model. The medieval doctors have just repackaged their cruel ministrations with warm and fuzzy labels. The challenge for critics is to keep up the pressure, exposing this façade and unifying around a concrete set of meaningful alternative goals and policies—real transparency, real democracy, and a real commitment to fight poverty.

ARTICLE 19

Economic Debacle in Argentina
The IMF Strikes Again

BY ARTHUR MacEWAN

March/April 2002

In the days just before Christmas 2001, with increasing cutbacks in social programs and an official unemployment rate approaching 20%, Argentinians took to the streets in protest. At the time, Argentina was in the midst of its fourth year of recession. The immediate spark for the unrest was the government's latest economic policies, which restricted the amount of money people could withdraw from their bank accounts. Political demonstrations and the looting of grocery stores quickly spread across the country.

The government declared a state of siege, but police often stood by and watched the looting "with their hands behind their backs." There was little the government could do. Within a day after the demonstrations began, principal economic minister Domingo Cavallo had resigned; a few days later, President Fernando de la Rúa stepped down.

In the wake of the resignations, a hastily assembled interim government immediately defaulted on $155 billion of Argentina's foreign debt, the largest debt default in history. The new government also promised a public works jobs program and announced plans to issue a new currency, the argentino, that would circulate alongside the Argentine peso and the U.S. dollar. As economic instability deepened, however, the argentino plan was abandoned. And the new public works program did little to address the fact that per capita income had dropped by 14% since 1998. Unable to win the popular support it needed, the new government quickly dissolved. A new president, Eduardo Duhalde, was sworn in on January 1, 2002; he was the fifth president to serve in two weeks.

As of this writing (mid-February), Argentina still faces widespread political and economic uncertainty. In the short run, many anticipate more unemployment, severe inflation, or both. Also, Argentina's currency remains highly unstable. After experimenting with several different exchange rates, the Duhalde government is now permitting the peso to "float." The peso has already dropped from its previous value (one to the dollar) down to two to the dollar on the open market, and further devaluation is widely anticipated.

Argentina's experience leading into the current debacle provides one more lesson regarding the perils of "free market" ideology, and specifically the economic policies that the International Monetary Fund (IMF) pushes on governments around the globe. In Argentina, as in other places, these policies have been embraced by local elites, who see their fortunes (both real and metaphoric) as tied to the deregulation of commerce and the curtailment of social programs. Yet the claims that these policies bring economic growth and widespread well-being have been thoroughly discredited, as events in Argentina have shown.

FROM GOOD TO BAD TO UGLY

Not long ago, Argentina was the poster child for the conservative economic policies of the IMF. From the late 1980s onward, a series of loans gave the IMF the leverage to guide Argentine policymakers in privatizing state enterprises, liberalizing foreign trade and investment, and tightening government fiscal and monetary policy. During the 1990s, the country's economy seemed to do well, with real per capita income growing at the very rapid annual rate of about 4.5%.

The rapid economic growth through most of the 1990s, however, was built on weak foundations. That growth, while substantial, appears to have resulted largely from an increasing accumulation of international obligations (debt to private banks, the IMF, and foreign governments, as well as direct foreign investment), fortuitous expansion of foreign markets for Argentine exports, and short-term injections of government revenues from the sale of state enterprises. Before the end of the decade, things began to fall apart.

Argentina's current problems are all the more severe because in the early 1990s, in the name of fighting inflation, the government created a "currency board." The board was charged with regulating the country's currency so that the Argentine peso would exchange one-to-one with the U.S. dollar. To assure this fixed exchange rate, the board kept a supply of dollars on reserve, and could not expand the supply of pesos without an equivalent increase in the dollars that it held. The currency board system appeared attractive because of absurd rates of inflation in the 1980s, with price increases of up to 200% a month. By restricting the growth of the money supply, the system brought inflation rates to heel.

Although the currency board system had virtually eliminated inflation in Argentina by the mid-1990s, it had also eliminated flexibility in monetary policy. When the current recession began to develop in the late 1990s, the government could not stimulate economic activity by expanding the money supply.

Worse yet, as the economy continued to spiral downward, the inflow of dollars slowed, forcing the currency board to restrict the country's money supply even further. And still worse, in the late 1990s, the U.S. dollar appreciated against other currencies, which meant (because of the one-to-one rule) that the peso also increased in value. As a result, the price of Argentine exports rose, further weakening world demand for Argentina's goods.

As Argentina entered into the lasting downturn of the period since 1998, the IMF continued, unwavering, in its financial support. The IMF provided "small" loans, such as $3 billion in early 1998 when the country's economic difficulties began to appear. As the crisis deepened, the IMF increased its support, supplying a loan of $13.7 billion and arranging $26 billion more from other sources at the end of 2000. As conditions worsened further in 2001, the IMF pledged another $8 billion.

However, the IMF coupled its largesse with the condition that the Argentine government maintain its severe monetary policy and continue to tighten its fiscal policy by eliminating its budget deficit. (The IMF considers deficit reduction to be the key to macroeconomic stability and, in turn, the key to economic growth.)

The Argentine government undertook deficit reduction with a vengeance. With the economy in a nosedive and tax revenues plummeting, the only way to balance the budget was to drastically cut government spending. In early July 2001, just before making a major government bond offering, Argentine officials announced budget cuts totaling $1.6 billion (about 3% of the federal budget), which they hoped would reassure investors and allow interest rates to fall. Apparently, however, investors saw the cuts as another sign of worsening crisis, and the bonds could only be sold at high interest rates (14%, as compared to 9% on similar bonds sold just a few weeks before the announcement of budget cuts). By December 2001, the effort to balance the budget required cuts that were far more severe; the government announced a drastic reduction of $9.2 billion in spending, or about 18% of its entire budget.

With these cutbacks, the government both eviscerated social programs and reduced overall demand. In mid-December 2001, the government announced that it would cut the salaries of public employees by 20% and reduce pension payments. At the same time, as the worsening crisis raised fears that Argentina would abandon the currency board system and devalue the peso, the government moved to prevent people from trading their pesos for dollars by limiting bank withdrawals. These steps were the final straws, and in the week before Christmas, all hell broke loose.

WHO BENEFITS FROM IMF POLICIES?

Argentina is just the latest example of how IMF policies have failed to establish the basis for long-term economic growth in low-income countries. IMF policies usually do succeed in curtailing inflation, as they did in Argentina in the mid-1990s, because sharp cuts in government spending and restrictions on the money supply tend to yield reduced price increases. Also, as the Argentine case illustrates, adopting IMF programs can open the door to large influxes of foreign loans—from the Fund itself, the World Bank, the governments of the United States and other high-income countries, and (with the IMF's approval) internationally operating banks. But nowhere, including Argentina, has the IMF policy package led to stable, sustained economic expansion.

What IMF policies do often lead to, though, is growing inequality. Officially, the IMF laments that its policies—specifically reductions in government spending—have a severe negative impact on low-income groups (because they generate high rates of unemployment and lead to the gutting of social programs). Yet IMF officials rationalize their mania for spending cuts in times of crisis by claiming that balanced budgets are the foundation of long-term economic stability and growth.

Nonsense. In recessions, moderate government deficits, like those in Argentina in recent years, are a desirable policy because they boost spending, which counteracts the downturn; balanced budgets in such circumstances tend to exacerbate downturns. Also, curtailing social spending—on education, health care, infrastructure projects—cuts the legs out from under long-term economic progress.

Yet the IMF sticks to its policies, probably because those policies serve important and powerful interests in the U.S. and world economies. The IMF is controlled by the governments of the high-income countries that finance its operations. The U.S. government, with over 18% of the voting shares in the Fund, has by far the greatest influence. Indeed, over the years, the IMF has operated largely as a branch of the U.S. foreign policy apparatus, attempting to create a context that assures the well-being of U.S. interests—which is to say the interests of U.S.-based internationally operating firms. Since the same context serves the interests of firms based in Europe, Japan, and elsewhere, the U.S. government generally has the support of its allied governments in directing the IMF.

To serve those interests, the IMF tells governments that a key to economic growth lies in providing unrestricted access for imports and foreign investment. In fact, virtually all experience suggests the opposite. Britain, the United States, Japan, the countries of Western Europe, Taiwan, South Korea—all built the foundations for successful economic growth not on "free trade," but on government regulation of trade. The IMF gets around the inconvenient facts of history by conflating free trade with extensive engagement in the international economy. But the two are not the same. Yes, successful development has always been accompanied by extensive international engagement, but through regulated commerce, not free trade.

During the 1980s and 1990s, the IMF pushed governments in low-income countries to liberalize their capital markets, claiming that capital controls were anathema to development. Then came 1997, when the open capital markets of East Asian countries were instruments of disaster. In the aftermath of 1997, it seemed clear that the real winners from open capital markets were financial firms based in the United States and other high-income countries.

These same financial firms have also been the winners of another component in the IMF policy package. "Fiscal responsibility," according to the IMF, means that governments must give the highest priority to repaying their international debts. However, experience does not support the contention that, when governments fail to pay foreign debts, they bring on financial disaster. Instead, experience suggests that, at times, defaulting on foreign debt can be an effective, positive policy option. It is the banks operating out of New York and other financial centers, not people in low-income countries, that gain from giving first priority to debt repayment.

The IMF's advocacy of privatization offers one more way to open the world economy more fully to U.S.-based firms. When state enterprises in low-income countries are sold, they are often bought by large internationally operating firms, able to move in quickly with their huge supply of capital. Of course, in Argentina and elsewhere, local business groups have often benefited directly from privatization, sometimes on their own and sometimes as junior partners of firms based abroad. Either way, this enlargement of the private sphere works in favor of private firms. The problem here is not that privatization is always inappropriate, but simply that, contrary to IMF nostrums, it is not always appropriate. Privatization is especially problematic when it only replaces an inefficient government monopoly with a private monopoly yielding huge profits for its owners. Moreover, the record from Mexico City to Moscow demonstrates that privatization is often a hugely corrupt process.

FORGING AN ARGENTINE ALTERNATIVE?

The recent political upheaval in Argentina lends new strength to the argument that IMF policies not only fail to bolster economic development but also lead to social and political disintegration. It also provides new opportunities to call for alternative strategies that support democratic, egalitarian forms of economic development. Such strategies would promote investment in social programs and other public services, the expansion of government revenues (raising taxes), and regulations to keep the private sector from being guided simply by private profits. These strategies, unlike those of the IMF, would establish a foundation for long-run economic expansion—and economic equality.

Could such strategies succeed in Argentina? The demonstrations that brought down the de la Rúa government seem to have brought together unemployed people, workers, and large segments of the middle class, at least for a time. Sporadic rioting continues, and in Buenos Aires, scores of neighborhood-based assemblies, attracting thousands of participants, are calling for a more democratic political system as well as issuing demands for economic change.

Nonetheless, positive changes will be difficult to attain. Although the Argentine government did default on the debt (a key element in repudiating the policies of the IMF), it did so as an act of desperation, not in a controlled manner that might yield the greatest advantage. Also, while deputy economic minister Jorge Todesca has been harshly critical of the IMF, he is also trying to appease foreign investors, saying that the government is "not thinking of" nationalizing the banking system or establishing price controls.

Externally, there are substantial political barriers to an alternative model of economic growth. At the end of December 2001, even as a new spate of rioting broke out in Buenos Aires, President Bush told the Argentine government to seek guidance from the IMF and "to work closely with" the Fund in developing its economic plans. In early February 2002, the finance ministers of the G-7 (the world's seven wealthiest industrial nations) rejected Argentina's request for a $20 billion loan, saying that the IMF must be on board in order to bring about a "sustainable" plan. Argentina's economic minister, Jorge Remes Lenicov, then met with IMF officials in Washington, D.C.

And the IMF is unlikely to change its program in any significant way. Indeed, as Argentinians took to the streets in response to their long suffering under the aegis of the IMF, the IMF disclaimed all responsibility. "The economic program of Argentina was designed by the government of Argentina and the objective of eliminating the budget deficit was approved by the Congress of Argentina," declared the IMF's spokesperson on December 21, 2001. Continued pressure from the U.S. government, combined with the IMF's persistence in pursuing its discredited policies, will make progressive change difficult.

Also, powerful elites in Argentina will reinforce the barriers to change. In spite of the current difficulties, Argentina's economic policies of the past 15 years have delivered substantial benefits to the country's business elite, especially those whose incomes derive from the financial sector and primary product exports (grain and beef). Those policies have allowed the elite to strengthen their position in their own country and to secure their roles as junior partners with U.S.-based and other internationally operating firms. Changing policies will therefore require shifting the balance of power within Argentina, and that will be no easy task.

A version of this article appeared in Foreign Policy in Focus www.foreignpolicy-infocus.org, 2 January 2002.

CHAPTER 5

Labor in the International Economy

ARTICLE 20

Sweatshops 101

Lessons in Monitoring Apparel Production Around the World

BY DARA O'ROURKE

September/October 2001

N avy blue sweatshirts bearing a single foreign word, Michigan, and a well-known logo, the Nike swoosh, were piled high in a small room off the main factory floor. After cutting, stitching, and embroidering by the 1,100 workers outside, the sweatshirts landed in the spot-cleaning room, where six young Indonesian women prepared the garments for shipment to student stores and NikeTowns across America. The women spent hour after hour using chemical solvents to rid the sweatshirts of smudges and stains. With poor ventilation, ill-fitting respiratory protection, no gloves, and no chemical hazard training, the women sprayed solvents and aerosol cleaners containing benzene, methylene chloride, and perchloroethylene, all carcinogens, on the garments.

It used to be that the only thing people wondered when you wore a Harvard or Michigan sweatshirt was whether you had actually gone there. More and more, though, people are wondering out loud where that sweatshirt was made, and whether any workers were exploited in making it. Students, labor activists, and human-rights groups have spearheaded a movement demanding to know what really lies beneath their university logos, and whether our public universities and private colleges are profiting from global sweatshop production.

WHERE WAS THAT SWEATSHIRT MADE?

So far, few universities have been able to answer these questions. Universities generally don't even know where their products are produced, let alone whether workers were endangered to produce them. Indeed, with global outsourcing many brand name companies cannot trace the supply chains which lead to the student store, and are blissfully ignorant of conditions in these factories.

Under pressure from student activists across the country, a small group of university administrators decided it was time to find out more about the garments bearing their schools' names and logos. As part of a collaborative research project, called the "Independent University Initiative" (IUI), funded by Harvard University, the University of Notre Dame, Ohio State University, the University of California, and the University of Michigan, I joined a team investigating where and under what conditions university garments were being made. Its report is available at web.mit.edu/dorourke/www. The team included staff from the business association Business for Social Responsibility, the non-profit Investor Responsibility Research Center, and the accounting firm PricewaterhouseCoopers (PwC). PwC was responsible for auditing the labor conditions in each of the factories included in the study. At the request of student activists, I joined the team as an outside evaluator.

The IUI research team evaluated garment manufacturing for the top apparel companies licensing the logos of these five universities. It looked at factories subcontracted by nine companies, including Adidas, Champion, and Nike. The nine alone outsource university apparel to over 180 factories in 26 countries. This may sound like a lot, but it is actually the tip of the global production iceberg. Americans bought about $2.5 billion worth of university-logo garments in 1999. Overall, however, U.S. apparel sales totaled over $180 billion. There are an estimated 80,000 factories around the world producing garments for the U.S. market. The university garment industry is important not so much for its size, but for the critical opening it provides onto the larger industry.

The research team visited factories in the top seven countries producing apparel for the nine companies: China, El Salvador, Korea, Mexico, Pakistan, Thailand, and the United States. It inspected 13 work sites in all. I personally inspected factories for the project in China and Korea, and then inspected factories in Indonesia on my own to see what things looked like outside the official process. Through this research I discovered not only exploitative and hazardous working conditions, but also an official monitoring process designed to gloss over the biggest problems of the apparel industry. PwC auditors found minor violations of labor laws and codes of conduct, but missed major labor problems including serious health and safety hazards, barriers to freedom of association, and violations of overtime and wage laws. This was a learning experience I call "Sweatshops 101."

Lesson #1   Global Outsourcing

The garment industry is extremely complicated and highly disaggregated. The industry has multiple layers of licensees, brokers, jobbers, importer-exporters, component suppliers, and subcontractors on top of subcontractors.

The University of Michigan does not manufacture any of the products bearing its name. Nor does Notre Dame nor Harvard nor any other university. These schools simply license their names to apparel makers and other companies for a percentage of the sale—generally around 7% of the retail price for each T-shirt, sweatshirt, or key chain. Until recently, the universities had little interest in even knowing who produced their goods. If they tracked this at all, it was to catch companies using their logos without paying the licensing fee.

Sometimes the companies that license university names and logos own the factories where the apparel is produced. But more often the licensees simply contract production out to factories in developing countries. Nike owns none of the hundreds of factories that produce its garments and athletic shoes.

A sweatshirt factory itself may have multiple subcontractors who produce the fabric, embroider the logo, or stitch sub-components. This global supply chain stretches from the university administration building, to the corporate office of the licensee companies, to large-scale factories in China and Mexico, to small scale sub-contractor factories everywhere in between, and in some cases, all the way to women stitching garments in their living rooms.

Lesson #2   The Global Shell Game

The global garment industry is highly mobile, with contracts continuously shifting from subcontractor to subcontractor within and between countries. Licensees can move production between subcontractors after one year, one month, or even as little as one week.

It took the university research team three months to get from the licensee companies a list of the factories producing university-logo garments. However, because the actual factories producing university goods at any one time change so fast, by the time I had planned a trip to China and Korea to visit factories, the lists were essentially obsolete. One licensee in Korea had replaced eight of its eleven factories with new factories by the time I arrived in town. Over a four month period, the company had contracted with 21 different factories. A range of factors—including price competition between contractors, changes in fashions (and factories capable of filling orders), fluctuations in exchange rates, and changing import quotas for different countries—is responsible for this constant state of flux.

Even after double-checking with a licensee, in almost every country the project team would arrive at the factory gates only to be told that the factories we planned to inspect were no longer producing university goods. Of course, some of this may have been the licensees playing games. Faced with inspections, some may have decided to shift production out of the chosen factory, or at least to tell us that it had been shifted.

Some of the largest, most profitable apparel firms in the world, known for their management prowess, however, simply did not know where their products were being produced. When asked how many factories Disney had around the world, company execs guessed there were 1,500 to 1,800 factories producing their garments, toys, videos, and other goods. As it turns out, they were only off by an order of magnitude. So far the company has counted over 20,000 factories around the world producing Disney-branded goods. Only recent exposés by labor, human rights, and environmental activists have convinced these companies that they need better control over their supply chains.

Lesson #3 Normal Operating Conditions

The day an inspector visits a factory is not a normal day. Any factory that has prior knowledge of an inspection is very likely to make changes on the day of the visit.

In a Nike-contracted shoe factory in Indonesia I visited in June 2000, all of the workers in the hot press section of the plant (a particularly dangerous area) were wearing brand new black dress shoes on the day of our inspection. One of the workers explained they had been given the shoes that morning and were expected to return them at the end of the shift. Managers often give workers new protective equipment—such as gloves, respirators, and even shoes—on the day of an inspection. However, as the workers have no training in how to even use this equipment, it is common to see brand-new respirators being worn below workers' noses, around their necks, or even upside down.

At one factory the university team visited in Mexico, the factory manager wanted to guarantee that the inspectors would find his factory spotless. So he locked all of the bathrooms on the day of the inspection. Workers were not allowed to use the bathrooms until the project team showed up, hours into the work day.

Licensees and subcontractors often try to subvert monitoring. They block auditors from inspecting on certain days or from visiting certain parts of a plant, claim production has moved, feign ignorance of factory locations, keep multiple sets of books on wages and hours, coach workers on responses to interviews, and threaten workers against complaining to inspectors. The university research team was unable to get around many of these obstructions.

Lesson #4 Conditions in University Factories

Factories producing university apparel often violate local laws and university codes of conduct on maximum hours of work, minimum and overtime wages, freedom of association, and health and safety protections.

In a 300-worker apparel plant in Shanghai, the university team found that many of the workers were working far in excess of maximum overtime laws.

A quick review of timecards found women working over 315 hours in a month and 20 consecutive days without a day off. The legal maximum in China is only 204 hours per month, with at least one day off in seven. A sample of 25 workers showed that the average overtime worked was 101 hours, while the legal limit is 36 hours per month. One manager explained these gross violations with a shrug, saying, "Timecards are just used to make sure workers show up on time. Workers are actually paid based on a piece rate system."

The factory also had a wide range of health and safety problems, including a lack of guarding on sewing and cutting machines, high levels of cotton dust in one section of the plant, several blocked aisles and fire exits, no running water in certain toilets, no information for workers on the hazardous chemicals they were using, and a lack of protective equipment for the workers.

Living conditions for the workers who lived in a dormitory on site were also poor. The dormitory had 12 women packed into each room on six bunk beds. Each floor had four rooms (48 women) and only one bathroom. These bathrooms had only two shower heads and four toilet stalls each, and no dividers between them.

And what of workers' rights to complain or demand better conditions? The union in this factory was openly being run by the management. While 70% of workers were "members" of the union, one manager explained, "We don't have U.S.-style unions here." No workers had ever tried to take control of this group or to form an independent union.

Lesson #5   The Challenges of Monitoring

Finding a dozen factories is relatively easy compared to the job of tracking the thousands of rapidly changing factories that produce university goods each year. Systematically monitoring and evaluating their practices on wages, hours, discrimination, and health and safety issues is an even bigger challenge.

Most universities don't have the capacity to individually monitor the conditions in "their" factories, so some are joining together to create cooperative monitoring programs. The concept behind "independent monitoring" is to have a consulting firm or non-governmental organization inspect and evaluate a factory's compliance with a code of conduct. There are now two major university monitoring systems. The Fair Labor Association (FLA) now has over 157 universities as members, and the Worker Rights Consortium (WRC) has over 80 affiliated universities. (The four smaller monitoring initiatives are Social Accountability International (SA8000), the Ethical Trading Initiative, the Clean Clothes Campaign, and the Worldwide Responsible Apparel Production (WRAP) program.)

The FLA emerged from the Clinton-convened "White House Apparel Industry Partnership" in 1998. It is supported by a small group of apparel companies including Nike, Reebok, adidas, Levi-Strauss, Liz Claiborne, and Philips Van Heusen. Students and labor-rights advocates have criticized the group for being industry-dominated and for allowing companies to monitor only 10% of their factories each year, to use monitors that the companies pay directly, to control when and where monitors inspect, and to restrict the information released to the public after the audits.

The United Students Against Sweatshops (USAS) and UNITE (the largest garment-workers' union in the United States) founded the WRC in 1999 as an alternative to the FLA. The WRC promotes systems for verifying factory conditions after workers have complained or after inspections have occurred, and to create greater public disclosure of conditions. The WRC differs from the FLA in that it refuses to certify that any company meets a code of conduct. The group argues that because of the problems of monitoring, it is simply not possible to systematically monitor or certify a company's compliance. Some universities and companies have criticized the WRC as being a haphazard "gotcha" monitoring system whose governing body excludes the very companies that must be part of solving these problems.

Both groups profess to support the International Labour Organization's core labor standards, including upholding workers' rights to freedom of association and collective bargaining, and prohibiting forced labor, child labor, and discrimination in the workplace. The WRC, however, goes further in advocating that workers be paid a "living wage," and that women's rights receive particular attention. Both programs assert a strong role for local NGOs, unions, and workers. However, the two have widely varying levels of transparency and public disclosure, and very different systems of sanctions and penalties.

Lesson #6   How Not To Monitor

Corporate-sponsored monitoring systems seem almost designed to miss the most critical issues in the factories they inspect. Auditors often act as if they are on the side of management rather than the workers.

PricewaterhouseCoopers (PwC) is the largest private monitor of codes of conduct and corporate labor practices in the world. The company performed over 6,000 factory audits in the year 2000, including monitoring for Nike, Disney, Walmart, and the Gap. (PwC recently announced that they were spinning off their labor monitoring services into a firm called Global Social Compliance.) PwC monitors for many of the top university licensees, and was hired as the monitor for the university project. Like other corporate monitors, the company has been criticized for covering up problems and assuaging the public conscience about sweatshop conditions that have not really been resolved.

PwC's monitoring systems epitomize current corporate monitoring efforts. The firm sends two auditors—who are actually financial accountants with minimal training on labor issues—into each factory for eight hours. The auditors use a checklist and a standard interview form to evaluate legal compliance, wages and benefits, working hours, freedom of association and collective bargaining, child labor, forced labor, disciplinary practices, and health and safety.

On the university project, PwC auditors failed to adequately examine any major issue in the factories I saw them inspect. In factories in Korea and Indonesia, PwC auditors completely missed exposure to toxic chemicals, something which could eventually cost workers their lives from cancer. In Korea, the auditors saw no problem in managers violating overtime wage laws. In China, the auditors went so far as to recommend ways for the managers to circumvent local laws on overtime hours, essentially providing advice on how to break university codes of conduct. And the auditors in Korea simply skipped the questions on workers' right to organize in their worker interviews, explaining, "They don't have a union in this factory, so those questions aren't relevant."

The PwC auditing method is biased towards managers. Before an inspection, PwC auditors send managers a questionnaire explaining what will be inspected. They prepare managers at an opening meeting before each inspection. In the Chinese factory, they asked managers to enter wages and hours data into the PwC spreadsheet. Even the worker interviews were biased towards the managers. PwC auditors asked the managers to help them select workers to be interviewed, had the managers bring their personnel files, and then had the managers bring the workers into the office used for the interviews. The managers knew who was being interviewed, for how long, and on what issues. Workers knew this as well, and answered questions accordingly.

The final reports that PwC delivered to its clients gave a largely sanitized picture of the factories inspected. This is unsurprising, considering PwC's business interest in providing companies with "acceptable" audits.

WHERE TO BEGIN?

Universities face increasing public pressure to guarantee that workers are not being injured or exploited to produce their insignia products. They have no system, however, to track apparel production around the world, and often no idea where their production is occurring. Monitoring systems are still in their fledgling stages, so universities are starting from a difficult position, albeit one they have profited from for years.

What can universities do about this? They should do what they are best at: produce information. They should take the lead in demanding that corporations—beginning with those they do business with—open themselves up to public inspection and evaluation. Universities have done this before, such as during the anti-apartheid campaign for South Africa. By doing this on the sweatshop issue, universities could spur a critical dialogue on labor issues around the world.

To start, the universities could establish a central coordinating office to collect and compare information on factory performance for member universities' licensees. (The WRC has proposed such a model.) This new office would be responsible for keeping records on licensee compliance, for making this information available over the Internet, for registering local NGOs and worker organizations to conduct independent verifications of factory conditions, and for assessing sanctions.

Such a program would allow universities to evaluate different strategies for improving conditions in different parts of the world. This would avoid the danger of locking in one code of conduct or one certification system. In place of sporadic media exposés embarrassing one company at a time, we would have an international system of disclosure and learning—benchmarking good performers, identifying and targeting the worst performers, and motivating improvement.

It is clearly not enough to expose one company at a time, nor to count on industry-paid consulting firms to monitor labor conditions. The building blocks of a new system depend on information. This fits the mission of universities. Universities should focus on information gathering and dissemination, and most importantly, on learning. If the universities learn nothing else from "Sweatshops 101," it is that they still have a lot of homework do to—and their next test will be coming soon.

ARTICLE 21

Immigrant Workers in the Crosshairs

BY DAVID BACON

January/February 2003

Erlinda Valencia came from the Philippines almost two decades ago. Like many Filipina immigrants living in the San Francisco Bay area, she found a job at the airport, screening passengers' baggage.

For 14 years she worked for Argenbright Security, the baggage-screening contractor used by airlines across the country. For most of that time, it was a minimum-wage job, and she could barely support her family working 40 hours a week. Then, two years ago, organizers from the Service Employees International Union (SEIU) began talking to the screeners. Erlinda Valencia decided to get involved, and eventually became a leader in the campaign that brought in the union. "We were very happy," she remembers. "It seemed to us all that for the first time, we had a real future." The new contract the union negotiated raised wages to over $10 an hour, and workers say harassment by managers began to decrease.

Erlinda Valencia's experience reflected a major national shift in immigrant workers' organizing. In recent years, immigrant workers made hard-fought gains in their rights at work, and in using these rights to organize unions and fight for better wages and conditions. Despite the hostile reaction embodied in measures like California's Propositions 187 and 227, which sought to penalize undocumented immigrants and ban bilingual education, the political and economic clout of immigrants has increased, in large part because of successful labor organizing efforts. Some, like the janitors' strike in Los Angeles, have become well-known.

As a result, the AFL-CIO changed its position on immigration, and began calling for the repeal of employer sanctions, the federal law making it illegal for an undocumented worker to hold a job. The national movement for amnesty for undocumented workers began to grow, and the U.S. and Mexican governments started to negotiate over variants of the proposal. Under pressure from unions and immigrant rights organizations, the Immigration and Naturalization Service (INS) reduced the number of raids it carried out from 17,000 in 1997 to 953 in 2000.

Then the airplanes hit the twin towers in New York and the Pentagon in Washington. The mainstream media universally portrayed the September 11 attacks as the actions of immigrants. Political figures across the board proposed restrictions on immigration (by students, for instance) and crackdowns against undocumented workers, despite the fact that none of this would have prevented the attacks. The movement towards amnesty, and away from immigration raids and heavy-handed enforcement tactics, halted abruptly. Many public agencies, from local police departments to the Social Security Administration, which previously faced pressure to stop aiding the INS, took up immigration enforcement as a new responsibility. The Bush administration took advantage of the anti-immigrant fever to undermine the rights of workers, especially the foreign-born. The nativist scapegoating also provided a rationale for attacks on civil liberties, including the open use of racial profiling, indefinite detention, and other repressive measures.

EVERYTHING CHANGES—FOR TRANSPORTATION WORKERS

Screeners like Erlinda Valencia were among the first, and hardest, hit. Media and politicians blamed the screeners for allowing terrorists to board airplanes in Boston and New York with box cutters and plastic knives, despite the fact that these items were permitted at the time. But the whispered undercurrent beneath the criticism, that the screeners were undependable, and possibly even disloyal, was part of the rising anti-immigrant fever which swept the country.

Screeners in California airports, like those in many states where immigrants are a big part of the population, are mostly from other countries. In fact, the low pay for screeners was one of the factors that led to the concentration of immigrants and people of color in those jobs. In the search for scapegoats, they were easy targets.

In short order, Congress passed legislation setting up a new Transportation Security Authority (TSA) to oversee baggage and passenger screening at airports, and requiring that screeners be federal government employees. That could have been a good thing for Valencia and her coworkers, since federal employees have decent salaries, and often, because of civil service, lots of job security. Federal regulations protect their right to belong to unions, as well—at least they used to.

The TSA, however, was made part of the recently established Homeland Security Department. Legislation passed after the November elections—and after some Democrats did an about face and voted for it—allows Homeland Security Czar Tom Ridge to suspend civil-service regulations in any part of the new department. By doing so, he can eliminate workers' union rights, allow discrimination and favoritism, and even abolish protection for whistleblowers.

In the anti-immigrant fever of the times, moreover, Congress required that screeners be citizens. Valencia had never become one, because of a Catch-22 in U.S. immigration law. She is petitioning for visas for family members in the Philippines. As a citizen, however, she would actually have to wait longer to petition for them than she has to as a legal resident.

At the San Francisco airport, over 800 screeners were non-citizens. The INS, however, refused to establish any fast-track to citizenship, to help them qualify for the new federalized jobs. So just as she and her coworkers finally made the job bearable and capable of supporting a family, she lost it in November, when the citizenship requirement went into effect nationwide. "It's so unfair," she said. "I've done this job for 14 years, and we're all really good at it. Instead of wanting us to continue, they're going to hire people with no experience at all, and we'll probably have to train them too. You can fly the airplane, even if you're not a citizen, and you can carry a rifle in the airport as a member of the National Guard doing security, without being a citizen either. But you can't check the bags of the passengers."

In recent years, screeners working for private contractors like Argenbright have organized unions at airports in a number of cities, including San Francisco and Los Angeles. By federalizing the workforce, the government was also, in effect, busting those unions and tearing up their newly won contracts. The act creating the Homeland Security Department—which, with 170,000 employees, will be the largest in the federal government—may be invoked to prevent the new screener workforce from forming new unions and bargaining with the TSA. The American Federation of Government Employees, which represents federal workers, has protested against the exemption of the TSA from federal regulations recognizing employees' collective bargaining rights, and announced its intention of organizing the new workforce. But it does not challenge the citizenship requirement for screeners.

TAKING THE "WAR" TO THE WORKPLACE

Valencia was caught up in a wave of anti-immigrant legislation and repression that has profoundly affected immigrants and workers across the country in the wake of the September 11 terrorist attacks. The INS has launched a series of large-scale raids—Operation Tarmac. In airports around the country, the agency has told employers to provide the I-9 form for their employees. Using this information, agents have organized raids to pick up workers, and demanded that employers terminate those it says lack legal status. Close to 1,000 workers have been affected.

Initially, the INS stated publicly that it would only concentrate on workers who had access to the planes themselves, using aviation security as a pretext (hence the name Operation Tarmac). But once the raids got going, the crackdown expanded to workers in food preparation, and even in food service within passenger areas of the airports. A late-August raid at the Seattle-Tacoma International Airport led to the arrest of workers at the Sky Chef facility, which prepares on-board meals for airlines. The Hotel Employees and Restaurant Employees International Union (HERE), which is negotiating a contract with the company, claims that workers were called to an employee meeting, where they were met by INS agents in company uniforms. Some arrested workers had worked as long as 10 years at the facility, which ironically is owned by a foreign airline, Lufthansa.

Another 81 airport workers were arrested in raids on the Los Angeles, Orange County, Ontario (Calif.), Palm Springs, and Long Beach airports on August 22. The detained immigrants were working in janitorial, food service, maintenance, and baggage handling jobs. They were picked up because they apparently were using Social Security numbers which didn't match the INS database. While federal authorities admit that none of them—in fact none of the people arrested in any Operation Tarmac raid—are accused of terrorist activity, U.S. Attorney Debra Yang claimed that "we now realize that we must strengthen security at our local airports in order to ensure the safety of the traveling public." Eliseo Medina, executive vice-president of the SEIU, which has mounted organizing drives among many of the workers in Southern California airports, called the arrests unwarranted. "These people aren't terrorists," he fumed. "They only want to work." Unions like the Communications Workers of America (CWA) have protested Operation Tarmac raids in Washington, D.C., and elsewhere.

While the anti-immigrant campaign may have started at U.S. airports, it has now expanded far beyond their gates. The agency taking the new anti-immigrant attitude most to heart has been the Social Security Administration (SSA). Following the September 11 attacks, the SSA has flooded U.S. workplaces with "no-match letters," which the agency sends to employers informing them of employees whose Social Security numbers don't correspond to the SSA database.

In the last few years, employers have used no-match letters to fire immigrant workers during union organizing drives, or to intimidate those attempting to enforce worker protection laws. Until September 11, unions were making some headway in preventing these abuses. Two years ago, San Francisco's hotel union, HERE Local 2, won an important arbitrator's decision, which held that finding the name of a worker in a no-match letter was not, by itself, sufficient reason for terminating her. In addition, pressure on the SSA resulted in the inclusion, in the text of the letter, of a similar caveat, saying that inclusion in a no-match list was not to be taken as evidence of lack of immigration status.

In the wake of September 11, however, SSA has consciously embraced the no-match letter as an immigration-enforcement device. In 2001, the agency sent out 110,000 letters, and only when there were more than ten no-matches at a company or if the no-matches represented at least 10% of a company's total workforce. This year it plans to increase the number of letters to 750,000, and all it takes is one no-match to generate a letter. The pretext is September 11: "Concerns about national security, along with the growing problem of identity theft, have caused us to accelerate our efforts," according to SSA Commissioner Jo Anne Barnhart. The Internal Revenue Service has also sharply increased the number of letters sent to employers questioning incorrect numbers, and has threatened to begin fining employers who provide them. As in the case of Valencia and the screeners, however, there is no logic that connects a worker's immigration status with national security. And proponents of these changes don't even bother trying to produce an explanation that does.

The new attitude at Social Security marks an important change. In Nebraska in 1998, Operation Vanguard, a large-scale INS program to enforce employer sanctions, relied on the SSA's database to sift out the names of possible undocumented immigrants from the rolls of all the state's meatpacking employees. Over 3,000 people lost their jobs as a result. The INS had plans to extend the operation to other states, but was unable to do so when the SSA expressed misgivings about the INS's use of its database, and denied further access. The SSA had faced pressure from immigrants' rights groups and labor unions, who questioned why information intended to ensure that workers receive retirement and disability benefits was suddenly being used to take their jobs. After September 11, 2001, such objections were brushed aside.

The net effect of the new enforcement efforts has been to turn the Social Security card into a *de facto* national ID card, especially for employment, without any act of Congress creating one. Immigrant rights and civil liberties advocates have fought for years against the creation of a national ID, saying that it would inevitably lead to abuse by government and employers, and that it would eventually become a kind of internal passport. And Congress has been unwilling to establish such a national identification system, at least until September 11.

AN INJURY TO ALL

The wave of repression against immigrant workers hasn't just affected immigrants themselves. Limitations on workers' rights affect all workers. But because immigrants have been in the forefront of organizing unions and fighting sweatshop conditions, the threat against them has increased the danger that such conditions will spread, and affect workers throughout the labor force.

THE *HOFFMAN* CASE

The Supreme Court jumped onto the anti-immigrant bandwagon last spring, in the case of José Castro, a man fired from the Hoffman Plastics plant in Los Angeles for his union activity. Castro admitted in court proceedings that he was undocumented. In a previous decision in the 1980s, the Supreme Court had held that undocumented workers fired for organizing unions could not be legally reinstated to their jobs, the normal remedy for citizens and legal residents. But all fired workers, including the undocumented, were still entitled to back pay for the time they were out of work as a result of the illegal firing.

In the Hoffman decision, the current court eliminated employers' liability for back pay. The decision rewarded employers seeking to stop union organizing efforts among immigrant workers—the very people who have built a decade-long track record of labor activism, often organizing themselves even when unions showed little interest. The bosses can now terminate undocumented workers without fear of any monetary consequences. Some employers have tried to argue that the *Hoffman* decision also disqualifies undocumented workers from minimum wage, safety and health, and other labor standards and worker protection laws. In California, state authorities have thrown out this argument and the legislature passed a bill emphasizing that state laws would be applied without such an immigration test. But Bush and the new Congress may seek to spread Hoffman's impact.

INS enforcement has increased the pressure on undocumented workers to avoid anything that could antagonize their employers, whether organizing a union, asking for a raise, or filing a complaint about unpaid overtime. There are almost 8 million undocumented people in the United States—4% of the urban workforce, and over half of all farm workers—according to a recent study by the Pew Hispanic Trust. When it becomes more risky and difficult for these workers to organize and join unions, or even to hold a job at all, they settle for lower wages. And when the price of immigrant labor goes down as a result, so do wages for other workers.

Attacks on immigrant workers have an especially big effect on unions trying to organize industries where immigrants are a large part of the workforce. The Operation Tarmac raids, for instance, hurt hotel unions' efforts to organize food service workers. The unions organizing immigrants are some of the most progressive in the labor movement. Unions like the Hotel Employees and Restaurant Employees have been disproportionately hit by the anti-immigrant offensive. Other unions, like the Teamsters and Laborers, have also led immigrant rights activity in many local areas, and suffered the impact of no-match letters and raids. Although the Bush administration has courted these unions' national leaders, the relationship doesn't seem to have provided any political leverage for stopping anti-immigrant abuses.

ORGANIZING A FIGHTBACK

Today, employers illegally fire workers for union activity in 31% of all union organizing campaigns, affecting immigrant and native-born workers alike. Companies treat the cost of legal battles, reinstatement, and back pay as a cost of doing business, and many consider it cheaper than signing a union contract. Labor rights for all workers need to be strengthened, not weakened. But, as former National Labor Relations Board chair William Gould IV points out, "There's a basic conflict between U.S. labor law and U.S. immigration law." In its recent *Hoffman* decision (see box), the Supreme Court has held that the enforcement of employer sanctions, which makes it illegal for an undocumented immigrant to hold a job, is more important than the right of that worker to join a union and resist exploitation on the job.

Despite the decision, however, and the growing anti-immigrant climate, immigrants workers are still organizing. In May, four hundred workers won a hard-fought union election at the ConAgra beef plant in Omaha, a city where INS raids destroyed immigrant-based union committees only a few years ago. New Jersey recycling workers at KTI also finally won a union vote, on their fourth attempt to join the Laborers Union, which is also organizing successful campaigns among asbestos workers on Long Island. HERE won a 22-year battle for a contract at San Francisco's Flagship Marriott Hotel, the hotel chain's first corporate-managed property to sign a union agreement.

The union-based efforts for amnesty and the repeal of employer sanctions were dealt a serious blow by the post-September 11 climate, but there are signs of renewed forward movement. SEIU Local 790, in cooperation with Filipinos for Affirmative Action and the Phillip Veracruz Justice Project, led efforts to fight for screeners' jobs at the San Francisco airport. The SEIU also initiated a national postcard campaign, called A Million Voices for Justice, to restart the national campaign for amnesty. In August, the SEIU and the ACLU sued the Department of Transportation over the citizenship requirement, and in mid-November Federal District Court Judge Robert Takasugi ruled the requirement illegal. The decision, however, only applies to the nine workers in whose names the suit was filed. Lawyers for the plaintiffs hope to broaden it to a class-action, while federal authorities predictably announced they would appeal.

Last summer, HERE announced plans for a Freedom Ride on Washington, D.C., for immigrant rights. The union deliberately chose the name and used the language of the civil rights movement in an effort to establish a greater level of unity between African Americans, Latinos, and Asian-Americans. HERE officials also said they intended to challenge the color line—employers have kept African-Americans out of hotel employment, while hiring immigrants at lower wages—in hotels across the country. Massive layoffs and the economic downturn in tourism made plans to challenge hiring discrimination a moot point, but in the spring, HERE announced that it would again begin organizing its Freedom Ride, and set it for fall 2003.

And while Erlinda Valencia was one of the nine named plaintiffs in the suit against the citizenship requirement, the favorable court decision only means, at best, that she can take a test to qualify for her old job. If she takes it and passes, she will be put on a list of eligible potential employees. Her old job at the airport and those of her coworkers have already been filled. Preliminary studies indicate that many new hires are ex-members of the military and law enforcement agencies, and that the new workforce does not include nearly as many immigrants or people of color as the old one.

Valencia, like may other former screeners, has found herself looking for another job. The labor councils, unions, and immigrant rights activists who supported the screeners mounted food drives, tried to help former screeners get retraining, and tried to help them find stable new employment. But the larger challenge, they believe, is building a political movement to roll back the anti-immigrant atmosphere in which Valencia, and many like her, have become ensnared.

ARTICLE 22

The "Race to the Bottom" in Imported Clothes

BY ROBERT J. S. ROSS

January/February 2002, updated July/August 2002 and August 2003

Unions and labor-rights activists have long argued that investors and corporations seek out the places where unions are weakest, labor protections are least enforced, workers are most repressed and, as a consequence, labor is cheapest. Political leaders around the world, therefore, try to hold down what they antiseptically call "costs of production" in an attempt to attract the proverbial golden goose of capital investment. In much of Europe, this may take the form of cutting back on employers' payroll taxes or severance costs. In places

MAJOR CLOTHING PRODUCING COUNTRIES INCREASING THEIR SHARE
OF U.S. CLOTHING IMPORTS, 1998–2001

Country	Average Hourly Wage in Clothing Manufacture, 1998
Bangladesh	$0.15
Burma (Myanmar)	$0.04
Cambodia	$0.20
El Salvador	$0.59
Guatemala	$0.44
Indonesia	$0.13
Mexico	$0.52
Nicaragua	$0.23
Pakistan	$0.23
Peru	$0.90
Thailand	$0.78
Turkey	$2.50

Source: U.S. Department of Labor, Office of International Economic Affairs, International Labor Affairs Bureau, February 2000; National Labor Committee; OTEXA; Major Shippers Report, YE 7/2001

like Burma (Myanmar), it takes the form of virtual forced labor under a brutally repressive military dictatorship. Labor activists call this process the "race to the bottom."

If there really is such a "race," we would expect export production to shift from higher-wage countries to lower-wage countries. Of course, many other factors—non-wage costs, production quality, etc.—influence "sourcing," so production will not necessarily shift instantly to the lowest-wage country. We can identify general trends, however, by calculating the average wage of workers producing goods exported to the United States, and seeing how that average wage changes over time.

CALCULATING THE AVERAGE WAGE

I constructed just such a measure for the production of imported clothing. First, I found data on the average garment-industry wage for each of the top 34 countries exporting clothing to the United States (accounting for about 94% of U.S. imports) in 1998. Then, I "weighted" the average wage for each country according to the percentage of U.S. imports coming from that country. This allowed me to calculate an average hourly wage, for a given year, for imported garments in general. Next, I recalculated this average wage based on the changed import percentages for a later year. In this way, I was able to determine whether export production was indeed shifting to lower-wage countries.

I made one final adjustment to these figures to account for the "transshipment" of garments from China to Hong Kong. As a consequence of the Multi-Fiber Agreement and its successor, the Agreement on Textiles and Clothing, imports to the United States from many countries are capped (until 2005, when the WTO agreement calls for the end of the MFA/ATC quotas). To evade these quotas, some countries, including the People's Republic of China (PRC), first ship clothing to jurisdictions that are under quota. There, some minor or fictitious process is performed, and the clothing is then shipped to the United States. According to official statistics, China and Hong Kong each produce slightly over 7% of all clothing imported to the United States. Some portion of the flow attributed to Hong Kong, however, is really made in the PRC.

A reasonable estimate of the amount of transshipment from the PRC to Hong Kong comes from the U.S. Customs Service's Textile Transshipment Team. Its members visited 55 Hong Kong garment factories in January 1999, and 51 more in September 1999. On both trips, inspectors found nearly 50% of the factories visited suspected of transshipment. Based on these findings, it would seem reasonable to assign 50% of U.S. imports from Hong Kong to the PRC. Since Hong Kong wages are estimated at $4.35 per hour, and PRC wages are estimated at between $0.23 and $0.33 per hour, such a shift would have a measurable impact on the estimated average hourly wage of workers who make imported clothing.

Using this method, I calculated an average hourly wage of $1.87 for U.S. apparel imports in 1998, based on U.S. Department of Labor data. When I supplemented these data with the National Labor Committee's reports from workers, the average wage came out to $1.75. I then recalculated the average wage based

AVERAGE HOURLY WAGE (US$) IN THE PRODUCTION OF IMPORTED CLOTHING

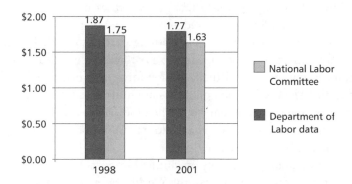

Source: U.S. Department of Labor, Office of International Economic Affairs, International Labor Affairs Bureau, February 2000; National Labor Committee; OTEXA; Major Shippers Report, YE 7/2001

on the changed percentages of imported garments that came from the same 34 countries in 2001. (The 1998 wage data are the latest available, so I had to use them again for my 2001 calculations.) Since 1998, the mix of U.S. clothing imports has changed. Indonesia, Bangladesh, Guatemala, Nicaragua, Peru, and Burma—all low-wage countries—have increased their shares. Meanwhile, Canada, Italy, the United Kingdom, and Israel have declined. As a result of these shifts, the average wage declined to $1.77, based on the Department of Labor data, or to $1.63 based on the National Labor Committee reports. Either way, the average wage fell by about 5.5%-6.5%.

THE RACE IS ON

This is a rough estimate, given the varying ways in which different countries report wages, as well as varying degrees of honesty in governments' data. Adjusting for transshipment also introduces uncertainty: although we have a good estimate of the proportion of factories involved in transshipment, that doesn't tell us exactly how much clothing is transshipped from China through Hong Kong. And it is certainly a disadvantage that, since new wage figures (in dollars per hour or other standard form) have not been calculated for 2001, we cannot take changed wages in individual countries into account in recalculating the general average wage for 2001. It is unlikely, however, that increased export production in low-wage countries—especially those where repression limits workers' bargaining power—has boosted wages very much. Imperfect though these calculations may be, they do suggest that a "race to the bottom" is really happening.

Worldwide, apparel production has been shifting dramatically to low-wage countries in recent years. Much of this shift has been to China, and most of that to its loosely regulated "Special Economic Zones." In China's clothing industry, the hours are long, workers toil in grim compounds, and union rights are nonexistent. Guangdong Province, bordering Hong Kong, is notorious for high accident rates and a bleak landscape of foreign-owned factories and dormitories.

Meanwhile, Mexico's exports to the United States increased dramatically in the 1990s. NAFTA really has worked—for U.S. retailers and importers. Close enough to major U.S. markets so that clothing can be delivered to warehouses one or two days after completion, Mexico's *maquila* factories are notorious for their hostility to unions and for the lack of enforcement of Mexico's pretty good labor laws. Official Mexican data on wages are undependable because employers falsely report paying the minimum wage when they really don't. Since the passage of NAFTA, apparel workers' wages have more than doubled, according to official figures—but living costs have tripled.

By 2005, all remaining restraints on clothing imports to the United States will expire. With China now a member of the World Trade Organization, experts believe its share of world production and exports will increase even faster than it has in recent years. The race for the rich-country markets is on, with China, Mexico, and the Caribbean going head-to-head for the U.S. market—or neck-in-neck in the race to the bottom.

RESOURCES *Forced labour in Myanmar (Burma): Report of the Commission of Inquiry appointed under article 26 of the Constitution of the International Labour Organization to examine the observance by Myanmar of the Forced Labour Convention*,1930 (No.29) Geneva, 2 July 1998; John Hooper and Kate Connolly, "Focus: Germany in Turmoil: Is the party over?" *The Observer*, August 26, 2001; International Labour Office, *Labour Practices in the Footwear, Leather, Textiles and Clothing Industries: Report for Discussion at the Tripartite Meeting on Labour Practices in the Footwear, Leather, Textiles and Clothing Industries*, Geneva, October 2000; Gregory K. Schoepfle, *Wage, Benefits, Poverty Line, and Meeting Workers' Needs in the Apparel and Footwear Industries of Selected Countries*, U.S. Department of Labor, Office of International Economic Affairs, International Labor Affairs Bureau, February 2000; National Labor Committee <www.nlcnet.org>; OTEXA: Major Shippers Report, YE 7/2001 <otexa.ita.doc.gov/msr/catv1.htm>; U.S. Customs Service, Textile Transshipment Team, *1999 Textile Transshipment Report*, March 2000 <www.customs.ustreas.gov/quotas/ttr/index99.htm>; *U.S. Statistical Abstract*, 2000; International Labor Organization: LABORSTA <laborsta.ilo.org>.

ARTICLE 23

Maquiladora Bosses Play the China Card

BY DAVID BACON

September/October 2003

For decades, U.S. workers have been told their wages are too high—and that high labor costs could force employers to move operations to Mexico. Now Mexican workers, whose numbers on the border have mushroomed in the last three decades, are on the receiving end of the same threat. This time the bogeyman is China.

Last November at the Asia Pacific Economic Conference in Cabo San Lucas, employers in Mexico declared that they are losing a wage competition with China, and warned that plants would close and move as a result. "With the advances of the giant Asian power," says Rolando González Barrón, national president of the Maquila Export Industry Association, "all these companies are trying to compete with China with cheap labor." He advises factory owners to move to southern Mexico, where wages are much lower. "The border has no possibility of competing with China."

González Barrón heads the organization for the owners and managers of *maquiladoras*, the mostly foreign-owned factories that have proliferated on the United States-Mexico border. Until the current economic crisis hit two years ago, the maquiladora industry employed over 1.3 million workers in over 2,000 factories (almost all in northern Mexico), according to the association. But the years since 2001 have seen massive job losses in the industry. González Barrón announced a year ago that 300,000 workers had been laid off along the border in 2001 and the first months of 2002. Marco Antonio Tomás of Mexico City's Center for Labor Research puts the number laid off to date at 400,000.

There is no doubt that border plants are facing a sharp economic slowdown. But there is cause to doubt the China explanation. The rising chorus claiming that Chinese competition threatens maquila workers' job security obscures a basic fact. The maquiladora plants all produce products for the U.S. market, and when consumers in the north stop buying, workers from Tijuana to Matamoros lose their jobs by the thousands. When the U.S. economy catches a cold, the saying goes, Mexico comes down with pneumonia. While the maquiladora industry would like workers to look east to China to find the source of their problems—the China "threat" gives employers a powerful justification for cutting wages and undermining organizing efforts—"where we really need to look is north," says Nelly Benítez, a former worker at Sony's huge plant in Nuevo Laredo.

The U.S. media often repeat the line coming from the maquiladora industry, ignoring the more fundamental problem of Mexico's dependence on the U.S. economy. Mary Jordan, writing in the *Washington Post* on July 15, said that "owners of maquiladora assembly plants who flocked to Mexico in recent decades to take advantage of cheap labor are now leaving for China, Malaysia, and Guatemala. That has cost Mexico tens of thousands of jobs—exacerbating the oversupply of workers that keeps wages down."

For all the talk of the China threat, only two actual plant closures have been cited as evidence by the media. One, a factory making computer monitors for Philips North America in Juárez, shut over the summer of 2002, costing about

---

MAQUILADORAS

Starting in 1964 under the Border Industrialization Program, the Mexico and U.S. governments encouraged foreign companies to build plants, called maquiladoras, on the Mexican side of the border. The program eliminated the restrictions on foreign ownership that had limited the ability of U.S. corporations to take advantage of low wages in Mexico. Maquiladoras are permitted to bring in materials, equipment, and replacement parts duty free. There are over 3,000 maquiladoras in Mexico; the majority are owned by U.S. interests and are situated within 30 miles of the border.

600 jobs. Production moved to Suzhou, China. Philips, however, has another 12 border plants, and increased investment in many of them last year. The other big monitor and television manufacturers, including Sony, Samsung, and Thomson, also continued to produce in Mexico. In the other cited case, Canon closed an older facility making inkjet printers, moving production to southeast Asia.

Relocating many maquiladora operations to China would not be practical or economical, however. For Mattel, product size and transportation cost are the primary considerations. Mattel produces many small toys in China, but produces its "large cube" items, like jungle gyms and tricycles, in Mexico. Thomas Debrowski, Mattel vice-president for operations, told *New York Times* reporter Daniel Altman that "if you want to be competitive in large-cube products, and you want to source it in China, you're going to go broke pretty quick."

Rick Clancy, senior vice-president for corporate communications at Sony Electronics, said that while employment levels at its plants in Nuevo Laredo, Mexicali, Tijuana, and Pittsburgh all vary from time to time, they produce products that the company isn't likely to produce elsewhere. The plants in Mexicali and Tijuana have begun producing digital flat panel displays and high definition televisions—state-of-the-art products. The Nuevo Laredo complex, which produces recording media, has begun to produce lithium ion batteries for laptop computers as well. "While labor costs are lower in China," Clancy says, "Mexico is beneficial because of its highly-skilled labor, its location close to the U.S. border, and the fact that we can operate these facilities in integration with each other."

There is no question that corporations can and do move production of many items from country to country in search of low labor costs. For labor-intensive products like clothing, the low level of capital investment required to set up operations makes them easy to close and move.

In other industries, like semiconductor manufacturing, corporations such as Intel and National Semiconductor have not moved offshore those parts of their production process that require high levels of capital investment and ready access to a sophisticated industrial infrastructure. These operations have largely remained in the United States and in other highly industrialized countries. The more labor-intensive assembly and test operations, however, are moved to less-developed ones where wages are lower. And even those operations are now being automated at breakneck speed.

ALCOA'S WARNING TO WORKERS

Alcoa Fujikura, Ltd. (AFL) played the China card directly after workers at its factory in Puebla sent a solidarity message to their coworkers at the Alcoa plant in Piedras Negras, who were involved in a bitter conflict with the company. Jake Siewart, company vice-president in Pittsburgh, sent the Puebla workers a letter from Alcoa executive Alan Belda, which enthused that "all the automotive operations of Alcoa Fujikura Limited in Mexico offer attractive pay and benefits pack-

A CLOSER LOOK AT MEXICO'S "INFLATED" WAGES

In their campaign to lower border wages, the maquiladora owners have been helped by media accounts that inflate the existing wage level. A *New York Times* article by Elizabeth Malkin in November 2002, for instance, stated that "Mexico can no longer compete on low wages alone. Mexican wages for workers in the maquiladora sector range from about $2 to $2.50 an hour, including many benefits and labor taxes. Figures on Chinese labor costs are less reliable, but they range from 35 cents to as much as $1 an hour if all benefits and taxes are paid." This would give maquiladora workers an average daily wage of $16 to $25, depending on hours worked.

According to Martha Ojeda, director of the Coalition for Justice in the Maquiladoras, however, the government-mandated minimum wage for maquiladora workers on the border is just 42 pesos daily, or about $4.20. She estimates that a majority of maquiladora workers earn close to this wage. A 2001 survey conducted by SEDEPAC, a community organization of maquiladora workers in Torreón and Ciudad Acuña, found that a normal maquiladora worker made 320–350 pesos a week ($32–35). Yet according to the same survey, it takes 1,500 pesos a week ($150) to provide food, housing, and transportation for a family of four. "We asked people, 'How do you survive when there's such a huge gap?'" says SEDEPAC director Betty Robles. "Many told us that two and three families share a couple of rooms, pooling income to cover rent and basic needs."

The Center for Reflection, Education and Action (CREA), a religious research group, conducted another study cosponsored by the Coalition for Justice in the Maquiladoras and the Interfaith Center for Corporate Responsibility. CREA found that at the minimum wage, it took a maquiladora worker in Juárez almost an hour to earn enough money to buy a kilo (2.2 pounds) of rice, and a worker in Tijuana an hour and a half. By comparison, a dockworker driving a container crane in California's San Pedro harbor could buy the rice after 3 minutes at work. Even an undocumented worker at minimum wage only has to labor 12 minutes for it in Los Angeles.

Yet another study by the Economics Faculty of the National Autonomous University in Mexico City says Mexican wages have lost over 80% of their buying power. Twenty years ago, researchers say, the minimum wage could pay for 93.5% of a family's basic necessities, while today it only buys 19.3%.

ages." Belda went on to warn, however, that the company's "Mexican workers earn approximately $3,300 dollars a year, not counting benefits ... [while equivalent] Chinese workers make about $2,000."

The union at the Puebla plant, which supplies wire harnesses to the nearby Volkswagen assembly facility, analyzed the company's claims, with the help of Huberto Juárez, a professor at the Autonomous University of Puebla who has studied the auto industry in Mexico for two decades. First, they found that labor costs in Mexico only make up 7.4% of total sales. In other words, even if what Belda said was true, the actual difference in cost was very small.

But they also found that the company's wage figures for its Mexican workforce just weren't true. The average worker at Alcoa Fujikura in Puebla makes $6.16 (U.S.) a day, or 89 cents an hour. That's a yearly average of $2,241.20 (at the rate of exchange in January 2003) or only about 10% more than the company itself quoted for equivalent Chinese wages.

"We know that the companies are beating the drum about the 'wage race to the bottom,' using the Chinese as a threat to put downward pressure on wages in many parts of the world," the union study explained. "But the low salaries are here [in Mexico], earned by workers who without any doubt are producing at a world-class level. But they don't live, as the company pretends, in world-class conditions."

The study went on to document that the typical Alcoa Fujikura worker in the city is a young woman between 18 and 28 years old. Only about 30% of them are married. Many are single mothers. Considering that about three-quarters of them earn less than 76 pesos a day (about $7.60), their wages "are not enough to offer a decent life." Ninety-five percent of the workers the union surveyed were supporting at least one dependent and said their earnings weren't enough to cover basic necessities for their families. Over 40% said they could not afford to eat chicken even once a week.

Nevertheless, when the companies play the China card, maquiladora workers say they get the message. Nelly Benítez, who worked at Sony's Nuevo Laredo plant, says "the company began threatening to move to China when they began lowering the wages and benefits in 2001. Weekly salaries were reduced from about 800 pesos to 600 pesos [for a six-day week, or from about $13 to $10 per day]. We used to get a ride to and from work on company buses, since almost no one owns a car, and often we get off work late at night. Now we can only get a ride one way, not both."

Benítez says that Sony is still bringing new machines into the plant to make batteries and microcassettes. But after starting production, the number of people working each machine is then cut. "For example, if they start with five on a machine, they'll eventually fire three, and the other two have to continue running it."

Until the recession hit, each of Sony's four plants employed about 2,600 people, permanent company employees. Now, say Benítez and Tomás, the number has been reduced to 1,500 apiece. The majority are temporary hires, laid off right before they acquire permanent status under Mexican law, at the end of 90 days. "They never became permanent employees," Benítez says, and therefore have no status under labor law and no right to severance pay or housing benefits.

"PROMOTING A POLICY OF FEAR"

According to Martha Ojeda, director of the Coalition for Justice in the Maquiladoras, the China threat is being used far beyond the maquiladora industry. The World Bank and the administration of President Vicente Fox have proposed modifying Mexican labor law to eliminate many of its historic protections for workers. "They're promoting a policy of fear, in which workers are told that it's better to see five pesos in wages cut to three, than to lose their jobs entirely," Ojeda explains. "This is combined now with an effort to change the labor law itself. If we don't accept their reform, the companies say they'll take their investment elsewhere."

The reforms under discussion would promote the kinds of restructuring seen in the Sony plant. "Companies want the unlimited ability to hire temporary workers, who never acquire seniority, benefits, or labor rights," Ojeda adds. "This is what already exists in the maquiladoras. They're using the maquiladoras as the model for what they want to do with workers in the rest of the economy."

The steady progression of economic reforms over the last two decades, of which maquiladora development was an important element, created conditions of increased poverty. Despite promises that a rising tide would lift all boats, in Mexico, the number of billionaires has multiplied and the incomes of working people have fallen.

Government businesses were sold to private investors, who cut labor costs by laying off thousands of workers. Privatization undermined public-sector unions. While three-quarters of the workforce in Mexico belonged to unions three decades ago, less than 30% do today. U.S. companies were also permitted to own land and factories anywhere in Mexico, without Mexican partners. Prices on basic goods were decontrolled, and government subsidies on food and services for workers and the poor were cut back or ended altogether.

Mexico was a laboratory for the economic reforms that have transformed the economies of developing countries away from policies encouraging national development toward ones opening up the economy for transnational investors. "For the Mexican government, the revenue from maquiladora production is pivotal," explains Harley Shaiken, head of the Center for Latin American Studies at the University of California at Berkeley. "Maquiladoras furnish the second-largest source of foreign exchange for the Mexican economy, after oil. This has created a culture in which anything favoring maquiladora production is emphasized, while the human cost is not addressed. The Mexican government has created an investment climate that depends on a vast number of low-wage earners. This climate gets all the government's attention, while the consumer climate—the ability of people to buy what they produce—is sacrificed."

The threat of plant relocation serves an important purpose, therefore, in the economic reform processs. Its message to workers is: "Shut up and work harder. You're already too expensive. If you ask for more, if you organize a union and strike, if you demand costly ventilation and pollution control equipment, factories will move offshore."

In the logic of reform, no labor is cheap enough. If workers lose their jobs, it's not because of Mexico's neoliberal economic policy or its increased dependence on production for the U.S. market. According to maquiladora managers and policy makers, workers have no one to blame but themselves.

CHAPTER 6

Economic Development

ARTICLE 24

Fields of Free Trade

Mexico's Small Farmers in a Global Economy

BY TIMOTHY A. WISE

November/December 2003

I n Cancún, Mexico, on the stifling afternoon of September 10, 2003, Korean
farm leader Lee Kyung Hae scaled the police barricades, which were keeping 10,000 protesting farmers from storming the World Trade Organization
(WTO) talks, and thrust a knife into his own heart. His self-sacrifice proved to
be a catalyst for the disparate protesters and a solemn reminder of the toll trade
liberalization has taken on the world's poorest farmers. When the talks collapsed
four days later, it became clear that the ship of free trade had foundered badly on
the shoals of its captains' hypocrisy on farm policy.

Mexican farmers provided the protests' largest contingent, and not just because
the meeting took place on their own embattled soil. Based on their experiences
under the North American Free Trade Agreement (NAFTA) and the free-trade
model that it embodies, they had a lot to say. Farmers of maize and other grains,
who produce for subsistence and for local and regional markets, have been hardest hit by liberalization, with imports from the United States driving prices down
to unsustainable levels. But much of the export sector has suffered as well, with
gains in industrial tomato farming more than offset by sharp declines in coffee,
Mexico's most important export crop in both employment and output.

Mexico's small-scale farmers came together last winter to demand that their government renegotiate NAFTA's agricultural provisions and establish new policies for the countryside. While they have thus far failed to win a commitment from the pro-free trade administration of Vicente Fox to renegotiate NAFTA, last spring they secured new funds for rural development and a promise to assess the agreement's impact on small farmers and to take measures to defend and promote the sector. Whether the movement can hold Fox to those promises remains to be seen, but the farmers' rejection of the neoliberal model is here to stay.

A closer look at the experiences of Mexican farmers of corn and coffee—the country's largest domestic and export crops which directly support some 20 million of the country's 100 million people—illustrates the perils of agricultural trade liberalization. Farmers' responses to the crisis and their policy proposals present a useful starting point for an alternative approach to rural development, one that recognizes the limits of trade, the importance of domestic food sources, and the value of peasant production.

UNREALIZED PROMISES

Although some policy-makers still point to Mexico as a success story, there is a growing consensus that the free trade experiment—which began well before NAFTA's inception in 1994—has not lived up to expectations. Its failures are all the more striking given Mexico's indisputable success in transforming one of the world's most protected economies into one of the most open and in attracting the foreign investment needed to capitalize such a transformation. Since 1985, when Mexico began its rapid liberalization process, exports have doubled and foreign direct investment has nearly tripled. According to the promises of free-trade proponents, with inflation in check, Mexico should have reaped the rewards of liberalization. It hasn't. Growth has been slow, job creation has been sluggish, wages have declined, poverty has increased, and the environment has taken a beating. (See "Free Trade's Unkept Promises.")

In many ways, Mexico got what NAFTA promised: trade and investment. Unfortunately, these have not translated into benefits for the Mexican population as a whole or into improvements in the country's fragile environment. And there is little question that rural Mexico has suffered the greatest decline.

NAFTA VERSUS MAIZE

When NAFTA was negotiated, Mexico's leaders promised the agreement would help modernize the countryside, converting low-yield peasant plots into highly productive commercial farms growing fruits, vegetables, and other export crops for the U.S. market. Farmers who could not modernize or export would be absorbed as workers into the rising export industrial sector and the expanding service sector. Sensitive to the important role of corn in Mexico's culture and econo-

FREE TRADE'S UNKEPT PROMISES

NAFTA took effect in 1994, but the "neoliberal" experiment began in the mid-1980s following Mexico's 1982 debt crisis. Ten years into NAFTA and nearly twenty years into neoliberalism, the track record, drawn from official World Bank and Mexican government figures, is poor:

- **Economic growth has been slow.** Since 1985, Mexico has seen average annual per capita real growth of just 1%, compared to 3.4% from 1960 to 1980.

- **Job growth has been sluggish.** There has been little job creation, falling far short of the demand from young people entering the labor force. Manufacturing, one of the few sectors to show significant economic growth, has registered only marginal net job creation since NAFTA took effect.

- **The new jobs are not good jobs.** Nearly half of all new formal-sector jobs created under NAFTA do not include any of the benefits mandated by Mexican law (social security, vacations, holidays, etc.). One-third of the economically active population works in the informal sector.

- **Wages have declined.** The real minimum wage is down 60% since 1982, 23% since NAFTA's inception. Wages in all sectors have followed suit.

- **Poverty has increased.** According to Mexico's most respected poverty researchers, the number of households living in poverty has grown 80% since 1984, with nearly 80% of Mexico's people now below the poverty line, up from 59% in 1984. Income distribution has become more lopsided, making Mexico one of the hemisphere's most unequal societies.

- **The rural sector is in crisis.** Four-fifths of rural Mexicans live in poverty, over half in extreme poverty. Migration levels remain high despite unprecedented risks due to increased U.S. border patrols.

- **Imports surpass exports.** The export boom has been outpaced by an import boom, in part due to intrafirm trade within multinationals.

- **The environment has deteriorated.** The Mexican government estimates that from 1985 to 1999, the economic costs of environmental degradation amounted to 10% of annual GDP, or $36 billion per year. These costs dwarf economic growth, which amounted to only $9.4 billion annually.

my—over 3 million farmers grow corn, triple the employment in the *maquiladora* export assembly sector—NAFTA included a 15-year phase-out period for corn tariffs along with strict import quotas. Such a phased "tariff-rate quota" system was designed to ensure a gradual transition to competition with more developed and highly subsidized U.S. producers.

Farmers were confronted with a far different reality. After negotiating these protections for its corn farmers, the Mexican government proceeded to throw them overboard. Citing supply shortages for basic grains, the government unilaterally approved imports over NAFTA's quotas and then declined to collect tariffs. The decision reflected the growing power of agribusiness interests within Mexico, which coveted access to cheaper and lower-quality U.S. corn. The livestock industry wanted cheap feed, the beverage industry sought inexpensive corn sweetener, and a growing processed-food industry wanted to reduce its input costs for flour.

The result was free-trade shock treatment for corn farmers. Instead of a difficult long-term adjustment to competition with U.S. farmers, they faced the near-impossible challenge of fully liberalized trade just three years into NAFTA. Imports doubled and the price of corn fell nearly 50%. At the same time, the Mexican government was phasing out its price-support system, the final step in bringing Mexico into compliance with the Uruguay Round Agreement on Agriculture (URAA). Though CONASUPO, the main government agency managing supplies and prices, did not fold until 1998, price supports for most crops were eliminated in 1989. Corn and beans saw support into the mid-1990s, though at reduced levels. Facing fiscal pressures after the peso crisis and bailout of the banking sector, the government also reduced other rural support and modernization programs.

Corn farmers and other grain growers responded with an aggressive effort to stay on the land. Their organization, the National Association of Commercial Enterprises (ANEC), brings together over 180,000 producers, mostly small- and medium-scale landowners working 25 acres or less and selling the majority of their produce in local and regional markets. ANEC has bought abandoned state storage facilities, developed its own marketing infrastructure, promoted regional trade, and fostered sustainable agriculture practices. It is estimated that members earn prices 10% to 12% higher than the free market can provide.

"We do not and will not accept that we are mere surplus, that we are not productive, not competitive, that we are a burden for the country," said an ANEC leader at the group's 2000 General Assembly. "We are productive now ... we can be more productive in the future ... but only if the role of the small and medium peasant producers is revalued." Despite ANEC's success in revaluing the contributions of small farmers, the import flood still threatens to drown many growers, with producer prices below the cost of production.

DISINTEREST AND DISINVESTMENT

The farm crisis is not simply a problem of imports, or even of the structural imbalances between the United States' industrial agriculture and Mexico's more traditional farming. In corn fields, those differences are stark, with the United States farming nearly four times the acreage at over three times the yield, resulting in eleven times Mexico's output. That glut of American corn, which is subsidized at a per-acre level at least triple that of Mexico, sells at less than half the price of Mexico's traditional maize. Such disparities prompted farmers' initial demand to exclude corn from NAFTA, a position the government later watered down to the 15-year tariff-rate quota and a vague U.S. promise to consider reducing its farm subsidies.

At the heart of the crisis, though, is a long-term structural decline in international prices for agricultural and other non-oil commodities. According to the World Bank, real prices for non-oil commodities have fallen by an average of 50% since 1980 to their lowest levels in a century. Global overproduction has been fed by rising productivity in industrial agriculture and the neoliberal mantra to export, export, export. For many developing countries, World Bank and International Monetary Fund policies have mandated a deepening dependency on a few commodities and a turn away from the diversification that characterized Latin American development strategies in the 1960s and 1970s. This dependency, in turn, makes countries particularly vulnerable when commodity prices fall sharply.

Small farmers are even more vulnerable when their government abandons them. True to its neoliberal ideals and its URAA commitments, the Mexican government dismantled most of the agencies that had bought and sold farm produce, provided credit and technical assistance, and administered price supports and subsidies. The percentage of the government budget devoted to agriculture fell by half, to just 4.6% of outlays. Farm subsidies dropped 58% in real terms. The promised modernization of Mexican agriculture through public investment withered on the free-trade vine. New irrigation, an explicit government goal prior to NAFTA, never materialized, with the amount of new irrigated land falling from 100,000 acres in 1991 to a post-NAFTA average of just 17,000 acres per year. Lending by both government and private-sector rural credit programs declined 75% after 1994, when NAFTA took effect, while rural bankruptcies increased sixfold.

Nor did foreign investment, the free-trade elixir for all development ills, step in to slow the bleeding. A paltry 0.2% of the $128 billion in foreign direct investment that flowed into Mexico from 1994 to 2002 went to agriculture. Just three activities—hog farming, horticulture (fruits and vegetables), and flowers—claimed 94% of that total, and almost 90% ended up in the two Mexican states that already had the most modern agriculture.

According to one government-commissioned study, overall investment levels as a percentage of agricultural GDP declined from a healthy 11% in 1980 to 6% in 1985, then dropped to 3% just prior to NAFTA's signing. They have remained under 2% since NAFTA took effect. If its goal was to modernize Mexican agriculture, the liberalization project has been a dismal failure.

WINNING THROUGH EXPORTS?

In a free-trade world it is almost a given that if you're not part of the trading, you're part of the problem. NAFTA's apologists could claim that Mexico's inefficient grain farmers were just not competitive in a market freed of distortions. As the cold logic of comparative advantage separated the high-value wheat (or, in this case, corn) from the uncompetitive chaff, they needed to find more productive uses for their labor or their land. With few prospects for efficiency gains on poor lands suffering disinvestment and a rural credit vacuum, farmers who wanted to stay in agriculture would have to switch crops and export.

For small farmers in Mexico's rugged highlands, coffee might have seemed a likely solution. It was already the country's largest export crop, and the second largest commodity export after oil. Before NAFTA, Mexico was the world's fourth largest coffee producer, and its shade-grown arabica beans were highly valued on the international market. Better still, there would be no competition with U.S. producers.

So much for economic theory. Mexico's coffee farmers have been living their own free-trade nightmare, and it has little to do with NAFTA. In 1989, the U.S. and Mexican governments pulled out of the International Coffee Agreement (ICA), a supply-management arrangement between major producing and consuming countries that had kept supplies and prices at relatively stable and sustainable levels. The target price had been $1.20 to $1.40 per pound. Such "market-distorting" schemes are proscribed by the Organization for Economic Cooperation and Development and the Agreement on Agriculture of the GATT (General Agreement on Tariffs and Trade), the precursor to the WTO.

The result was as predictable as it was devastating to small coffee farmers. Prices plummeted to below the costs of production (about $0.60 a pound in Mexico) as stored coffee flooded the market and free competition among producing countries bid down prices. Five years of low prices (1989-94) ended temporarily when destructive frosts in Brazil in 1994 and 1997 killed off coffee trees in the world's largest producing nation. But when Brazil's new, high-yield coffee plantations came back on the market, prices fell even lower.

The market was further glutted by the entry of Vietnam, which grew from a virtual nonproducer in 1990 into the second largest coffee producer in the world by 2000. The World Bank and other development agencies had heavily promoted coffee as a viable export crop for small farmers in Vietnam and elsewhere, offering loans and other inducements. It worked, but by 2000, depressed prices had even low-cost producers in Vietnam scrambling to survive. By 2002, even the lowest-cost producers were unable to recoup their production costs.

Mexico's coffee farmers were especially hard hit by the price drop. They grow some of the world's best coffee, but at costs higher than many of their competitors. The sector is dominated by small farmers on shady hillside plots, with yields lower than Brazil's ecologically damaging but high-yield plantations. And the Mexican government added neoliberal insult to free-trade injury by eliminating INMECAFE, the Mexican coffee institute that had marketed and promoted Mexican coffee from its 285,000 producers.

In one of Mexico's poorest coffee-growing states, the Coffee Producers of Oaxaca (CEPCO), a grassroots organization of nearly 30,000 small-scale producers from nine indigenous groups, responded to the crisis with an impressive array of independent initiatives designed to "appropriate the production process for the producers." The members created their own credit union, mobilized women farmers, and promoted direct sales from their collective to marketers and consumers in the fair-trade movement. CEPCO campaigns encouraged farmers to produce certified organic coffee, bringing substantially higher prices for some 8,000 member families.

International market prices now hover around $0.50 a pound (and producers usually get far less than that). Organic fair-trade coffee pays producers $1.41 a pound, a dramatic price premium. But while the fair-trade and organic markets are growing quickly, they still account for a very small percentage of the market—currently about 3%. As even the most ardent fair-trade advocates acknowledge, niche markets can't solve a worldwide overproduction problem that affects far more producers than fair-trade consumers could ever sustain.

CEPCO's organic producers aside, most Mexican coffee farmers are in dire straits. Even high-quality arabica beans now receive low prices from international buyers. The national coffee farmer association in Mexico reports a 40% decline in coffee production in the past three years, a 55% decline in coffee exports, and a 70% decline in income from coffee sales. Many producers are letting the beans rot on the trees, since it makes little economic sense to harvest them. Clearly, if there is going to be a solution to coffee farmers' free-trade woes, it will come from a reversal of free-trade policies. An international coalition of coffee farmer organizations has called for a return to supply management and international assistance in keeping the lowest quality coffee off the market.

MOBILIZING FOR CHANGE

CEPCO's and ANEC's efforts have not been enough to reverse the overwhelming impacts of unregulated globalization and the Mexican government's abandonment of small-scale farmers. That is why coffee and corn growers have joined other farmers' groups in demanding policies and trade agreements that recognize and value the social, economic, and environmental contributions of small producers. Their demands are hardly radical, but their implications are entirely subversive to the neoliberal model. The farmers' movement has demanded:

1. A moratorium on the agricultural provisions of NAFTA, if not their renegotiation;
2. Emergency and long-term agricultural development programs;
3. Viable rural credit institutions providing adequate and affordable credit;
4. Government investment in rural infrastructure and communities;
5. Food safety and quality for Mexican consumers (a response to the importation of genetically modified corn from the United States);
6. Recognition of the rights of indigenous communities.

The April 2003 agreement with the Fox administration represented one important battle in a longer war. In the long run, the farmers' movement is demanding a return to an inclusive government development strategy in which trade and foreign investment are but two of many economic means to an end. They are not the ends in themselves.

If the WTO meetings in Cancún are any indication, farmers will continue to be a thorn in the side of the liberalization juggernaut. Via Campesina, an international farmer alliance that claims over 100 million members, put the issue front and center in Cancún. Arguing that agricultural products are more than just commodities and rural communities are more than just laborers, the group demanded that agriculture be removed from the WTO. They advanced the new concept of "food sovereignty"—the right of every country to decide how it will meet the food needs of its people, free of the strictures of WTO rules.

With negotiations on the proposed Free Trade Area of the Americas slated for November 2003, we can look forward to further conflict. Current drafts include significant agricultural liberalization, following through on the U.S. promise that the Free Trade Area of the Americas will be a "NAFTA for the hemisphere." Before signing any deal, the peoples of Latin America and the Caribbean would do well to talk to Mexico's farmers.

SOURCES Timothy A. Wise, Hilda Salazar, and Laura Carlsen, *Confronting Globalization: Economic Integration and Popular Resistance in Mexico* (Kumarian Press 2003); Timothy A. Wise, "NAFTA's Untold Stories: Mexico's Grassroots Responses to Economic Integration," (Interhemispheric Resource Center, June 10, 2003); Charis Gresser and Sophia Tickell, "Mugged: Poverty in Your Coffee Cup," (Oxfam Int'l, 2002); Alejandro Nadal, "The Environmental and Social Impacts of Economic Liberalization on Corn Production in Mexico," (Oxfam GB and WWF International, September 2000).

ARTICLE 25

Fair Trade and Farm Subsidies: How Big a Deal? Two Views

November/December 2003

In September, the global free-trade express was derailed—at least temporarily—when the World Trade Organization talks in Cancún, Mexico, collapsed. At the time, the inconsistency of the United States and other rich countries—pressing poor countries to adopt free trade while continuing to subsidize and protect selected domestic sectors, especially agriculture—received wide attention for the first time. Where does ending agricultural subsidies and trade barriers in the rich countries rank as a strategy for achieving global economic justice? Dollars & Sense asked progressive researchers on different sides of this question to make their case.

Make Trade Fair

BY GAWAIN KRIPKE

Trade can be a powerful engine for economic growth in developing countries and can help pull millions of people out of poverty. Trade also offers an avenue of growth that relies less than other development strategies on the fickle charity of wealthy countries or the self-interest of multinational corporations. However, current trade rules create enormous obstacles that prevent people in developing countries from realizing the benefits of trade. A growing number of advocacy organizations are now tackling this fundamental problem, hoping to open a route out of poverty for tens of millions of people who have few other prospects.

WHY TRADE?

Poor countries have few options for improving the welfare of their people and generating economic growth. Large debt burdens limit the ability of governments in the developing world to make investments and provide education, clean water, and other critical services. Despite some recent progress on the crushing problem of debt, only about 15% of the global South's $300 billion in unpayable debt has been eliminated.

Poor countries have traditionally looked to foreign aid and private investment to drive economic development. Both of these are proving inadequate. To reach the goals of the United Nations' current Millenium Development campaign, including reducing hunger and providing universal primary education, wealthy countries would have to increase their foreign aid from a paltry 0.23% of GDP to 0.7%. Instead, foreign aid flows are stagnant and are losing value against inflation and population growth. In 2001, the United States spent just 0.11% of GDP on foreign aid.

Likewise, although global foreign direct investment soared to unprecedented levels in the late 1990s, most developing countries are not attractive to foreign investors. The bulk of foreign private investment in the developing world, more than 76%, goes to ten large countries including China, Brazil, and Mexico. For the majority of developing countries, particularly the poorest, foreign investment remains a modest contributor to economic growth, on a par with official foreign aid. Sub-Saharan Africa, with the highest concentration of the world's poor, attracted only $14 billion in 2001.

In this environment, trade offers an important potential source of economic growth for developing countries. Relatively modest gains in their share of global trade could yield large benefits for developing countries. Gaining an additional 1% share of the $8 trillion global export market, for example, would generate more revenue than all current foreign aid spending.

But today, poor countries are bit players in the global trade game. More than 40% of the world's population lives in low-income countries, but these countries generate only 3% of global exports. Despite exhortations from the United States and other wealthy countries to export, many of the poorest countries are actually losing share in export markets. Africa generated a mere 2.4% of world exports of goods in 2001, down from 3.1% in 1990.

Many factors contribute to the poorest countries' inability to gain a foothold in export trade, but the core problem is that the playing field is heavily tilted against them. This is particularly true in the farm sector. The majority of the global South population lives in rural areas and depends on agriculture for survival. Moreover, poverty is concentrated in the countryside: more than three-quarters of the world's poorest people, the 1.1 billion who live on less than one dollar a day, live in rural areas. This means that agriculture must be at the center of trade, development, and poverty-reduction strategies throughout the developing world.

Two examples demonstrate the unfair rules of the global trading system in agriculture.

"IT'S NOT WHITE GOLD ANYMORE"

Cotton is an important crop in Central and West Africa. More than two million households depend directly on the crop for their livelihoods, with millions more indirectly involved. Despite serious social and environmental problems that have accompanied the expansion of cotton cultivation, cotton provides families with desperately needed cash for health care, education, and even food. The cotton crop can make a big difference in reducing poverty. For example, a 2002 World Bank study found a strong link between cotton prices and rural welfare in Benin, a poor West African country.

Cotton is important at a macroeconomic level as well; in 11 African countries, it accounts for more than one-quarter of export revenue. But since the mid-1990s, the cotton market has experienced chronic price depression. Though prices have rebounded in recent months, they remain below the long-term average of $0.72 a pound. Lower prices mean less export revenue for African countries and lower incomes for African cotton farmers.

But not for U.S. cotton farmers. Thanks to farm subsidies, U.S. cotton producers are insulated from the market and have produced bumper crops that depress prices worldwide. The global price of cotton is 20% lower than it would be without U.S. subsidies, according to an analysis by the International Cotton Advisory Committee. Oxfam estimates that in 2001, as a result of U.S. cotton subsidies, eight countries in Africa lost approximately $300 million—about one-quarter of the total amount the U.S. Agency for International Development will spend in Africa next year.

DUMPING ON OUR NEIGHBOR

Mexico has been growing corn (or maize) for 10,000 years. Today, nearly three million Mexican farmers grow corn, but they are facing a crisis due to sharply declining prices. Real prices for corn have fallen 70% since 1994. Poverty is widespread in corn-growing areas like Chiapas, Oaxaca, and Guerrero. Every year, large numbers of rural Mexicans leave the land and migrate to the cities or to the United States to try to earn a living.

The price drops are due to increased U.S. corn exports to Mexico, which have more than tripled since 1994. These exports result in large part from U.S. government policies that encourage overproduction. While Mexican farmers struggle to keep their farms and support their families, the United States pours up to $10 billion annually into subsidies for U.S. corn producers. By comparison, the entire Mexican government budget for agriculture is $1 billion. Between 2000 and 2002, a metric ton of American corn sold on export markets for $20 less than the average cost to produce it. The United States controls nearly 70% of the global corn market, so this dumping has a huge impact on prices and on small-scale corn farmers in Mexico.

To be fair, the Mexican government shares some of the responsibility for the crisis facing corn farmers. Although the North American Free Trade Agreement (NAFTA) opened trade between the United States and Mexico, the Mexican government voluntarily lowered tariffs on corn beyond what was required by NAFTA. As NAFTA is fully phased in, though, Mexico will lose the option of raising tariffs to safeguard poor farmers from a flood of subsidized corn.

WHAT DO POOR COUNTRIES WANT?

Cotton and corn illustrate the problems that current trade regimes pose for developing countries and particularly for the world's poorest people. African countries want to engage in global trade but are crowded out by subsidized cotton from the United States. The livelihood of Mexican corn farmers is undermined by dumped U.S. corn. In both of these cases, and many more, it's all perfectly legal. WTO and NAFTA rules provide near impunity to rich countries that subsidize agriculture, and increasingly restrict developing countries' ability to safeguard their farmers and promote development.

How much do subsidies and trade barriers in the rich countries really cost the developing world? One study estimates that developing countries lose $24 billion annually in agricultural income—not a trivial amount. In today's political climate, it's hard to see where else these countries are going to find $24 billion to promote their economic development.

The benefits of higher prices for farmers in the developing world have to be balanced against the potential cost to consumers, both North and South. However, it's important to remember that many Northern consumers actually pay more for food *because of* subsidies. In fact, they often pay twice: first in higher food costs, and then in taxes to pay for the subsidies. Consumers in poor countries will pay more for food if farm commodity prices rise, but the majority of people who work in agriculture will benefit. Since poverty is concentrated in rural areas, the gains to agricultural producers are particularly important.

However, some low-income countries are net food importers and could face difficulties if prices rise. Assuring affordable food is critical, but this goal can be achieved much more cheaply and efficiently than by spending $100 billion on farm subsidies in the rich countries. The World Bank says that low-income countries that depend on food imports faced a net agricultural trade deficit of $2.8 billion in 2000-2001. The savings realized from reducing agricultural subsidies could easily cover this shortfall.

Each country faces different challenges. Developing countries, in particular, need flexibility to develop appropriate solutions to address their economic, humanitarian, and development situations. Broad-stroke solutions inevitably fail to address specific circumstances. But the complexity of the issues must not be used as an excuse for inaction by policy-makers. Failure to act to lift trade barriers and agricultural subsidies will only mean growing inequity, continuing poverty, and endless injustice.

SOURCES   Xinshen Diao, Eugenio Diaz-Bonilla, and Sherman Robinson, "How Much Does It Hurt? The Impact of Agricultural Trade Policies on Developing Countries," (International Food Policy Research Institute, Washington, D.C., 2003); "Global Development Finance: Striving for Stability in Development Finance," (World Bank, 2003); Lyuba Zarksy and Kevin Gallagher, "Searching for the Holy Grail? Making FDI Work for Sustainable Development,"(Tufts Global Development and Environment Institute/WWF, March 2003); Oxfam's website on trade issues <www.maketradefair.com>.

False Promises on Trade

BY DEAN BAKER AND MARK WEISBROT

Farmers throughout the Third World are suffering not from too much free trade, but from not enough. That's the impression you get from most media coverage of the recent World Trade Organization (WTO) meetings in Cancún. The *New York Times, Washington Post,* and other major news outlets devoted huge amounts of space to news pieces and editorials arguing that agricultural subsidies in rich countries are a major cause of poverty in the developing world. If only these subsidies were eliminated, and the doors to imports from developing countries opened, the argument goes, then the playing field would be level and genuinely free trade would work its magic on poverty in the Third World. The media decided that agricultural subsidies were the major theme of the trade talks even if evidence indicated that other issues—for example, patent and copyright protection, rules on investment, or developing countries' right to regulate imports—would have more impact on the well-being of people in those countries.

There is certainly some element of truth in the argument that agricultural subsidies and barriers to imports can hurt farmers in developing countries. There are unquestionably farmers in a number of developing countries who have been undersold and even put out of business by imports whose prices are artificially low thanks to subsidies the rich countries pay their farmers. It is also true that many of these subsidy programs are poorly targeted, benefiting primarily large farmers and often encouraging environmentally harmful farming practices.

However, the media have massively overstated the potential gains that poor countries might get from the elimination of farm subsidies and import barriers. The risk of this exaggeration is that it encourages policy-makers and concerned nongovernmental organizations (NGOs) to focus their energies on an issue that is largely peripheral to economic development and to ignore much more important matters.

To put the issue in perspective: the World Bank, one of the most powerful advocates of removing most trade barriers, has estimated the gains from removing all the rich countries' remaining barriers to trade in manufactured and farm products *and* ending agricultural subsidies. The total estimated gain to low- and middle-income countries, when the changes are phased in by 2015, is an extra 0.6% of GDP. In other words, an African country with an annual income of $500 per person would see that figure rise to $503 as a result of removing these barriers and subsidies.

SIMPLISTIC TALK ON SUBSIDIES

The media often claim that the rich countries give $300 billion annually in agricultural subsidies to their farmers. In fact, this is not the amount of money paid by governments to farmers, which is actually less than $100 billion. The $300 billion figure is an estimate of the excess cost to consumers in rich nations that results from all market barriers in agriculture. Most of this cost is attributable to higher food prices that result from planting restrictions, import tariffs, and quotas.

The distinction is important, because not all of the $300 billion ends up in the pockets of farmers in rich nations. Some of it goes to exporters in developing nations, as when sugar producers in Brazil or Nicaragua are able to sell their sugar in the United States for an amount that is close to three times the world price. The higher price that U.S. consumers pay for this sugar is part of the $300 billion that many accounts mistakenly describe as subsidies to farmers in rich countries.

Another significant misrepresentation is the idea that cheap imports from the rich nations are always bad for developing countries. When subsides from rich countries lower the price of agricultural imports to developing countries, consumers in those countries benefit. This is one reason why a recent World Bank study found that the removal of *all* trade barriers and subsidies in the United States would have no net effect on growth in sub-Saharan Africa.

In addition, removing the rich countries' subsidies or barriers will not level the playing field—since there will still often be large differences in productivity—and thus will not save developing countries from the economic and social upheavals that such "free trade" agreements as the WTO have in store for them. These agreements envision a massive displacement of people employed in agriculture, as farmers in developing countries are pushed out by international competition. It took the United States 100 years, from 1870 to 1970, to reduce agricultural employment from 53% to under 5% of the labor force, and the transition nonetheless caused considerable social unrest. To compress such a process into a period of a few years or even a decade, by removing remaining agricultural trade barriers in poor countries, is a recipe for social explosion.

It is important to realize that in terms of the effect on developing countries, low agricultural prices due to subsidies for rich-country farmers have the exact same impact as low agricultural prices that stem from productivity gains. If the opponents of agricultural subsidies consider the former to be harmful to the developing countries, then they should be equally concerned about the impact of productivity gains in the agricultural sectors of rich countries.

Insofar as cheap food imports might have a negative impact on a developing country's economy, the problem can be easily remedied by an import tariff. In this situation, the developing world would gain the most if those countries that benefit from cheap imported food have access to it, while those that are better served by protecting their domestic agricultural sector are allowed to impose tariffs without fear of retaliation from rich nations. This would make much more sense, and cause much less harm, than simply removing all trade barriers and subsidies on both sides of the North-South economic divide. The concept of a "level playing field" is a false one. Mexican corn farmers, for example, are not going to be able to compete with U.S. agribusiness, subsidies or no subsidies, nor should they have to.

It is of course good that such institutions as the *New York Times* are pointing out the hypocrisy of governments in the United States, Europe, and Japan in insisting that developing countries remove trade barriers and subsidies while keeping some of their own. And the subsidy issue was exploited very skillfully by developing-country governments and NGOs at the recent Cancún talks. The end result—the collapse of the talks—was a great thing for the developing world. So were the ties that were forged among countries such as those in the group of 22, enabling them to stand up to the rich countries. But the WTO remedy of eliminating subsidies and trade barriers across the board will not save developing countries from most of the harm caused by current policies. Just the opposite: the removal of import restrictions in the developing world could wipe out tens of millions of farmers and cause enormous economic damage.

AVOIDING THE KEY ISSUES

While reducing agricultural protection and subsidies just in the rich countries might in general be a good thing for developing countries, the gross exaggeration of its importance has real consequences, because it can divert attention from issues of far more pressing concern. One such issue is the role that the IMF continues to play as enforcer of a creditors' cartel in the developing world, threatening any country that defies its edicts with a cutoff of access to international credit. One of the most devastated recent victims of the IMF's measures has been Argentina, which saw its economy thrown into a depression after the failure of a decade of neoliberal economic policies. The IMF's harsh treatment of Argentina last year, while it was suffering from the worst depression in its history, is widely viewed in the developing world as a warning to other countries that might deviate from the IMF's recommendations. One result is that Brazil's new president, elected with an overwhelming mandate for change, must struggle to promote growth in the face of 22% interest rates demanded by the IMF's monetary experts.

Similarly, most of sub-Saharan Africa is suffering from an unpayable debt burden. While there has been some limited relief offered in recent years, the remaining debt service burden is still more than the debtor countries in that region spend on health care or education. The list of problems that the current world economic order imposes on developing countries is long: bans on the industrial policies that led to successful development in the West, the imposition of patents on drugs and copyrights on computer software and recorded material, inappropriate macroeconomic policies imposed by the IMF and the World Bank. All of these factors are likely to have far more severe consequences for the development prospects of poor countries than the agricultural policies of rich countries.

SOURCES Elena Ianchovichina, Aaditya Mattoo, and Marcelo Olareaga, "Unrestricted Market Access for Sub-Saharan Africa: How much is it worth and who pays," (World Bank, April 2001); Mark Weisbrot and Dean Baker, "The Relative Impact of Trade Liberalization on Developing Countries," (Center for Economic and Policy Research, June 2002).

ARTICLE 26

The Mercurial Economics of the Phantom Palestinian State

BY KAREN PFEIFER

January/February 2002

If by some miracle of history and politics an independent Palestinian state were created alongside Israel, what would its economy be like? As many former colonies well know, an autonomous political entity, no matter how small, must have control over its own economic development to ensure true independence. Does that mean that a small economy must close itself off? This path has always been difficult, as Tunisia and Jordan, the closest analogues to the Palestinian economy in the Arab world, have clearly shown. And in this age of growing international economic integration, autonomous development has become virtually impossible even for large economies such as Egypt's. What chance, then, for tiny Palestine?

Ironic as it may seem, the appropriate, and not altogether far-fetched, model for the economy of a would-be Palestine is Israel. The Israeli government is certainly in control of its economic policy—effectively managing tariffs and public investment in infrastructure, for example—and has developed institutions similar to those of Western Europe for its citizens, such as banking and labor law (which do not, however, apply to Palestinians in the occupied territories). Like the United States and Western Europe, Israel protected and nurtured its agricultural and industrial base in the earlier years of development, allowing the service and export production sectors to grow gradually out of that base—albeit with generous and regular doses of external aid. In the last 15 years, Israel has thrived with its borders relatively open to flows of goods and services and labor and capital, and has become remarkably similar in both structure and standard of living to the "developed" economies of the West (see table). It is no empty boast that contemporary Israel, with help from its friends, was able to build a modern, developed society from modest beginnings in only 50 years.

If the Israelis could do it in their part of that stony and dry but beautiful land, 78% of historic Palestine, then perhaps the Palestinians could do it too in the 22% that would be left to them in the West Bank and Gaza (WBG). After all, they have the classic advantage of the late developers, namely, a well-developed Israel on one side and a moderately well-developed Jordan on the other, to serve as their partners in trade and investment. That expectation was the essence of the many hopeful projections put forth by the parties to the Oslo Accords in 1993, signed by Palestinian and Israeli officials and presented to the world as a breakthrough peace agreement.

With international agencies and non-governmental organizations pledging aid, the hope was that the Oslo Accords would mark the beginning of real economic development for WBG.

Alas, the exact opposite has come to pass. The material basis for an independent Palestinian state actually eroded between 1993 and 2000, largely because of the powers retained by the Israeli military authority during its continued occupation of WBG under these "interim accords." The accords were supposed to last just five years and lead to "final status negotiations," with a vague promise to eventually realize some version of the two-state solution. Far from solving the Israel/Palestine conflict, the Oslo agreement put off discussion of fundamental issues such as the official borders between the "two states," the future of Jerusalem, reversing Jewish settlement in WBG, and the fate of the four million Palestinians in diaspora. It also legitimized and protected Israel's control of the flow of goods and resources into and out of these territories, and enabled Israel to keep right on creating "facts on the ground" in WBG, such as road-building, land confiscation, and more settlements.

THE GEOGRAPHY OF "FACTS ON THE GROUND"

As Israeli correspondent Amira Hass recently explained in the *New York Times* (9/2/01), "Israelis and Palestinians are in a single geographic state, 'from the Mediterranean Sea to the Jordan River,' controlled by one government, but they live under two separate and unequal systems of rights and laws." Even the smallest

BASIC ECONOMIC FACTS
ISRAEL COMPARED TO THE WEST BANK AND GAZA

	Israel	West Bank and Gaza
Population (2000)	6 million	2.9 million
Population Growth Rate (average per year, 1990-2000)	2.9%	3.9%
Gross National Income per capita (2000)	$16,310	$1,610
GDP per capita growth (1999-2000)	3.5%	−9.6%
Under-5 mortality rate (1999)	8 per 1000	26 per 1000

Source: *World Development Report 2002*, Table 1 (p. 232) for Israel and Table 1a (p. 240) for the West Bank and Gaza.

export-oriented economy would need a contiguous geographical area for its own domestic market. However, the occupying power's land confiscations and home demolitions, establishment of a complex system of bypass roads in the West Bank, and settlement construction and expansion in the territories, have both shrunk the area left to a Palestinian domestic market and carved it into small, isolated enclaves. Furthermore, the 1.8 million Palestinians in the West Bank and the more than one million in Gaza remain physically unconnected with each other.

Between October 1993 and August 2001, Israel built at least 40 new settle-ments in the West Bank, including the eastern part of Jerusalem, and has consoli-dated others into territorial blocks containing 50,000 or so inhabitants each. It built 90,000 new housing units, not only in the settlements but also in (what is no longer Arab) "Arab East Jerusalem." All of this new living space has accom-modated the doubling of the settler population, from 200,000 to 400,000, in just seven years. Only 6,000 of those settlers live in Gaza, in closed communities bris-tling with barbed wire and armed patrols, but their settlements cover 25% of the land area and most of the shoreline. These areas are all off-limits to Palestinians,

THE ECONOMIC PROGRAM OF THE
PALESTINIAN NATIONAL AUTHORITY

In the 1998 report Palestine: Building the Foundations for Economic Growth, *the Palestinian Economic Council for Development and Reconstruction (PECDAR) out-lines an economic-development strategy based on the view that "the private sector must provide the engine for economic growth" and that "government should be limited to creating the appropriate investment climate." PECDAR, the main eco-nomic-development agency of the Palestinian National Authority (PNA), explains that this strategy was "prepared with the support of the World Bank" for a 1996 Paris conference with potential aid donors. The following points are taken from the 1998 PECDAR report.*   —Eds.

On State Intervention
The State should adopt a selectively interventionist role. International experience has discredited both the minimalist and the All-encompassing State as models. Intervention to address problems of market failure—if well designed, focused, and limited—can be beneficial to growth. If, on the other hand, such interventions are ill conceived or hostile to market discipline, they will prove disastrous.

On Private Enterprise
The PNA is implementing a private sector led development strategy. Private ini-tiative will provide the engine for growth and will be the major force in developing the economy. To that end, the PNA will seek to transfer economic activity to the

private sector. It will stimulate growth in the enterprise sector both directly and, more importantly, by creating an enabling environment for investment.

On Export Orientation
Given Palestine's small size and poor endowment base, the PNA has adopted an outward looking economic strategy. Encouraging private investment is, among other things, designed to create a healthy export sector. This will ensure full utilization of Palestine's specialized human and physical resources and will encourage domestic and foreign investment to take advantage of international market opportunities.

On Welfare Expenditures
The creation of a dynamic and successful economy is not an end in itself but a means to allow people to live prosperous, dignified and fulfilled lives. Concern for the weaker members of society, and those who experience difficulty in competing effectively in the market place, is therefore the hallmark of a civilized society.

Source: *Palestine: Building the Foundations for Economic Growth,* Palestinian Economic Council for Development and Reconstruction (PECDAR), 1998.

except for the fortunate few who are employed there, and the economic costs to the rest are high—for example, to Gazan fishermen whose ability to contribute to the livelihood of their families has been decimated.

From the point of view of Israeli "security," these many settlements should not be isolated from one another or unreachable in times of crisis from Israel proper (i.e., the internationally recognized Israel within the "Green Line" boundaries that predated the June 1967 war). This quixotic quest for "security" led to the construction of a network of broad, modern U.S.-style highways and bypass roads to connect them all together and to Israel. The term "bypass" conveys the illusion that settlers can use this system without ever having to cross paths with the irksome but now-invisible natives. However, the roads may result in less security for Israeli settlers, since traveling on them makes settlers easier targets for Palestinian guerrilla attacks.

These roads serve both military and commercial functions for the Israelis—many settlers commute to work within Israel proper, for example—while Palestinians are permitted neither to use these roads for travel nor to cross them to go from one Palestinian enclave to another. Instead, Palestinians have to drive over unpaved back roads or wait in long lines to go through (and often to not go through) military checkpoints, frequently having to change taxis three or four times just to travel a few miles when the taxi drivers themselves are not allowed through.

RESOURCES: LAND, WATER AND INFRASTRUCTURE

Besides needing a contiguous area, a small developing economy would also need to be in control of its natural resources and of the space for its population to expand. However, to enable the development of settlements and the road system, and to minimize sacrifice on the part of the 5.5 million people living within the Green Line, the Israeli authorities expropriated resources in the occupied territories, indeed at an accelerated pace after 1993. For example, large areas of "uncultivated" land (used by the Palestinians for grazing their goats and sheep) were taken to lay the beds for the roadways and to secure open spaces for Israelis' recreation in the present, and for more development in the future. Between October 1993 and August 2001, the Israeli government confiscated more than 70,000 acres of "empty" land, plus an additional 200 square kilometers of planted Palestinian agricultural land abutting the expanding settlements, and uprooted 282,000 fruit and olive trees in the West Bank.

Under Israeli occupation, Palestinians must obtain permits to build new homes or expand existing ones to accommodate growing families. The Palestinian population in WBG has one of the fastest rates of growth in the world, 3.9% per year in the 1990s. The Israeli authorities insist that Palestinians provide proof of land ownership, and even when they do provide the most modern legal deeds signed by Israelis themselves, it can still take years to get a building permit. Even the Palestinian areas under the "self-rule" created by the Oslo Accords still require Israeli permits for building.

After 1993, and contrary to what most people expected from the vaunted accords, the Israeli authorities tightened up on these practices. Palestinian families defied the rules of occupation, expecting liberation, and went ahead and built or expanded homes anyway. In response, the Israeli armed forces intensified the technique they had previously used mainly to punish political militants—home demolitions. Between 1993 and 2001, Israeli soldiers demolished at least 674 Palestinian homes, some of them two or three times because the obstinate natives kept rebuilding. Meanwhile, neighboring Jewish settlements were granted generous government subsidies and grew apace on the hilltops overlooking Palestinian-populated areas.

Israel/Palestine is a land where water is scarce and needs to be prudently rationed. The Israelis know this well; one of their main technical accomplishments and gifts to the world was the invention of drip irrigation—a technique that inhibits waste by delivering water to the crops in exact quantities, through pipes a few feet above the ground and usually during the night. The main sources of fresh water for all of historic Palestine are the Sea of Galilee (Lake Tiberias), the Jordan River, and two aquifers located almost entirely in the West Bank, under the Judean and Samarian Hills.

About one-third of the water used in Israel proper comes from the latter source. That is, Israel simply appropriates this resource from the occupied territory without compensation. Furthermore, water is inequitably distributed: Israelis consume 280 liters per person per day (for all purposes, including irrigation) while Palestinians consume about 90 in the West Bank and just 60 in Gaza. Many settlements have large swimming pools and green lawns in the dry season, while the water is turned off for days on end in Palestinian cities, villages and refugee camps. Palestinian standards of personal and household cleanliness, including in refugee camps, are high, but a full bath or shower is considered sheer luxury in humid, stultifyingly hot, overcrowded Gaza in the summertime.

While the Israeli authorities in the territories have invested in infrastructure mainly to service the Jewish settlements and build up Jerusalem, other modern necessities continued to be scarce for Palestinians in the occupied territories in the late 1990s. For every 13 kilowatts of electricity used by Palestinians, Israelis use 82. Palestinians have 3.1 phones for every 100 people; Israelis have 37. Palestinians have 80 meters of paved roads per 100 people; Israelis have 266. All Israeli households have indoor plumbing, as compared to 25% of Palestinians. Israeli electric power systems fail just 4% of the time, while Palestinian systems fail 30% of the time.

LABOR AND CAPITAL

In today's world, an underdeveloped small economy is not viable without labor and capital mobility, since it cannot realistically employ all of its labor force in diverse occupations or provide enough capital on its own to industrialize. The stark reality for Palestinians is that, given the dearth of investment and job opportunities within the territories, their best bet for a decent standard of living is to work in Israel or abroad. After all, Israel's gross national income per capita was ten times that of WBG in 2000 (see table).

Instead of becoming easier after Oslo, working in Israel and even in WBG became more difficult. The Israeli authorities have retained the ability to unilaterally restrict, whether for security or other reasons, the number of Palestinian workers who may cross into Israel to work. Indeed, the number of legal work permits for Palestinians actually declined after Oslo, from 165,000 in 1987 to 100,000 under the Paris Protocol of 1994, and the actual number issued by 1998 was less than 50,000. (The numbers are probably twice as high if informal workers—those without legal permits—are counted, still over a fifth of the Palestinian labor force in 1999.) Israel has also continued to impose border closures between the territories and Israel at will, collectively punishing Palestinians by preventing them from going to work. Israel still maintains checkpoints that impede travel within and between the territories—especially into Jerusalem, the commercial, educational, religious, and cultural heart of the West Bank.

As the number of Palestinians working in Israel dropped after 1993, the territories' economies shrank and annual real gross domestic product (GDP) growth was, on average, negative. GDP growth jumped to 6% in 1999 because of a temporary 15% surge in employment in Israel and the settlements, and because of a sharp one-time 12% increase in external donor aid. But then it fell again between 1999 and 2000 by a stunning 9.6% (see table).

The concept of the Jewish state, where only Jews (from anywhere in the world) can become citizens, assumes the maintenance of a Jewish majority and embodies fears that the Palestinians could win the demographic war (see table). After Oslo, Israel retained the ability to perpetually deny the right of return to expatriate Palestinians and refuses to negotiate over any but the most marginal adjustments via "family reunification" plans. Going to work abroad has serious risks, because, once out, a Palestinian—especially a young male ready to return and start a family—can find it very difficult to get back in.

The ingathering of skilled and experienced expatriate Palestinian labor and accumulated diaspora capital could dramatically improve the economic prospects of a Palestinian state (just as the inflow of Jewish labor and capital helped to rapidly build the new Israel). But Israel's policies systematically undermine the development potential of the Palestinian economy. Consider that industry accounted for about 9% of Palestinian GDP in the 1990s, while agriculture contributed another 14%, construction 16%, and public services 12%. The remaining 50% came from other "services," like commerce and transportation, and personal services like home repairs and barbering—most provided on a very small scale via self-employment.

Finally, a small, developing economy needs to have access to relatively unfettered trade in goods and services, to sell exports to earn foreign exchange, and to import the items it cannot produce itself. It needs to be able to purchase the inputs that enhance productivity in agriculture, manufacturing, and services like communications. Its government needs to be able to tax income and products, or to issue bonds, in order to pay for social services like transportation. It needs a set of legal institutions and regulations that encourage investment, by either the public or the private sector, for the production of manufactured goods and necessary services. It needs financial institutions that can recycle savings and create credit to stimulate new investment of all sorts.

After Oslo, and particularly after the follow-up economic negotiations that resulted in the Paris Protocol of 1994, Israel did not reduce but actually enhanced its power to subordinate or suppress Palestinian trade and agriculture in favor of its own producers and exporters. Whereas WBG exports to Israel were 37% of their imports from Israel in 1987, exports had fallen to just 26% of imports by 1999—the reverse of what was expected from Oslo. Held up at Israeli military checkpoints, Gaza's fresh flowers wilted in greater numbers, and lorry-loads of West Bank fruits and vegetables were left to rot, as they waited in vain for export to Europe or, via Jordan, to the Arab world. Problems in banking and finance remained unsolved as well. At the start of the occupation in 1967, Israel closed down existing financial institutions (mainly Jordanian) in favor of Israeli banks, thereby inhibiting the emergence of a Palestinian banking system that would directly serve savers and investors in the occupied territories. Palestinians either hoarded their savings in gold or sent them out to banks in Amman. After 1993, banks were again allowed to set up shop in WBG and accept deposits. But few of these are locally owned, and, due to lack of deposit insurance and regulatory oversight, they have been unwilling to lend to finance new investment in productive activity in Palestine.

The Geneva Conventions forbid an occupying military force from expropriating resources in the territory it occupies, from transplanting its own population into that territory, and from interfering with the freedom of movement and pursuit of livelihood by the indigenous population. These conventions are international laws agreed upon by the community of nations in the aftermath of World War II. They presumably govern the behavior of Israel in the Palestinian territories it has occupied since 1967. Yet the world allows Israel to act with impunity. Meanwhile, to note a contrasting example, the Iraqi occupiers of Kuwait are still being punished ten years after being forcibly expelled.

CONCLUSION

Israeli penetration of the West Bank and Gaza is now so deep and so complex that it is hard to conjure the shape of a just and peaceful two-state solution, let alone how Palestine could have a viable economy. This harsh reality is the underlying material cause of the Palestinian uprising that began in September 2000, the "second intifada" against Israeli occupation, a collective and anarchic expression of seven years of mounting rage and frustration at the false promises of Oslo.

Despite the deadly and futile violence of 2000-01, a few rays of hope remain. In addition to the work of international and Palestinian voluntary organizations and NGOs in the WBG, such as the Union of Palestinian Medical Relief Committees (UPMRC), there is also a peace movement that bridges the Israeli/Palestinian divide. Organizations like Bat Shalom and New Profile, and the network of the Women in Black, continue to bring attention to the inequities of Israeli occupation of WBG and press to reform Israeli society in a less militaristic and racist direction. Magazines such as *Challenge* and *News from Within* give voice to a small but growing peaceful civil rights movement in both Israel and Palestine. Noting the similarities between apartheid, South Africa's much reviled strict segregation of the races, and Israel's discriminatory treatment of both Arab Israelis and Palestinians in WBG, activists hope to promote understanding of Israel's abuse of power, even under the Oslo Accords. These groups struggle to define a new, politically democratic, and more economically equitable vision for the resolution of the Israel/Palestine conflict.

RESOURCES   For a discussion of the issues in defining "Palestinians in diaspora" and controversies over how to count them, see Elia Zureik, *Palestinian Refugees and the Peace Process,* Institute for Palestine Studies, Washington, D.C., 1996.

ARTICLE 27

A Palestinian Labor Leader Speaks Out
Interview with Mohammed Saleh Aruri

BY ALEX HOGAN

May/June 2003

I n the three years since the current *intifada*, or uprising, began, the already-frag-
ile Palestinian economy has nearly broken down. Under military and economic
siege, entire economic sectors have collapsed. Unemployment runs well over
50%, with 411,000 people out of work. Almost half of the population lives on
less than $2 a day, and food shortages have struck certain areas. The besieged and
directionless Palestinian Authority (PA) appears unable to meet the staggering
crisis.

In this context, the Palestine General Federation of Trade Unions (PGFTU) is
focused on the literal survival of its members and their families. As one of the largest nongovernmental organizations in Palestine, the PGFTU is responding to the
mass deprivation by stepping into a role previously fulfilled by the PA: providing
an economic and social safety net for its members. The federation delivers unemployment and health insurance benefits to tens of thousands.

PGFTU also continues its long-term struggle to build a movement for workers' rights in Palestine, and recently succeeded in pushing the PA to establish a set
of working labor laws. With 500,000 public and private worker-members in the
West Bank and Gaza strip, PGFTU represents 75% of the Palestinian workforce.
That's a unionization level most unions in the West would envy. But its members
have faced conditions that no one would envy.

Since the beginning of the occupation following the 1967 war, Palestinian labor played a role in the Israeli economy roughly similar to that played by Mexican
labor in California. Palestinian territories provided a supply of low-wage labor
for Israeli employers. Like many Mexican immigrant workers in the United States,
Palestinians who work in Israel lacked basic rights and government protections
once they crossed the border. They constituted the most easily exploited and ex-
pendable segment of the Israeli labor force.

On and off throughout these decades, prior to the closure of the border three
years ago, thousands of Palestinians would spend up to five hours a day in checkpoints in order to find work as day laborers in Israel in construction, agriculture,
and service industries. Before 2000, 40% of all employed Palestinians worked in
Israel. Work was usually temporary, with a high dismissal rate. Palestinians work-

ing in Israel were taxed up to 20% of their salary, despite being ineligible for most Israeli government benefits. Exorbitant court fees prevented most Palestinians from bringing charges against their employers.

Since the 1993 Oslo Accord between Israel and the Palestine Liberation Organization (PLO), efforts to strengthen the Palestinian economy have been undercut by both Israeli restrictions and reoccupation and by the corruption of the Palestinian Authority bureaucracy. The PA's favoritism and nepotism, particularly its practice of building monopolies (both state-owned and private) run by a handful of Yasir Arafat's close associates, have stunted economic development. Further, the Palestinian economy suffers from stringent Israeli tax policy and the theft of Palestinian natural resources, including water, by settlers.

Israel's periodic closures—or the shutting down of borders between Israel and the Palestinian Territories—have devastated sectors that rely heavily on trade with Israel. Since 1993, closures cost Palestinian agriculture and building industries over $2 billion. Most of all, the closures have devastated people's capacity to earn even a meager living.

In addition to the economic siege, the PGFTU is subject to the intense level of violence and repression faced by all popular organizations in Palestine since the reoccupation. On March 7, 2002, Israeli jets bombed PGFTU headquarters, destroying it, and prompting a letter of condemnation to Israeli Prime Minister Ariel Sharon from the International Confederation of Free Trade Unions. Amazingly, no one was killed. Constant curfews and military checkpoints have made it extremely difficult to organize even local branch meetings. And as an independent union, the PGFTU is often in conflict with the PA over workers' rights, in particular over labor legislation and the rights of public workers whose unions are tightly controlled by the PA.

Over the last few years, the PGFTU has been engaged in an aggressive effort to build international labor solidarity to keep this struggling union going. The union recently unveiled a multifaceted strategic plan that aims to build union-wide democratic elections, reestablish the union's administrative infrastructure, and provide training for members. PGFTU leaders have toured Europe and Asia, visiting with unions to describe their plans and present their case. In the United Kingdom, they helped members of the Trade Union Congress, the U.K.'s national labor federation, establish a Palestinian-labor solidarity network.

This winter, PGFTU members made their first trip to the United States. The group spoke with labor activists throughout the country. I spoke with Mohammed Saleh Aruri, a member of the PGFTU's Executive Committee, during his stop in Detroit. Mr. Aruri started his work in the labor movement in 1980 when he started a union at a water company in Jerusalem. He served as chairman of his local and was later elected to the council of the PGFTU. In 1996, he was elected to the union federation Executive Committee. Mr. Aruri now works at the PGFTU office in Ramallah.   —*Alex Hogan*

• • • • •

Q: How has the situation changed for the Palestinian labor movement since the beginning of the *intifada* over three years ago?

ARURI: Since the beginning of the *intifada*, the Israeli government has placed Palestinian cities, refugee camps, and villages under siege. The rings of checkpoints permit no one to leave their village, or city, to get to their workplace in Palestine or in Israel.

Palestinian workers who were employed before the *intifada* at worksites inside Israel have been fired—130,000 workers all together. And more than 150,000 were laid off from their jobs in the occupied territories of the West Bank and Gaza. One reason is that since the *intifada*, the Israeli army often won't even let workers leave their homes. Also, many factories and worksites have been destroyed in the fighting, and the remaining ones face the problem of getting materials shipped in from outside their city. For example, we can't transport materials to Jenin or Nablus or Gaza because of Israeli checkpoints. So, many of these factories have closed.

More than 65% of Palestinians are living below the poverty line—around 2 million people.

Q: How has the PGFTU dealt with this? How have you organized to deal with the crisis?

ARURI: From the beginning of the *intifada*, we started an emergency program. We gave out unemployment benefits to workers amounting to $150 each. So far we have doled out benefits to more than 225,000 of our unemployed members. We also gave free health insurance to over 400,000 unemployed members and their families. And we give out emergency food rations.

We are in the process of filing over 100,000 legal cases against Israeli employers for unjust termination of our members.

Q: The laid-off Palestinians have not received any kind of unemployment or other benefits from Israel or the companies they were working for?

ARURI: No. None. We have also filed over 100,000 cases with the Palestinian Authority against Palestinian employers because they have not given any of their workers any kind of unemployment benefits, either.

We have a very big list of unemployed workers waiting for emergency benefits from us because we don't have enough money to help all our unemployed members. We have a limited amount collected from our friends and unions in Arab countries and Europe, but it is not enough.

Q: What is the PGFTU relationship with other political forces and parties, like Fatah?

ARURI: In the PGFTU there are many active unionists from all the parties. On our Executive Committee, we have representatives from six parties: the Fatah movement, the Palestine Democratic Union, the Popular Front for the Liberation of Palestine, the Democratic Front for the Liberation of Palestine, the Palestinian People Party, and the Popular Struggle Front. But only 30% of our members are members of any of the six mentioned parties. The majority of our members are unaffiliated.

Q: What about Hamas?

ARURI: We don't have any members from the Islamic fronts in the leadership of our unions. They had their own unions before the *intifada*: one in Ramallah and the other in Nablus. But during the *intifada* [Hamas] closed down their union. Most of their former members have approached us about joining, and many did join, because of our ability to provide vital services as I talked about earlier. Now we represent over three-quarters of the Palestinian workforce.

Q: What kind of organizing force does the PGFTU have?

ARURI: We have a staff of 76, plus hundreds of active members working with us as volunteers. In addition, many university students work closely with us. All our workers' committees in workplaces, factories, villages, and offices work as our organizers.

Q: What is the PGFTU relationship with Histadrut (the National Labor Federation of Israel)?

ARURI: After the Olso agreement, we signed our own agreement with Histadrut in 1995. It stated that Histadrut must return back half of membership dues taken from Palestinian workers who were working in Israel. (All workers who live inside Palestine are considered part of the PGFTU's jurisdiction, whether they are working in Palestine or Israel. Up until 1995, however, Histadrut took membership fees from Palestinian workers.) There were some other items in the agreements, but Histadrut has not as of yet returned all of the money owed to us. With the dire economic situation now in Palestine, we especially need that money to continue to provide needed services to our members. During the *intifada*, we haven't heard Histadrut's voice against Israeli government policies that hurt our members. Many of our members have been killed and wounded by Israeli soldiers. To give an example, two months ago, Israeli soldiers killed six workers from a village near Hebron because they tried to reach their workplace, a stone factory, just outside their village. Before that, five workers were killed in the morning at a refugee camp near Nablus. On their way to work, soldiers fired at their taxi, killing or wounded all those in the car.

Q: And Histadrut has not said anything about this?

ARURI: Yeah, they have said nothing.

Q: What about other groups in Israel?

ARURI: We have very good relations with some unionists in the Labor Party, and also with activists from the Communist Party, the Democratic Front, and Peace Now. They support the Palestinian right to have an independent state within the pre-1967-war borders.

Q: What do you see as the PGFTU role in the wider struggle for Palestinian self-determination?

ARURI: We struggle along with all our people, political parties, human rights, and peace organizations in Palestine against the last military occupation in the world, Israel's occupation of Palestine. Also, we struggle together all over the world with activists in Europe, Africa, Asia, and North America. We struggle against war in Palestine and we support justice and peace: a comprehensive peace in the Middle East that would allow our people—both Palestinian and Israeli—to live in peace and freedom. We want to let our children build their future in peace and security.

Q: What is the PGFTU's relationship with the Palestinian Authority?

ARURI: We are a nonprofit independent organization. We have our own decision-making processes and finances, independent of any government authority. We support all the Palestinian people and parties, including the PA, in their struggle against Israel's occupation. But we are sometimes against the PA in terms of struggles over labor rights. To give an example, we organized three large demonstrations—before the start of the *intifada*—against the PA's labor ministry and the Palestinian Legislation Council, to pressure them to take into account our positions on upcoming labor law legislation. We succeeded in getting many of our planks into the law and now we have the first set of labor laws in Palestine.

Q: In documents you sent out, you talk a lot about the PGFTU's strategic plan to democratize the PGFTU. What do you mean by that?

ARURI: According to our strategic plan, we want to have democratic elections at every level throughout our union as soon as possible, once Israel ends their occupation in our cities and removes all tanks and soldiers from our towns and villages. It is very difficult to have elections now because we are under siege. There are many checkpoints, so our members cannot go to meetings or conferences. Our executive committee can't even hold a meeting now. We are in touch by fax and e-mail with our branches, but we are under curfew so we have to communicate from our homes. How can we have an election in this situation?

Q: What do you feel the labor movement in the United States can do to help the labor movement in Palestine?

ARURI: We came here to talk with unionists and peace and human-rights activists about our struggle and to build support for a just peace in the Middle East—a struggle not only for human rights but for workers' rights. We feel that we are members in this big family: the international workers' movement. We are sure that our voice will reach the U.S. workers movement to place pressure on the government to implement the U.N. resolutions numbers 242 and 338, which call for the withdrawal of Israel from the occupied territories. All the people we have met here in the United States are very kind. All have promised to struggle together against war and to develop our relations. They have promised to send labor delegations to Palestine to see the reality of the situation, and to come back and speak with their unions' members about what they witnessed.

ARTICLE 28

Labor and Democracy in South Africa

BY FRANCO BARCHIESI

September/October 2001

Angelina is a street cleaner in the Soweto region of Johannesburg, South Africa, and a member of the South African Municipal Workers Union (SAMWU). She earns 2,300 rand (US$290) a month. Once she has paid for her health insurance, housing loan, transportation, water, electricity, and school fees for her four children, she is usually left with only about 1,300 rand, with which she pays for the basic necessities (food and clothing). Her husband was laid off two years ago, following a "restructuring" at the manufacturing company where he had worked. After 20 years in employment for the Johannesburg municipality, the only way Angelina makes it to the end of the month is by borrowing money from co-workers or from loan sharks in Soweto, who charge exorbitant interest rates.

The Greater Johannesburg Municipal Council recently announced a general restructuring of its operations, turning the waste collection department where Angelina works into a corporatized business utility. Now, service delivery will be driven by profitability, and jobs will be lost. Angelina knows that if she loses her job, the Unemployment Insurance Fund, to which the state contributes, will allow her to survive only for a few months, after which she will have to use money from her retirement fund and hope to find another job. Unemployment in South Africa stands at approximately 35% of the economically active population. So for many workers Angelina's age, defined as "unskilled" in the official labor statistics, finding a new job is often an unrealizable dream.

Many workers share Angelina's feelings about the "new South Africa." The African National Congress (ANC) government "was my government, which I have voted for," Angelina says. "It said we are going to live in peace and harmony in our country. Now I see only fear and crisis, and it is our government who is creating all these things. This government is hitting ... the working class. What I see is privatization, and this will go back to the days of apartheid. One person is going to do the job of ten people ... We thought we're going back to Canaan, but they're bringing us back to Egypt."

TOWARDS A "GLOBALIZED" SOUTH AFRICA

Since the end of apartheid and South Africa's transition to democracy, the country's organized labor movement has lived a paradoxical reality: while being recognized as an important actor in policy-making institutions, its once impressive strength at the grassroots has seriously eroded.

When the ANC won the first democratic elections, in 1994, millions of workers saw the victory not only as the landmark event in regaining political freedom, but also as the culmination of a decades-old struggle by the black working class against the racist state. In the course of this struggle, the trade unions emerged as the best organized and most powerful force opposing apartheid. Today, the Congress of South African Trade Unions (COSATU), the country's largest union federation, claims about two million members. The 1995 Labour Relations Act (LRA) extended for the first time the rights to organize and bargain collectively to South African trade unions. COSATU is now part of a formal alliance with the ruling ANC and the South African Communist Party (SACP). COSATU leaders have been elected to Parliament on the ANC list while maintaining pro-working class commitments. Organized labor has also been included, together with representatives of the government and of capital, in bargaining institutions where economic policies are debated.

The ANC, which won 67% of the vote in South Africa's last elections (1999), rose to power on the basis of massive working class support and a virtually unchallenged supremacy on the political left—a result of its 80-year history of opposition to state racism. The party was able to mobilize a broad array of class forces around themes of national liberation, non-racialism, and social equality. For the black working class, this meant not only the access to political and civil rights, but especially access to the social goods essential for full enjoyment of citizenship in a democratic state. Under the impulse of working-class struggles, "freedom" came to mean "that the people of our country can not only vote for a representative of their choice," as Murphy Morobe of the United Democratic Front (UDF) said in 1985, but also have "some direct control over where and how they live, eat, sleep, work, how they get to work, how they and their children are educated, what the content of that education is." Yet most black households, especially in the devastated rural areas, remain deprived.

Some of the social demands made their way into the programs of the new government, especially the Reconstruction and Development Programme (RDP), under which the ANC ran in the 1994 elections. Under the priority of "meeting basic needs" and modernizing infrastructures and human resources, the RDP promised a growth path leading to a general land reform, employment creation programs, an inclusive welfare system, and limitations to the power of financial corporations. However, the political and policy vagueness of these promises revealed a deep ideological and class rift within both the ANC-SACP-COSATU Alliance and the ANC itself.

The ANC's view of "national liberation" had historically prioritized interclass cooperation among the oppressed, rather than socialist transformation. The collapse of the Soviet bloc (once the ANC's most important ally) and the rise of neoliberalism worldwide tilted the balance of class power against the working class—and towards a more conservative interpretation of the RDP. This process was facilitated by the ANC's pragmatic "transitional" compromises with the apartheid regime and domestic capital, which led the party to abandon goals of radical social transformation. At the same time, technocratic views, promoted by right-wing think tanks and international financial institutions, gained increasing influence in the party. ANC leaders grew to consider working-class militancy and state intervention obstacles to growth in a neoliberal world. The government's Growth, Employment and Redistribution (GEAR) policy of 1996 codified the new strategy of market liberalization and the promotion of private investment, mainly directed at globally competitive industries, for which reduced working-class militancy is a key asset.

These changes are part of a broader view, expressed in President Thabo Mbeki's notion of a rising "African renaissance," which considers the successful globalization of South African capitalism the best way to raise the black population's living standards. This approach consists of boosting export-oriented industries, increasing South African investment throughout the Southern African region, and enhancing foreign investor confidence. Crucial to these ends—as Mbeki argued in 1998 in front of the Black Business Forum—was the creation of a black business elite, which would also become a source of support for the ANC government.

THE NEW INSECURITY

The South African government has been quick to open the country to competition, lowering its tariff protections five years before the timetable required under the General Agreement on Tariffs and Trade (GATT). In sectors that were highly protected by the old regime, such as clothing and appliances, this meant that nearly total liberalization replaced tariffs as high as 100%. As a consequence, industrial decline and unemployment are now widespread in many manufacturing regions.

Workers and union organizations have suffered harsh consequences. The "old" manufacturing industries, which under the apartheid regime had catered to the largely white domestic market, have all but collapsed. Approximately 600,000 permanent jobs have been lost during the first five years of ANC government, largely in sectors such as metals, chemicals, mining, and textiles. Meanwhile, new jobs largely take the form of precarious, temporary employment. These jobs generally do not include benefits such as retirement funds, medical insurance, or severance packages. Workers employed in these positions, usually in small or medium-sized companies, are vulnerable and extremely difficult to unionize.

Employers enjoy easy access to vast numbers of unemployed people in the black townships. This has led to a renewed exploitation of women and children, who often have to make up for income lost by laid-off adult male workers. George Magaseng is an organizer for the National Union of Metalworkers of South Africa (NUMSA), the country's biggest industrial union, with almost 200,000 members. In the East Rand, the core manufacturing area of the country, 80,000 industrial jobs have been lost since 1993 and NUMSA has lost 6,000 members (26% of its total membership) in the area over the past five years. Masageng has seen the reemergence in the East Rand of home-based family work for large corporations. Children "assemble small pieces, then the company comes and collects, paying them very poorly," he says. "They're taking advantage of the social situation of the workers. These people, due to the poverty situation, are compelled to accept [these] conditions."

Extreme poverty is no longer confined to those who have lost their jobs. "Flexible" forms of employment are creating a new group of working poor. Research conducted by the union-affiliated National Labour and Economic Development Institute (NALEDI) shows that most families living in official poverty have at least one employed member. The only alternative to precarious and low-paid jobs is the meager welfare system, which provides state pensions of 540 rand (US$68) per month for absolutely destitute elderly people. Meanwhile, workers face the increasing privatization of social services and infrastructure, especially at the local government level, due to the reduction in central government funding. Necessities such as water, electricity, and housing—rather than being social rights as the RDP promised—are quickly becoming unaffordable to millions of working-class people. Evictions and service disconnections, often executed with brutal force by the police or private companies hired by the municipalities, are the order of the day in many poor communities around the country.

A NEW STRUGGLE?

The decline of employment as the primary source of community, citizenship, and dignity is the main challenge facing South African labor today. COSATU maintains a strong vocal opposition to GEAR, but many grassroots labor activists criticize its participation in the ANC-led alliance and in state institutions that try to promote moderation on the part of labor. This sentiment has fueled militant industrial action in opposition to the union leadership—such as recent strikes at Volkswagen South Africa.

COSATU's own analysis often reflects these problems. The official document "Accelerating Transformation," prepared for the federation's 2000 congress, admits: "Economic policy has arguably been the area of greatest contestation during the first term. It would be fair to say that the economic policy debate currently stands at an impasse both in terms of process and in content. Although COSATU has made more interventions on economic questions than in any other area, it is also the area in which its submissions, with significant exceptions, have resulted in the fewest policy or legislative changes."

The decline in stable work and lack of access to services is not merely pushing the communities towards informal survival activities. It is also reshaping their demands and practices of resistance. In the past few years, communities have mobilized against the privatization of municipal services and for a more equitable access to social citizenship rights. At the forefront of these struggles have been organizations, known as as "new civics," like the Soweto Electricity Crisis Committee, which is opposing electricity disconnections; the Concerned Citizens' Group (CCG), which is fighting against evictions from former municipal housing in Durban; and the Treatment Action Campaign (TAC), which is campaigning for free access to AIDS medicines. The concept of "civics" harkens back to the pro-ANC community mobilization in black townships under apartheid. At the same time, the new generation of civics differs sharply from the "old" one, which had grown in the popular uprisings of the 1980s and has since been institutionalized in the ANC-aligned South African National Civic Organisation (SANCO), established in 1991.

As Ashwin Desai of the CCG points out, the new civics have reappropriated the slogans, strategies of direct action, and organizational models from the fight against apartheid. They also, however, express a growing rejection of the policies adopted by the ANC, and are much less likely to be represented by leaders from the historic liberation movements or from trade-union organizations. COSATU's support for many of these struggles, as in the case of the TAC, is constantly endangered by the unions' difficulties in representing unemployed and precarious workers, who constitute the backbone of these movements. The ANC's position towards these new movements, meanwhile, has been hostile, when not overtly repressive. ANC leaders have labeled the new civics "adventurist" and "counter-revolutionary," regarding them as threats to the party's hold on civil society organizing. Many disillusioned grassroots ANC members have joined the new civics—confronting ANC-dominated local authorities, which are often, as in the case of Durban, directly in charge of evictions, service disconnections, and law enforcement against "defaulters." ANC activists who chose to run as "independents" to represent new civics in the 2000 local government elections were generally expelled from the party.

Conflicting and not always progressive agendas are now scrambling for leadership among the grassroots communities. Populist leaders are trying to win community support with ethnic or xenophobic agendas. The right-wing parliamentary opposition, such as the Democratic Alliance, is also trying to build a base among the unemployed in the townships. Smaller left opposition parties have been active in some cases, like the Pan Africanist Congress (PAC) in the recent land occupation in Bredell (Johannesburg). They lack, however, a sustainable organizational base.

New organizations, like the Anti-Privatisation Forum (APF), are not only countering conservative or reactionary agendas, but are also working to create national movement for social rights and universal access to services. The APF, which was founded in Johannesburg, has gathered together many of the "new civics" and is expanding its connections with struggles and organizations in different regions. The organization has already gained the support of trade unions, such as the municipal workers' organization (SAMWU), in the frontline of the struggle against privatization of municipal services. SAMWU's "anti-privatization campaign"—recognizing the limitations of mere workplace-based actions—explicitly notes the importance of an alliance with community organizations. Once again, as in the struggle against apartheid, forging grassroots links at the community level will be critical for the South African labor movement.

ARTICLE 29

Korea's Neoliberal Restructuring

Miracle or Disaster?

BY JAMES CROTTY AND KANG-KOOK LEE

July/August 2001

Over the last two years, South Korea's economy has recovered from the 1997 East Asian economic crisis faster than anyone expected. Indeed, Korea has become the new poster child for the "free-market" or "neoliberal" economic restructuring that the International Monetary Fund (IMF) is peddling to a suspicious public in the developing world. In early 2000 the IMF touted Korea's "dramatic turnaround" after the crisis. Not only was Korea's output above what it had been before the crisis but, the IMF gleefully proclaimed, "Over the past two years bold policies and a commitment to reform have made Korea a more open, competitive, and market driven economy."

There is a more pessimistic interpretation of Korea's experience under IMF and U.S.-sponsored economic restructuring since late 1997. The harsh policies the IMF imposed on Korea immediately after the start of the Asian crisis actually caused the Korean economy's 1998 collapse. Now, three years later, Korea faces an unbalanced recovery of questionable durability and a labor movement badly, perhaps fatally, wounded by neoliberalism, while the majority of its people suffer rising insecurity and falling incomes. If the IMF and the U.S. government succeed in their drive to transform Korea from an East Asian-style state-guided economy to a market-driven, "globalized" economy, future progressive political movements will find it exceedingly difficult to create an efficient, egalitarian economic system designed to meet the needs of the majority of its people.

THE RISE AND FALL OF KOREA'S "EAST ASIAN" ECONOMIC MODEL

Following a 1961 coup, Korea's new military dictatorship adopted the economic development program pioneered by Japan that came to be known as the "East Asian model." The government took control over the broad contours of economic life, guiding and regulating markets to achieve state-set national development goals. It decided what new industries and technologies would receive priority, allocated financial capital to support these decisions, and regulated investment spending by powerful Korean conglomerates known as *chaebol*. Most important, the government tightly controlled the movement of money into and out of Korea.

Under state guidance, Korea became one of East Asia's "miracle" economies. Though the authoritarian government severely repressed the labor movement, Korea's economic performance was outstanding. From 1961 through 1996, real GDP growth averaged 8% a year. And the fruits of this incredible growth were widely shared. Real wages grew by 7% a year during this 35-year period. Renowned Cambridge University economist Ajit Singh called the East Asian model "the most successful economic development model in the history of the world."

About a decade ago, under intense pressure from the United States, the IMF, and large *chaebol* and elite families who had prospered under the old model but now wanted the freedom to use their wealth as they pleased, the Korean government began to relinquish its control over key economic processes. By the mid 1990s, it let firms invest as they pleased, reduced regulation of domestic bank activity, and let foreign banks and investors run short-term or "hot" money into and out of the country. Short-term foreign bank loans exploded between 1993 and 1996, fueling an over-heated investment boom. When it became clear in 1997 that the boom was over, these banks pulled out, demanding immediate repayment of some $60 billion in short-term loans, which pushed the Korean banking system near bankruptcy. The banks, in turn, cut loans to highly indebted domestic corporations, forcing them toward the brink of insolvency. Korea borrowed money from the IMF to pay its foreign creditors, and in return the IMF took effective control of the Korean economy, immediately imposing high interest rates and tight budgets to help restore foreign investor "confidence." These policies pushed the weakened economy over the edge, into 1998's state of collapse.

The Korean crisis occurred because the government stopped performing its traditional economic functions, making the economy vulnerable for the first time to volatile international financial flows. Yet the IMF did not urge Korea to restore control over capital flows to protect against another crisis. Instead, it took advantage of Korea's weakness to destroy what remained of its East Asian structure and replace it with a market-driven neoliberal system. Strong laws protecting job security were replaced by fire-at-will legislation. Remaining barriers to the entry of foreign goods, money, and corporate investment were eliminated. In the neoliberal future, global markets would make all important economic decisions without interference from the government.

THE NOT-SO-MIRACULOUS RECOVERY

It is not hard to assemble evidence in support of the IMF's triumphalist view of Korea's recovery. After falling almost 7% in 1998, Korea's real gross domestic product (GDP) grew by over 10% in 1999, and about 9% in 2000. The unemployment rate, which peaked at over 8% in early 1999, dipped below 4% in 2000. Before the crisis, Korea actually faced a large trade deficit. But the collapse of 1998 drastically reduced imports. That year, in the middle of the crisis, Korea showed a trade surplus of $40 billion—a record 13% of GDP. Since then, continued trade surpluses ($25 billion in 1999 and $12 billion and 2000) have helped restore the country's production and employment levels.

A closer look at the data, however, suggests that the recent Korean "miracle" may not be all that miraculous. In 2000, three years after the crisis hit, consumption was only 5% above its pre-crisis level, while fixed capital investment was still 9% lower. What domestic growth did take place in 1999 and 2000 was only possible because the Korean government brought down interest rates and increased government spending after the initial IMF-imposed austerity. But external agencies such as the IMF and the Organization for Economic Cooperation and Development (OECD) demanded a return to fiscal and monetary conservatism. In 2000, the Korean government actually ran a budget surplus equal to 1.1% of the country's GDP. Since Korea's public debt had risen from 17% to 39% of GDP in the last three years, the government is not in position to sustain its stimulus program much longer anyway.

The recovery appeared to have petered out by late 2000. Economic growth slowed dramatically in the year's fourth quarter. Investment in machinery and other equipment, which had been growing rapidly, declined in the last two months of the year. The unemployment rate is above 4% again, and climbing. The Korean Development Institute forecasts that GDP growth in 2001 will fall to 4%, and even less if U.S. growth slows.

THE IMPACT OF RESTRUCTURING ON LABOR AND SOCIAL SOLIDARITY

The United States had been trying for decades, with only limited success, to open Korea's prosperous economy to Western multinational firms and banks. The IMF takeover of Korea finally gave multinationals the opportunity they had long sought. However, these companies wanted no part of Korea's militant trade-union movement. To attract foreign investment, the Korean government and corporations would first have to drastically weaken Korean labor. One of the IMF's key demands was that the government repeal labor laws protecting workers from being fired and replaced. In February 1998, Korea, for the first time in the country's modern history, legalized mass firings and the creation of firms to lease temporary workers to other companies. Korea's *chaebol* were quick to take advantage of their new legal powers, firing about 30% of their workers. As demand picked up in 1999 and 2000, firms hired mostly part-time or temporary workers. As a result, the percentage of Korean employees with stable permanent or regular jobs, already by far the lowest in the industrialized world before the crisis, fell dramatically, from 58% in 1995 to 48% in 2000.

In January 1998, President-elect Kim Dae Jung promised workers a "U.S. style" social welfare system to compensate them for the rising economic insecurity that his policies were bound to create. Given the enormous cost of such a system and the ever-tighter constraint on government spending, this promise will never be kept. Social welfare spending did rise after the crisis—from less than 3% of

GDP in 1997 to over 7% in 1999—as unemployment, poverty, and homelessness increased and the government broadened coverage. Even under these dire circumstances, however, Korea's social welfare spending came nowhere near the Western European levels of 15 to 20% of GDP.

The militant and democratic Korean Confederation of Trade Unions (KCTU) made valiant efforts to slow the pace of neoliberal restructuring. Strike activity in 1998 and 1999, measured in number of work days lost to strikes, stood at almost three times the 1997 level, and militant labor actions continue to this day. The KCTU even tried to organize nationwide general strikes to break neoliberal momentum in 1998 and 1999. Unfortunately, resistance has thus far been unsuccessful.

President Kim turned against the labor movement immediately upon taking office, responding to worker activism with fierce repression, including the arrest of virtually all union leaders involved in strike activity (see James Crotty and Gary Dymski, "Can the Korean Labor Movement Defeat the IMF?" *Dollars & Sense* November/December 1998). In February 2001, the government crushed a large strike triggered by the firing of 1,700 Daewoo Motor workers, and issued arrest warrants for the strike's leaders. In April 2001, police attacked union members demanding access to their office at a Daewoo Motor factory. Even the conservative *Korea Times* deplored the scenes of "bloodied unionists being viciously attacked by riot police," and the conservative opposition political party called for the resignation of the government's Prime Minister.

The labor movement, however, is divided: The more conservative Federation of Korean Trade Unions has refused to join forces with the KCTU in its fight against restructuring, and the widening split in the workforce between permanent and temporary workers makes it difficult to maintain labor unity. The media is universally anti-labor, the middle class fears that labor activism will destabilize the fragile recovery, and the once-powerful progressive student movement no longer exists. While it would be premature to rule out a new outbreak of effective labor militancy, prospects for labor do not look good. In a June 2000 interview with one of the authors, KCTU President Dan Byung-Do observed that while resistance to neoliberal restructuring was on the rise, continued government, *chaebol*, and IMF-U.S. offensives against Korean workers were inevitable.

Korea is a country fiercely proud of its tradition of social solidarity. This is reflected in its long-term commitment to mass education and relative income equality. But Koreans have discovered that there are no exceptions to the rule that neoliberalism generates rising inequality wherever it is imposed. The real income of the top fifth of households rose right through the collapse of 1998, the recovery of 1999 and beyond, while the rest of Korea lost income in both 1998 and 1999. The income of the poorest fifth dropped by 18% over these two years. Not surprisingly, poverty has also worsened since the crisis. The household poverty rate, which stood at 5% in 1996, more than tripled by 1999.

RESTRUCTURING AND RISING FOREIGN ECONOMIC DOMINATION

Outgoing President Kim Young Sam signed the first restructuring agreement between the IMF and Korea in December 1997. According to the *New York Times*, President Clinton telephoned the wavering Korean president and told him "Korea would be 'severely punished' if the deal was not quickly reached." Incoming President Kim Dae Jung did not need outside pressure to cooperate with the IMF. Perhaps because he had been harshly treated by the military regime and the *chaebol*, Kim was a fervent neoliberal. In a 1985 book, written at Harvard under the influence of his U.S. mentors, he strongly criticized government interference with markets: "Maximum reliance on the market is the operating principle of my program." Resource allocation, he stressed, should be determined solely through unrestricted, globally open financial markets.

Kim believes that foreign investment is the key to future Korean prosperity. "What we need now, more than anything else, are foreign investors," he stated in an address to the U.S. Congress in 1999. "Market reforms and foreign investment are the only solution" to Korea's problems," he said. Kim predicted that "the crisis will be remembered as a blessing," because it would force Korea's economy open to foreign capital. Kim wants Korea to dance to the tune played by foreign stockholders and banks, a group shown by the Asian crisis to be astoundingly fickle.

The most pressing problem facing the incoming Kim government in late 1997 was the imminent collapse of the nation's banks. To deal with this threat, the government injected massive public funds into the banking system, effectively nationalizing most banks. Standard and Poor's estimate the ultimate cost at $125 billion, or about 30% of the country's 1999 GDP. President Kim used state control of the banks to dictate structural change to the heavily indebted *chaebol*. He threatened to cut off their credit unless they slashed their indebtedness by 60% within just two years. In near-depression conditions, firms could meet this demand only by the extensive sale of real assets and the large-scale issue of new stock. Since domestic firms were broke, this policy was guaranteed to dramatically increase foreign control of Korea's economy.

Just as President Kim intended, foreign investment poured in. After running between $1 billion and $2 billion for most of the 1990s, foreign direct investment (FDI)—which includes the construction or acquisition of factories or other real assets—totaled over $40 billion from 1998 through 2000. Net portfolio investment—which includes investment in stocks and other financial assets—totaled $22 billion over the same period. These figures, however, may understate the increase in foreign control, since the collapse of the Korean currency (the won) made asset purchases in foreign currency "fire sale" cheap. Most FDI took the form of acquisitions rather than the building of new facilities. Korea thus gained few additional real assets in return for this unprecedented transfer of corporate control to outsiders.

Opening the Korean stock market to global investors dramatically increased both foreign ownership (which almost tripled between 1997 and 2000, to over 30% of the value of Korean stocks) and stock-price volatility. The main Korean stock price index (equivalent to the United States' Dow Jones) went on a roller-coaster ride: tripling between late 1997 and mid 1999, then falling by half by the end of 2000, before rebounding in early 2001. Yet President Kim continues his effort to impose shareholder-guided capitalism in Korea, a system that forces managers to adapt investment strategies to hyperactive stock-price fluctuations—a far cry from the days when they adapted their strategies to long-term government development plans.

These capital inflows have added to Korea's holdings of foreign currencies, but they have a longer-run downside. Korea is losing control of its economic destiny. Major Korean financial institutions, previously used by Korean governments to guide credit in accordance with development plans, have been sold at bargain prices to foreign owners, who have no obligation to cooperate with the government. With the proposed sale of Seoul Bank to foreign interests this summer, control of six of Korea's nine commercial banks will be in the hands of outsiders. The *Korea Times* reports that foreign owned banks are "reluctant to extend loans to Korean enterprises." Meanwhile, the industries most responsible for Korea's export performance—such as semiconductors, telecommunications, and autos—have also fallen under foreign influence. Foreigners own 44% of Korean semiconductor shares and 21% of telecommunication shares, according to the *Korea Times*, and are the dominant stockholders in such important firms as Hyundai Motors, Hyundai Electronics, LG Chemical, and Samsung Electronics.

The situation in autos is especially disastrous. In 2000, Daimler-Chrysler gained significant influence over Hyundai Motors through the purchase of over 10% of its shares. And Kim, in his lust for foreign ownership, ordered Daewoo Motors, Korea's second largest auto maker, to be sold to foreign interests, even though Daewoo has become so weak that its sale will bring little money. In April 2001, the *Korea Herald* reported that a General Motors (GM) spokesman "demanded that Daewoo Motor be immediately sold to the U.S. car maker without charge." Daewoo has lost much of its value because government-controlled creditor banks starved it of operating funds to deliberately force management to impose firings and wage cuts on its fiercely militant unions, bringing them to heel. "Mass layoffs are inevitable," Kim said in January 1998, "because without them foreign investors will not come to Korea." GM refused to make an offer for Daewoo until the unions were broken. Daewoo cut employment by 6,100 since November, firings the *New York Times* says are designed "to make a deal more desirable to GM." The influential *Financial Times* in mid-2000 raised "the possibility that the entire [Korean auto] sector, the second largest in Asia, could soon be dominated by foreigners."

**KOREA'S ONLY HOPE FOR THE FUTURE IS TO DEFEAT
NEOLIBERAL RESTRUCTURING**

The widely advertised neoliberal Korean "miracle" is a fraud. The financial system remains fragile and subject to crisis even after the massive injection of public funds. Key corporations remain debt-ridden. Since Korea's financial markets have been liberalized to an even greater extent than in 1997, and foreign financial investment in Korea is both more important and more unstable, a renewed outbreak of financial crisis cannot be ruled out.

The neoliberal restructuring process has dismantled or badly weakened most of the policy tools the government used so effectively to impose social control over the Korean economy in the decades before the crisis. Indeed, this is largely what neoliberal restructuring *is*—the replacement of potentially democratic political control over the economy with market processes dominated by rich individuals and powerful companies. With a "flexible" labor market and weak unions, free cross-border capital flows, unregulated stock and bond markets, corporations independent of government influence, banks guided only by short-term profits, and foreign domination of finance and industry, what policy instruments will be available to future progressive governments to guide Korean economic development so that it meets the needs of all the country's people? This is the most serious long-term problem facing Korea.

The destruction of the policy tools traditionally used to guide the economy is not an easily reversible political process. State-regulated economic systems, whether in the West during the Golden Age of the 1950s and 1960s or in the East Asian "miracle" economies, were created in the aftermath of depression, revolution, or war. In the absence of a severe economic crisis, it will be extraordinarily difficult to put together the domestic political coalitions necessary to create such a system from scratch, even in the absence of external pressures and constraints. For a country as embedded in the global neoliberal system as Korea will be if the U.S. government, the IMF, President Kim, and their supporters have their way, it might well prove impossible. The battle for a progressive future for Korea has not yet been lost. The government has not yet lost its leverage over the economy, the union movement remains militant, and public support for neoliberal restructuring, and for President Kim himself, has declined dramatically of late. The *Far Eastern Economic Review* observed that "Kim now presides over a political disaster zone" and that opposition to the president now stands at 70%. Backing for the progressive Democratic Labor Party, though still weak, has been rising rapidly. But time is running short. To have any chance of success, a national offensive to defeat neoliberalism must begin soon.

ARTICLE 30

Is Decreasing Infant Mortality Due to Neoliberal Policies?

BY ARTHUR MACEWAN

July/August 2000

Dear Dr. Dollar,
  Defenders of the International Monetary Fund (IMF) and the World Bank, including U.S. Treasury Secretary Lawrence Summers, claim that during the past two decades there have been dramatic improvements in lowering infant-mortality rates and increasing longevity in Third World countries due to the IMF, World Bank, and neoliberal economic policies generally. What validity is there to this position?
                                                   — *Larry Siegel, Bedford Hills, NY*

Not much validity.
      In spite of the persistence of great inequality and poverty in the world, throughout the last 50 years infant-mortality rates have fallen and life expectancy has risen in almost all countries. The gains in many low-income countries are especially impressive. Yet these improvements were no greater in the 1980s and 1990s, when neoliberalism gained dominance, than in earlier periods, and they cannot be tied to the neoliberalism of the IMF and World Bank.

Public-health programs, such as inoculation against smallpox and improvements in sanitation, are responsible for most of these improvements. Yet these types of social programs are, to say the least, not central elements in the neoliberal agenda, which encourages government cutbacks and privatization. Of course, the neoliberals justify their approach by arguing that their policies lead to economic growth, which then leads to the expansion of social programs. Neoliberal policies, however, have not greatly improved economic growth, nor is there any automatic connection between economic growth and improvements in infant-mortality rates and longevity.

Chile is one case that might lend support to the claims made by supporters of the IMF and World Bank. In that country, where neoliberal policies were imposed by the military dictatorship in the mid-1970s, the infant-mortality rate fell from 77 per 1,000 live births in 1970 to 32 in 1980, to 16 in 1990, and to 11 in 1997. (Life expectancy data tell a similar tale, rising from 62.4 years in 1970 to 75.2 in

1997.) The substantial success of the 1970s, however, can hardly be attributed to the neoliberal model, since free-market policies were not instituted until the latter part of the decade and it takes time for economic policies to produce health results. Also, the improvements occurred at least in part because the dictatorship departed from its neoliberal policies, establishing government prenatal and neonatal programs.

Nowhere else in Latin America can advocates of neo-liberalism find support for their claims, even though the governments in the region have adopted neoliberal policies. For example, in Mexico, Brazil, Argentina, and Peru, infant-mortality rates and longevity figures have improved continuously, but no more than when "statist" policies were in force. Indeed, in Mexico improvements in the infant-mortality rate have slowed dramatically since 1990—precisely the years when neoliberal policies began having their impact on the country.

Also, to date, no other country in Latin America has matched the experience of Cuba. In 1997, the life expectancy in Cuba was 76 years and the infant-mortality rate was 7 per 1,000—the same as in the U.S. Whatever one thinks of Cuban economic policies, they can hardly be classified as neoliberal!

Outside of Latin America, it is hard to find evidence that would support the IMF and World Bank on the basis of these social indicators. On the one hand, there is the case of South Korea, where a military dictatorship achieved great success with capitalist development under a regime of strong state control of the economy. The infant-mortality rate fell from 46 in 1970 to 12 in 1990, and life expectancy rose from 60 to 70. On the other hand, in sub-Saharan Africa, where the IMF and World Bank have had major roles in recent years, social indicators remain dismal and the era of increased neoliberal influence has not been better than earlier decades. Life expectancy rose from 44 years in 1970, to 48 in 1980, inched up to 50 in 1990 and then to 51 in 1997; the infant-mortality rates for those years have been 137, 115, 100, and 91. (Neoliberalism, it seems, has done little to counter the AIDS epidemic.)

Shifting attention to the wealthy capitalist countries, it is interesting to compare the U.S. and Japan. In spite of Japan's relative economic stagnation since the end of the 1980s, in 1997 life expectancy was 80 and the infant-mortality rate was a remarkable 3.7 per 1,000. In the U.S., where we talk about the great economic expansion of the 1990s, the figures for 1997 were 76 for life expectancy and 7.1 for infant mortality. There are many differences between the two countries that could explain Japan's better social indicators. Still, one economic fact is probably most relevant here, as in other parts of the world: the distribution of income in Japan is much less unequal than in the U.S.

All the data I have used here are from World Bank sources!

ARTICLE 31

"Missing Women"

BY ALEJANDRO REUSS

May/June 2001

f you look down a column of population statistics for the world's 200-odd countries, the female-male split rarely seems to stray very far from 50-50. Women rarely make up less than 48% of a country's population, and they seldom account for more than 52%. This seemingly narrow band, however, hides a demographic catastrophe of holocaust proportions. In the world's most populous country, China, males outnumber females by about 40 million; in its second most populous, India, by about 30 million. In 1990, economist Amartya Sen calculated that, to bring the female-to-male ratio in China, India, and other countries up to the sub-Saharan African level (about 102 women per 100 men), one would have to add a total of over 107 million women to their populations. He dubbed this figure the number of "missing women."

COUNTRIES MISSING OVER ONE MILLION WOMEN

Country	Women per 100 men	Female pop. (in millions)	Expected female pop. (in millions)	Missing women (in millions)
China	93.8	599.4	654.3	54.9
India	93.7	473.9	517.7	43.7
Pakistan	92.9	63.4	69.8	6.5
Bangladesh	97.8	62.1	65.0	2.9
Indonesia	100.4	102.0	104.0	2.0
Philippines	94.4	37.3	38.8	1.5
Turkey	97.9	31.4	32.8	1.4
Total for countries listed				112.9

For the sake of simplicity, the sub-Saharan African average of about 102 women per 100 men is used as the benchmark female-to-male ratio. The expected female population is the number of women that, given the actual male population, would raise the country's female-to-male ratio to this level. The number of missing women is the difference between the expected female population and the actual female population. The source population data (total population of each country and women as a percentage of total population) are from the World Bank's *World Development Indicators CD-ROM*. All figures are for 1998.

CHANGE IS POSSIBLE

The gender disparities reflected in the missing women figures may be colossal, but they are not necessarily intractable. Studies of gender and mortality within India suggest that areas with higher rates of female education and labor-force participation tend to have higher female-to-male ratios as well. The two Indian states of Kerala and Uttar Pradesh, despite sharing very low per capita incomes and very high (40–50%) poverty rates, are polar opposites when it comes to missing women. The female-to-male ratio in Uttar Pradesh is about 88 (women per 100 men), while it is about 104 in Kerala.

Resources: Mamta Murthi, Anne-Catherine Guio, and Jean Dreze, "Mortality, Fertility, and Gender Bias in India: A District-Level Analysis," *Population and Development Review*, Vol. 21, Issue 4, 1995.

Sen used the concept of "missing women" to dramatize the wrenching consequences, in many parts of the world, of anti-female bias in nutrition, health care, and other basics of life. In China and other countries where there is a strong preference for male babies, sex-selective abortion and even infanticide of female babies undoubtedly contribute to the number of missing women. The figures mainly reflect, however, the enormous economic inequalities, hidden by official statistics focusing on total household income, within families.

Not all family members always enjoy an equal claim to a family's income. All too often, especially when an adult male controls the family's money income, women come after men in the family pecking order, and girl children come last of all—even when it comes to basics like food and visits to the doctor. In India, 11 more infant girls die per thousand born than boys per thousand born. In China, the difference is 13. These facts go a long way toward explaining why the two countries account for nearly three-fourths of the world's missing women. Today, anti-female bias may account for as many as 135 million missing women worldwide.

Sen adopted the sub-Saharan African figure as a benchmark for calculating the number of missing women because the region—having very low income, low overall life expectancy, high overall birth rates, etc.—resembled the areas he was studying. Other economists have since developed more sophisticated estimates of expected female-to-male ratios. Based on complex studies of age-specific mortality in females and males under conditions of equal treatment, these benchmarks vary from one country to another. While the total number of missing women can vary considerably depending on the standard one applies, however, it always numbers in the tens of millions. A 1994 study published in the journal *World Development*, for example, put the worldwide figure at about 89 million missing women.

Of course, the missing women data should not be taken to mean that there is no anti-female bias in areas where women are in the majority, like the United States and most of Europe. Rather, in the words of Amartya Sen, excess female mortality is "a crude and sharply visible aspect of gender inequality, which often manifests itself in more subtle and less gruesome forms."

RESOURCES Amartya Sen, "More Than 100 Million Women Are Missing," *New York Review of Books*, December 20, 1990; Amartya Sen, *Development as Freedom* (Alfred A. Knopf, 1999); Stephan Klasen, "'Missing Women' Reconsidered," *World Development* 22(7), 1994; United Nations, *The World's Women: Trends and Statistics*, 2000; World Bank, *World Development Indicators* CD-ROM, 2000.

CHAPTER 7

Environment, Health, and Agriculture

Business and Climate Change

Privatizing Environmental Regulation

BY DAVID L. LEVY

January/February 2001

H uman-caused emissions of greenhouse gases have "contributed substantially to the observed warming over the past 50 years" and, if left unchecked, could cause the earth's average surface temperature to rise between 2.7 and 11 degrees Fahrenheit. So concluded an October 2000 report of the Intergovernmental Panel on Climate Change (IPCC), the international group of scientists charged with assessing the causes, extent, and impacts of climate change. The IPCC's language is much stronger than in its previous report, issued five years ago, and the range of warming is nearly twice the previous estimate. Industries dependent on fossil fuels, however, did not react to the 2000 report with the stonewalling that once typified their public declarations on climate change.

Before the November 1997 Kyoto Protocol, an international agreement which established mandatory limits on the emission of greenhouse gases, large sectors of U.S. industry waged an intense and well-funded campaign against international regulation. Companies organized a strong industry association, the Global Climate Coalition (GCC), challenging the scientific basis for action and highlighting the economic costs of curtailing emissions. In the months leading up to the meeting of more than 150 country delegates in Kyoto, U.S. industry put $13 million into the Global Climate Information Project, a public relations campaign against any international agreement.

Even before Kyoto, however, the first signs of a major shift were visible in Europe. In May 1997, John Browne, the Group Chief Executive of oil giant British Petroleum (BP), declared publicly, "The time to consider the policy dimensions of climate change is not when the link between greenhouse gases and climate change is conclusively proven, but when the possibility cannot be discounted and is taken seriously by the society of which we are part." By 1998, U.S. industry was also showing a change in stance. The GCC was weakened by a series of defections: BP left in late 1997, Shell in April 1998, and Ford in December 1999. In 1998, General Motors joined an initiative of the World Resources Institute called "Safe Climate, Sound Business," agreeing that precautionary action needed to be taken on climate change. That same year, thirteen companies, including BP, Toyota, Boeing, Lockheed, and Enron, joined the newly formed Pew Center on Global Climate Change. The companies endorsed a series of newspaper advertisements stating that they "accept the views of most scientists that enough is known about the science and environmental impacts of climate change for us to take actions to address its consequences."

SMOKE AND MIRRORS?

Many environmentalists doubt the sincerity of big business's sudden conversion. Given the history of industry hostility to emission controls, changed public statements can easily be dismissed as cynical posturing or "greenwashing." In May 1999, for example, William Clay Ford, Jr., the new chairman of Ford Motor Company, proclaimed that "more and more, the marketplace will demand vehicles that are truly clean." At the same time, Ford continued to produce ever larger trucks and SUVs, like the 12-mile-per-gallon Expedition, contributing to the continuing decline in U.S. fuel economy. Even Shell and BP, the apostles of the new movement, have not curtailed their oil exploration or refining activities at all. The $100 million a year Shell has pledged to invest in renewables is only about 7% of the company's total annual expenditure on petroleum exploration and production.

Incomplete though the conversion may be, investments of hundreds of millions of dollars cannot be discounted as mere public relations. Since its acquisition of Amoco, BP has become the world's largest producer of solar photovoltaic panels, with plans to reach $1 billion in sales by 2010. Shell has also announced that it will invest $500 million in photovoltaics over five years as part of a new International Renewable Energy Division. In 1998, European automakers (including European subsidiaries of U.S.-based companies) accepted a "voluntary" agreement to reduce carbon emissions by about 25% over the following decade. European car companies have introduced very small, light-weight cars, like Daimler-Chrysler's SMART car, and invested substantial amounts in a range of technologies from diesel to fuel cells. Even the most ardent opponents of mandatory emission controls have begun to invest in low-emission technologies. In December 1997, Ford invested about $400 million in a fuel-cell joint venture with Daimler-Chrysler and the Canadian company Ballard. Texaco was the first major U.S. oil company to break ranks and proclaim the need for precautionary action on climate, and in May 2000 it invested $67 million in Electronic Conversion Devices, a company which develops advanced batteries and solar technology.

This shift suggests something more than mere PR "greenwashing," though less than a conversion to sustainable practice. It is not surprising that large sectors of industry viewed action on climate change as a major stategic threat. Controls on the emission of carbon dioxide, the main greenhouse gas, would raise the price of fuels and hurt the revenues and profits of oil, coal, and car companies, as well as other energy-intensive industries. The companies seem to have concluded, however, that open defiance of the climate-change consensus could jeopardize their long-run interests even more—causing them to lose political legitimacy and therefore the power to shape the eventual regulatory outcome. This change of attitude illustrates the resilience of capitalism and the strategies by which business attempts to sustain hegemony—a term used by the early-twentieth-century Italian Marxist Antonio Gramsci to describe a position of dominance based on consent, the projection of moral leadership, and an ability to present one's goals as the general interest. In the face of strong challenges from state institutions and civil society, companies are moving away from confrontation, and instead towards a strategy of accommodation, compromise, and cooptation.

EXPLAINING THE TURNAROUND

The change in Europe can be understood mostly as a response to political and social pressures. From a European perspective, the ratification of the Kyoto Protocol and the imposition of mandatory emission controls appear inevitable. European firms were concerned that, if they aggressively opposed emission controls, they might be jeopardizing their privileged access and influence with policy makers. In international negotiations, the European Union has called for bigger emission cuts than the United States, and European politicians were sensitive to charges that they talked tough but lacked the will to act. Therefore, they looked to industry for substantial, early emission reductions. The auto industry was already on the defensive for environmental reasons, even facing a total ban on cars in some cities. This complex of factors resulted in the European car industry's agreement to the "voluntary" emission reductions.

U.S. companies have, meanwhile, experienced growing pressure to respond to their competitors' moves in other countries. In the auto industry, Ford and General Motors (GM) saw Toyota launch the Prius, a hybrid electric-gasoline engine car, in Japan in 1998 and the United States in 2000. Honda leapfrogged Toyota, launching its own hybrid, Insight, in the U.S. market in December 1999.

While U.S. companies publicly expressed skepticism about the market potential for small, expensive, fuel-efficient cars, they stepped up their own plans for low-emission technologies. Companies often prefer to make mistakes together rather than risk ceding a major advantage to competitors. After Daimler-Chrysler announced a target date of 2004 for introducing a commercial fuel cell vehicle, Ford, GM, BMW, and Honda followed with similar announcements. Ford and GM's European subsidiaries had already agreed to substantial emission cuts, so these companies needed to develop the appropriate technologies anyway. When Ford announced in spring 2000 that it would improve the fuel economy of its SUVs by 25%, GM quickly followed suit.

Within the GCC, more companies were questioning the value of aggressively denying the climate problem. The public effort to challenge the legitimacy of the Intergovernmental Panel on Climate Change (IPCC) had little impact, and even threatened to backfire on industry. Environmental groups in Europe and the United States seized upon the lobbying and public relations efforts of the fossil fuel industry, issued a number of reports that documented industry support for climate skeptics, and attempted to frame the issue as big business using its money and power to distort the scientific debate. In the run-up to the Kyoto conference in December 1997, the GCC decided to shift strategy. Instead of challenging the science, industry's message shifted to the high cost and limited environmental effectiveness of an agreement that excludes developing countries from emission controls. After Kyoto, companies increasingly worried that they were losing political access. The Pew Center's Eileen Claussen was blunt in stating that "joining Pew gives companies credibility, and credibility means political access and influence."

In the years since Kyoto, companies have begun to reevaluate the threat posed to their economic interests by emission controls. In the oil industry, companies have come to realize that their primary markets for oil and gas will enjoy significant growth for at least 20 years. Rapid growth of car ownership in developing countries and the continued growth of vehicle-miles traveled in industrialized countries will offset the gradual introduction of low-emission car technologies. With global air travel growing at about 5% annually, aviation remains a strong market for the oil industry. Demand for natural gas, a relatively low-carbon fuel, is also booming worldwide, as small, efficient gas turbines replace large coal-fired electric power plants. In the auto industry, companies are realizing that they can stay in the business of making and selling cars, even if the power train undergoes radical change. Change is likely to be slow, in any event, because new technologies are expensive and could require massive investments in alternative fuel infrastructure.

The likelihood of stringent emission controls in the short term has also receded. Parties to the Kyoto Protocol only reached agreement in 1997 by deferring difficult decisions about implementation. It has therefore become easier for companies to win public sympathy and political credibility by expressing support for a weak and ineffective international treaty. As details have emerged, companies have realized that there will be plenty of room for fudging. The United States is planning to comply with its commitments on emissions by buying emissions credits from other countries. Russia and other East European countries, whose economies collapsed along with the Soviet Union, now emit far less carbon dioxide than in the 1990 baseline year, allowing them to sell billions of tons of carbon credits, labeled "hot air" by critics. The United States has resisted European efforts to restrict the percentage of a country's commitments that can be met by emissions trading. It has also pushed for credits rewarding hard-to-measure increases in "carbon uptake" (due to such factors as expanded forest lands).

There is still some danger that the whole process could collapse. It is becoming clear that even the modest emission-reduction targets established in Kyoto are unlikely to be met. The United States agreed to reduce emissions to 7% below 1990 levels by the "budget period" 2008-2012, but by 1999 its emissions were already 13.1% above 1990 levels. Although an agreement was reached in Kyoto, industry efforts have succeeded in blocking its ratification by the U.S. Senate. The Senate is unlikely to ratify the treaty without major revisions, which will be opposed by most other countries. Without the participation of the United States, which accounts for nearly one-quarter of global emissions, the Protocol is meaningless. According to one anonymous industry source, the GCC did not collapse; it was more a case of "mission accomplished; now we can avoid the political cost of membership."

THE PRIVATIZATION OF INTERNATIONAL ENVIRONMENTAL GOVERNANCE

Even as some environmentalists have welcomed industry's changed stance on climate change, some observers have expressed concern that increasing industry participation in shaping regulation amounts to the privatization of environmental governance. In fact, industry has been closely involved in international climate policy from the outset. The Business Council for Sustainable Development, a group of industrialists representing 48 of the world's largest multinational corporations, was particularly active at the U.N. Rio conference in 1992, and helped to ensure that the original Framework Convention on Climate Change contained no binding commitments.

Governments have encouraged industry involvement. In a 1996 speech announcing that the United States would no longer oppose binding international emission controls, U.S. State Department negotiator Tim Wirth proclaimed that "meeting this challenge requires that the genius of the private sector be brought to bear on the challenge of developing the technologies that are necessary to ensure our long term environmental and economic prosperity." The U.S. Environmental Protection Agency and Department of Energy have adopted the same stance. The Climate Wise program, jointly administered by the two agencies, bills itself as "a unique partnership that can help you turn energy efficiency and environmental performance into a corporate asset." At the international level, Intergovernmental Panel on Climate Change (IPCC) head Bob Watson attempted to head off criticism of its 2000 report by recruiting corporate experts as chapter authors and reviewers.

In the absence of an international mechanism to limit emissions, private bodies have been taking the initiative. The World Bank Prototype Carbon Fund (PCF) was established in 2000 as "public-private partnership" between a few national governments, including the Netherlands, Sweden, Japan, and Canada, and twenty-six companies, including Hydro Quebec, Daimler-Chrysler, Shell-Canada, BP-Amoco, and numerous Japanese firms. The fund's purpose is to raise $140 million for investments in renewables and efficiency in developing countries, projects that will earn carbon credits for the investing companies. The Environmental Defense Fund brought together seven large companies, including Dupont, Alcan, Shell and BP, in summer 2000 to form the "Partnership for Climate Action," whose purpose is to enable emission trading among its members.

THE PRICE OF ACCOMMODATION

Compared to the history of corporate denial and hostility, these moves appear to be constructive and proactive. The cost of this accommodation and compromise with industry, however, is a loss of democratic process and accountability. Dan Becker of the Sierra Club has sharply criticized the EDF's emissions trading initiative, saying it offered only modest reductions in greenhouse gases while undercutting efforts to write strong regulations on emission controls as part of the 1997 Kyoto treaty. Peter Utting, in a UN report called "Business Responsibility for Sustainable Development," concluded that "the most significant concern with some forms of voluntary initiatives and partnerships is that they may serve to weaken key drivers of corporate responsibility, namely governmental and intergovernmental regulation, the role of trade unions and collective bargaining, as well as more critical forms of NGO activism and civil society protest."

The new business strategy on climate issues includes a strong dose of public relations, but it is not all hot air. Companies also have to demonstrate some tangible progress toward reducing emissions in order to blunt demands for more stringent regulation, and to protect their market positions in the event that mandatory emissions controls become a reality. While this strategy may sustain the political access and legitimacy of business, however, it is unlikely to result in the sustainable development that business now claims to champion. The IPCC report notes that greenhouse gases need to be slashed by more than 50% to stabilize the climate; the Kyoto Protocol called for a 5% cut in industrialized countries, and that target is fast becoming unreachable. There is a still a long struggle ahead.

ARTICLE 33

Genetic Engineering and the Privatization of Seeds

BY ANURADHA MITTAL AND PETER ROSSET

March/April 2001

In 1998, angry farmers burned Monsanto-owned fields in Karnataka, India, starting a nationwide "Cremate Monsanto" campaign. The campaign demanded that biotech corporations like Monsanto, Novartis, and Pioneer leave the country. Farmers particularly targeted Monsanto because its field trials of the "terminator gene"—designed to prevent plants from producing seeds and so to make farmers buy new seed each year—created the danger of "genetic pollution" that would sterilize other crops in the area. That year, Indian citizens chose Quit India Day (August 9), the anniversary of Mahatma Gandhi's demand that British colonial rulers leave the country, to launch a "Monsanto Quit India" campaign. Ten thousand citizens from across the country sent the Quit India message to Monsanto's Indian headquarters, accusing the company of colonizing the food system.

In recent years, farmers across the world have echoed the Indian farmers' resistance to the biotech giants. In Brazil, the Landless Workers' Movement (MST) has set out to stop Monsanto soybeans. The MST has vowed to destroy any genetically engineered crops planted in the state of Rio Grande do Sul, where the state government has banned such crops. Meanwhile, in September 2000, more than 1,000 local farmers joined a "Long March for Biodiversity" across Thailand. "Rice, corn, and other staple crops, food crops, medicinal plants and all other life forms are significant genetic resources that shape our culture and lifestyle," the farmers declared. "We oppose any plan to transform these into genetically modified organisms."

INDUSTRIAL AGRICULTURE I: THE GREEN REVOLUTION

For thousands of years, small farmers everywhere have grown food for their local communities—planting diverse crops in healthy soil, recycling organic matter, and following nature's rainfall patterns. Good farming relied upon the farmer's accumulated knowledge of the local environment. Until the 1950s, most Third World agriculture was done this way.

The "Green Revolution" of the 1960s gradually replaced this kind of farming with monocultures (single-crop production) heavily dependent on chemical fertilizers, pesticides, and herbicides. The industrialization of agriculture made Third World countries increase exports to First World markets, in order to earn the foreign exchange they needed to pay for agrochemicals and farm machinery manufactured in the global North. Today, as much as 70% of basic grain production in the global South is the product of industrial farming.

The Green Revolution was an attempt by northern countries to export chemical- and machine-intensive U.S.-style agriculture to the Third World. After the Cuban revolution, northern policymakers worried that rampant hunger created the basis for "communist" revolution. Since the First World had no intention of redistributing the world's wealth, its answer was for First World science to "help" the Third World by giving it the means to produce more food. The Green Revolution was to substitute for the "red."

During the peak Green Revolution years, from 1970 to 1990, world food production per capita rose by 11%. Yet the number of people living in hunger (averaging less than the minimum daily caloric intake) continued to rise. In the Third World—excluding China—the hungry population increased by more than 11%, from 536 to 597 million. While hunger declined somewhat relative to total Third World population, the Green Revolution was certainly not the solution for world hunger that its proponents made it out to be.

Not only did the Green Revolution fail to remedy unequal access to food and food-producing resources, it actually contributed to inequality. The costs of improved seeds and fertilizers hit cash-poor small farmers the hardest. Unable to afford the new technology, many farmers lost their land. Over time, the industrialization of agriculture contributed to the replacement of farms with corporations, farmers with machines, mixed crops with monocultures, and local food security with global commerce.

INDUSTRIAL AGRICULTURE II: THE NEW BIOREVOLUTION

The same companies that promoted chemical-based agriculture are now bringing the world genetically engineered food and agriculture. Some of the leading pesticide companies of yesterday have become what today are euphemistically called "life sciences companies"—Aventis, Novartis, Syngenta, Monsanto, Dupont, and others. Through genetic engineering, these companies are now converting seeds into product-delivery systems. The crops produced by Monsanto's Roundup-Ready brand seeds, for example, tolerate only the company's Roundup brand herbicide.

The "life sciences" companies claim that they can solve the environmental problems of agriculture. For example, they promise to create a world free of pesticides by equipping each crop with its own "insecticidal genes." Many distinguished agriculture scientists, corporate bigwigs, and economists are jumping on the "biotechnology" bandwagon. They argue that, in a world where more than 830 million people go to bed hungry, biotechnology provides the only hope of feeding our burgeoning population, especially in the Third World.

In fact, since genetic engineering is based on the same old principles of industrial agriculture—monoculture, technology, and corporate control—it is likely to exacerbate the problems of ecological and social devastation:

- As long as chemical companies dominate the "life sciences" industry, the biotechnology they develop will only reinforce intensive chemical use. Corporations are currently developing plants whose genetic traits can be turned "on" or "off" by applying an external chemical, as well as crops that die if the correct chemical—made by the same company—is not applied.
- The biotechnology industry is releasing hundreds of thousands of genetically engineered organisms into the environment every year. These organisms can reproduce, cross-pollinate, mutate, and migrate. Each release of a genetically engineered organism is a round of ecological Russian roulette. Recently, Aventis' genetically engineered StarLink corn, a variety approved by the U.S. Department of Agriculture only for livestock consumption, entered the food supply by mixing in grain elevators and cross-pollination in the field.
- With the advent of genetic engineering, corporations are using new "intellectual property" rights to stake far-reaching claims of ownership over a vast array of biological resources. By controlling the ownership of seeds, the corporate giants force farmers to pay yearly for seeds they once saved from each harvest to the next planting. By making seed exchanges between farmers illegal, they also limit farmers' capacity to contribute to agricultural biodiversity.

THE FALSE PROMISE OF "GOLDEN RICE"

The biotech industry is taking great pains to advertise the humanitarian applications of genetic engineering. "[M]illions of people—many of them children—have lost their sight to vitamin A deficiency," says the Council for Biotechnology Information, an industry-funded public relations group. "But suppose rice consumers could obtain enough vitamin A and iron simply by eating dietary staples that are locally grown? ... Biotechnology is already producing some of these innovations." More than $10 million was spent over ten years to engineer vitamin A rice—hailed as the "Golden Rice"—at the Institute of Plant Sciences of the Swiss Federal Institute of Technology in Zurich. It will take millions more and another decade of research and development to produce vitamin A rice varieties that can actually be grown in farmers' fields.

In reality, the selling of vitamin A rice as a miracle cure for blindness depends on blindness to lower-cost and safer alternatives. Meat, liver, chicken, eggs, milk, butter, carrots, pumpkins, mangoes, spinach and other leafy green vegetables, and many other foods contain vitamin A. Women farmers in Bengal, an eastern Indian state, plant more than 100 varieties of green leafy vegetables. The promotion of monoculture and rising herbicide use, however, are destroying such sources of vitamin A. For example, bathua, a very popular leafy vegetable in northern India, has been pushed to extinction in areas of intensive herbicide use.

The long-run solutions to vitamin A deficiency—and other nutritional problems—are increased biodiversity in agriculture and increased food security for
poor people. In the meantime, there are better, safer, and more economical short-
run measures than genetically engineered foods. UNICEF, for example, gives high-
dose vitamin A capsules to poor children twice a year. The cost? Just two cents per
pill. (You can support the UNICEF Vitamin A project by calling 1-800-FOR-KIDS
or visiting <www. unicefusa.org>.)

INTELLECTUAL PROPERTY RIGHTS AND GENETIC ENGINEERING

In 1998, Monsanto surprised Saskatchewan farmer Percy Schmeiser by suing him
for doing what he has always done and, indeed, what farmers have done for millennia—save seeds for the next planting. Schmeiser is one of hundreds of Canadian
and U.S. farmers the company has sued for re-using genetically engineered seeds.
Monsanto has patented those seeds, and forbids farmers from saving them.

In recent years, Monsanto has spent over $8.5 billion acquiring seed and bio-
tech companies, and DuPont spent over $9.4 billion to acquire Pioneer Hi-Bred,
the world's largest seed company. Seed is the most important link in the food
chain. Over 1.4 billion people—primarily poor farmers—depend on farm-saved
seed for their livelihoods. While the "gene police" have not yet gone after farmers
in the Third World, it is probably only a matter of time.

If corporations like Monsanto have their way, genetic technology—like the
so-called "terminator" seeds—will soon render the "gene police" redundant. Far
from being designed to increase agricultural production, "terminator" technology
is meant to prevent unauthorized production—and increase seed-industry profits. Fortunately, worldwide protests, like the "Monsanto Quit India" campaign,
forced the company to put this technology on hold. Unfortunately, Monsanto
did not pledge to abandon "terminator" seeds permanently, and other companies
continue to develop similar systems.

FUTURE POSSIBLE

From the United States to India, small-scale ecological agriculture is proving itself
a viable alternative to chemical-intensive and bioengineered agriculture. In the
United States, the National Research Council found that "alternative farmers
often produce high per acre yields with significant reductions in costs per unit of
crop harvested," despite the fact that "many federal policies discourage adoption
of alternative practices." The Council concluded that "federal commodity programs must be restructured to help farmers realize the full benefits of the productivity gains possible through alternative practices."

Another study, published in the *American Journal of Alternative Agriculture*,
found that ecological farms in India were just as productive and profitable as
chemical ones. The author concluded that, if adopted on a national scale, ecologi-

cal farming would have "no negative impact on food security," and would reduce soil erosion and the depletion of soil fertility while greatly lessening dependence on external inputs.

The country where alternative agriculture has been put to its greatest test, however, is Cuba. Before 1989, Cuba had a model Green Revolution-style agricultural economy (an approach the Soviet Union had promoted as much as the United States). Cuban agriculture featured enormous production units, using vast quantities of imported chemicals and machinery to produce export crops, while the country imported over half its food.

Although the Cuban government's commitment to equity and favorable terms of trade offered by Eastern Europe protected Cubans from undernourishment, the collapse of the East bloc in 1989 exposed the vulnerability of this approach. Cuba plunged into its worst food crisis since the revolution. Consumption of calories and protein dropped by perhaps as much as 30%. Nevertheless, today Cubans are eating almost as well as they did before 1989, with much lower imports of food and agrochemicals. What happened?

Cut off from imports of food and agrochemicals, Cuba turned inward to create a more self-reliant agriculture based on higher crop prices to farmers, smaller production units, urban agriculture, and ecological principles. As a result of the trade embargo, food shortages, and the opening of farmers' markets, farmers began to receive much better prices for their products. Given this incentive to produce, they did so, even without Green Revolution-style inputs. The farmers received a huge boost from the reorientation of government education, research, and assistance toward alternative methods, as well as the rediscovery of traditional farming techniques.

While small farmers and cooperatives increased production, large-scale state farms stagnated. In response, the Cuban government parceled out the state farms to their former employees as smaller-scale production units. Finally, the government mobilized support for a growing urban agriculture movement—small-scale organic farming on vacant lots—which, together with the other changes, transformed Cuban cities and urban diets in just a few years.

WILL BIOTECHNOLOGY FEED THE WORLD?

The biotech industry pretends concern for hungry people in the Third World, holding up greater food production through genetic engineering as the solution to world hunger. If the Green Revolution has taught us one thing, however, it is that increased food production can—and often does—go hand in hand with more hunger, not less. Hunger in the modern world is not caused by a shortage of food, and cannot be eliminated by producing more. Enough food is already available to provide at least 4.3 pounds of food per person a day worldwide. The root of the hunger problem is not inadequate production but unequal access and distribution. This is why the second Green Revolution promised by the "life sciences" companies is no more likely to end hunger than the first.

The United States is the world's largest producer of surplus food. According to the U.S. Department of Agriculture, however, some 36 million of the country's people (including 14 million children) do not have adequate access to food. That's an increase of six million hungry people since the 1996 welfare reform, with its massive cuts in food stamp programs.

Even the world's "hungry countries" have enough food for all their people right now. In fact, about three quarters of the world's malnourished children live in countries with net food surpluses, much of which are being exported. India, for example, ranks among the top Third World agricultural exporters, and yet more than a third of the world's 830 million hungry people live there. Year after year, Indian governments have managed a sizeable food surplus by depriving the poor of their basic human right to food.

The poorest of the poor in the Third World are landless peasants, many of whom became landless because of policies that favor large, wealthy farmers. The high costs of genetically engineered seeds, "technology-use payments," and other inputs that small farmers will have to use under the new biotech agriculture will tighten the squeeze on already poor farmers, deepening rural poverty. If agriculture can play any role in alleviating hunger, it will only be to the extent that we reverse the existing bias toward wealthier and larger farmers, embrace land reform and sustainable agriculture, reduce inequality, and make small farmers the center of an economically vibrant rural economy.

ARTICLE 34

Environmental Justice in South Africa

Water Sanitation, Privatization, and the Legacy of Apartheid

BY HEIDI VOGT

March/April 2003

There's a new hero fighting on edge of illegality to get clean drinking water to Johannesburg's poor. The "struggle plumber" knows how to uninstall the blocks that prevent free water from flowing from central pipes into peoples' homes. Yes, that's against the law. But poor communities depend on the struggle plumbers to help them survive as water prices rise in South Africa.

The residents of the country's poor neighborhoods are fighting for access in the face of multinational corporations' increasing control of the water supply. The government's answer has been to send armed security guards to shut off the water. "Out of desperation people are reconnecting their water. The council can call them thieves but obviously people have become so desperate that they can't do without water," said Orlean Naidoo, who lives in the poor neighborhood of Bayview in Chatsworth.

The people who are struggling for water access find justification in the South African constitution, one of the most progressive in the world on basic economic rights. The constitution promises clean water to all its citizens as a right, not a privilege. "Everyone has the right to have access to sufficient food and water," reads the six-year-old document. Still, change is slow, infrastructure is spotty, and millions of South Africans are still waiting for this promise to translate into drinkable water.

PERILS OF PRIVATIZATION

The ongoing privatization of utilities in South Africa stands in the way. In 2000, the French company Suez Lyonnaise Des Eaux signed one of the largest water contracts in the world, taking over a large section of South Africa's water utilities. Others have followed: Multinationals Biwater, Vivendi, and Saur all now own a chunk of South Africa's water supply.

When private companies take over utility contracts, prices go up, water quality goes down, and the poor lose out. South Africans have seen the price increases firsthand. In 1995, Biwater signed a contract to supply the city of Nelspruit with water. Over the next five years, rates increased more than 400%.

But these costs have not deterred the advocates of "free market" water. In December 2002, the U.S. Agency for International Development (USAID) sponsored a report suggesting that the privatization of water utilities in South Africa could help bring the price of water under control. The report, written for USAID by the Washington consulting firm Padco, admits that "there have been failures" of water privatization, but claims that critics "ignore ... unforeseen changes" responsible for price increases. A copy of the report, originally commissioned for the South African government, found its way into the hands of private water companies interested in investing in South Africa. So the funding that was supposed to help bring clean water to South Africans has created a tool for multinationals to justify privatization—with the approval of the United States government.

The World Bank, unsurprisingly, is also on the water-privatization bandwagon. The Bank-approved "cost recovery" program in South Africa proceeds from the principle that water should be made available to people only if the company providing it can recover its costs plus a profit. Taxes are not to subsidize utility prices and those who can't pay are not to get services. Since the South Africam government introduced cost recovery as part of the Growth Employment and Redistribution (GEAR) program in 1996, more than 10 million people have had their water cut off. GEAR didn't meet mass opposition in South Africa when it was first introduced. But as the program began to take effect, jobs and services started disappearing, and protests started to become the norm for every new move towards privatization.

The poor (mostly black) majority has paid the price for South Africa's new economic model. By 2000, piped water had become too expensive for many residents of KwaZulu Natal—where unemployment hovers around 40%. When water was cut off, citizens resorted to drinking untreated water from rivers, ponds, and puddles. By the end of 2001, more than 100,000 residents had been infected with cholera, a disease virtually unseen in South Africa for decades. After the cholera outbreaks, the government decided to give 6,000 free liters of water a month to people who couldn't afford water. However, the people wouldn't get the free water until they had paid outstanding debts for water—which they didn't have the money for. "When water's a private commodity at a market rate, it's not rich white people in the suburbs that are going to suffer," says Sara Grusky of the California-based activist group Public Citizen, which is currently working with a number of community groups in South Africa on water issues.

Since the end of apartheid in 1994, pipes that used to supply the poorer neighborhoods of Johannesburg with free, clean water have been slowly replaced with pre-paid pumps. The pumps, which private multinationals are putting in place, are among the government's most controversial moves. In this system, each water pump has a counter that deducts units from a pre-paid card. This system eliminates the difficulty of issuing and collecting bills. It also means days without clean water for cash-strapped families. Since 1998, pre-paid water meters have been outlawed in Britain as a threat to public health. But pre-paid meters have not disappeared in South Africa. Suez Lyonnaise Des Eaux is currently beginning a pre-paid meter trial in Orange Free State.

So the struggle plumbers have gone to work. They've dismantled pre-pay meters and hacked into company pipes in the name of the right to water. A copper disk placed inside the pipes prevents water from flowing to those who haven't paid. The struggle plumbers open up the pipes and remove that disk.

The people of South Africa are also fighting back politically. Since 1999, the Congress of South African Trade Unions (COSATU) has held two-day general strikes to protest the privatization of utilities. In October 2002, COSATU led a demonstration of 70,000 in Johannesburg to protest job cuts and the commercialization of services. "COSATU remains opposed to the government selling off state companies which provide essential services to the community," spokesperson Patrick Craven told Afrol News. "We will continue to demand that the government ... maintain these organizations in the public sector and make them deliver affordable and accessible services, especially to the poor."

ARTICLE 35

Is the United States a Pollution Haven?

BY FRANK ACKERMAN

March/April 2003

Free trade, according to its critics, runs the risk of creating pollution havens—countries where lax environmental standards allow dirty industries to expand. Poor countries are the usual suspects; perhaps poverty drives them to desperate strategies, such as specializing in the most polluting industries.

But could the United States be a pollution haven? A look at agriculture under NAFTA, particularly the trade in corn, suggests that at least one polluting industry is thriving in the United States as a result of free trade.

In narrow economic terms, the United States is winning the corn market. U.S. corn exports to Mexico have doubled since 1994, NAFTA's first year, to more than five million tons annually. Cheap U.S. corn is undermining traditional production in Mexico; prices there have dropped 27% in just a few years, and a quarter of the corn consumed in Mexico is now grown in the United States. But in environmental terms, the U.S. victory comes at a great cost.

While the United States may not have more lax environmental *standards* than Mexico, when it comes to corn U.S. agriculture certainly uses more polluting *methods*. As it is grown in the United States, corn requires significantly more chemicals per acre than wheat or soybeans, the other two leading field crops. Runoff of excess nitrogen fertilizer causes water pollution, and has created a huge "dead zone" in the Gulf of Mexico around the mouth of the Mississippi River. Intensive application of toxic herbicides and insecticides threatens the health of farm workers, farming communities, and consumers. Genetically modified corn, which now accounts for about one-fifth of U.S. production, poses unknown long-term risks to consumers and to ecosystems.

Growing corn in very dry areas, where irrigation is required, causes more environmental problems. The United States also has a higher percentage of irrigated acreage than Mexico. While the traditional Corn Belt enjoys ample rainfall and does not need irrigation, 15% of U.S. corn acreage—almost all of it in Nebraska, Kansas, the Texas panhandle, and eastern Colorado—is now irrigated. These areas draw water from the Ogallala aquifer, a gigantic underground reservoir, much faster than the aquifer naturally refills. If present rates of overuse continue, the Ogallala, which now contains as much fresh water as Lake Huron, will be drained down to unusable levels within a few decades, causing a crisis for the huge areas of the plains states that depend on it for water supplies. Government subsidies, in years past, helped farmers buy the equipment needed to pump water out of the Ogallala, contributing to the impending crisis.

Moreover, the corn borer, a leading insect pest that likes to eat corn plants, flourishes best in dry climates. Thus the "irrigation states," particularly Texas and Colorado, are the hardest hit by corn borers. Corn growers in dry states have the greatest need for insecticides; they also have the greatest motivation to use genetically modified corn, which is designed to repel corn borers.

Sales to Mexico are particularly important to the United States because many countries are refusing to accept genetically modified corn. Europe no longer imports U.S. corn for this reason, and Japan and several East Asian countries may follow suit. Mexico prohibits growing genetically modified corn, but still allows it to be imported; it is one of the largest remaining markets where U.S. exports are not challenged on this issue.

Despite Mexico's ban, genetically modified corn was recently found growing in a remote rural area in the southern state of Oaxaca. As the ancestral home of corn, Mexico possesses a unique and irreplaceable genetic diversity. Although the extent of the problem is still uncertain, the unplanned and uncontrolled spread of artificially engineered plants from the United States could potentially contaminate Mexico's numerous naturally occurring corn varieties.

An even greater threat is the economic impact of cheap U.S. imports on peasant farmers and rural communities. Traditional farming practices, evolved over thousands of years, use combinations of different natural varieties of corn carefully matched to local conditions. Lose these traditions, and we will lose a living reservoir of biodiversity in the country of origin of one of the world's most important food grains.

The United States has won the North American corn market. But the cost looks increasingly unbearable when viewed through the lens of the U.S. environment, or of Mexico's biodiversity.

ARTICLE 36

Who's to Blame for Climate Change?

BY BEN BOOTHBY

March/April 2003

It's now an indisputable fact that the global climate is changing. Scientists have warned for decades that "greenhouse gases," mainly carbon dioxide (CO_2), were building up in the atmosphere and trapping the sun's heat. Over the course of the 20th century, as fossil-fuel pollution expanded, the amount of CO_2 in the atmosphere rose by about 30%, increasing temperatures and causing extreme weather patterns worldwide. The greenhouse danger is now so undeniable that even George W. Bush's "blue ribbon" scientific panel on climate change admitted that global temperatures are on the rise.

If we hope to combat global warming, we need to drastically reduce the levels of CO_2 released into the atmosphere. Scientists consider even the targets set by the Kyoto Protocol (the international agreement to limit greenhouse gas emissions) inadequate compared to the urgency of the problem. But the Bush administration reneged on the United States' commitment even to these minimal standards, on the pretext that the agreement "exempts 80 percent of the world including major population centers, such as China and India."

Bush's scapegoats, however, are hardly responsible for the climate-change crisis. China accounted for just 7% of the world's CO_2 emissions over the course of the 20th century; India, for only 2%. The United States, in contrast, accounted for more than 30% of the total. (See Graph 1.) Moreover, emissions levels in the United States continue to surge, rising every year between 1991 and 2000, the latest year for which data is available. According to the Department of Energy, the country's fossil-fuel-related CO_2 emissions increased by more than 2.7 percent between 1999 and 2000. In contrast, China reduced its emissions by almost 2.2% in 2000, its third straight year of reductions.

The United States' ruling elite has never been as big about taking responsibility for its actions (e.g., slavery, support for dictatorships, etc.), as it has been about posturing as a world leader. So it comes as no surprise that the United States remains number one in CO_2 emissions (in both total and per capita terms) year after year. (See Graph 2.) If any country is in a position—technologically and economically—to "lead by example" towards a sustainable future, it is the United States. Yet the U.S. government has steadfastly refused to adopt common-sense measures like raising fuel efficiency standards, reducing automobile use, lessening dependence on coal and petroleum, or promoting alternative-energy technologies.

Instead, less-developed countries with far fewer resources than the United States are leading in the reduction of greenhouse-gas emissions. "China's actions are nothing short of remarkable," notes a 2001 report by the World Resources Institute. "The world's most populous country reduced its emissions ... by 19 percent from 1997 to 1999. This is simply unprecedented, especially considering that China's economy grew rapidly over the same period." Now that India, too, has ratified the Kyoto Protocol, it seems that Bush will just have to find himself some new scapegoats.

GRAPH 1

PERCENTAGE OF WORLD CARBON EMISSIONS, 1900–1999

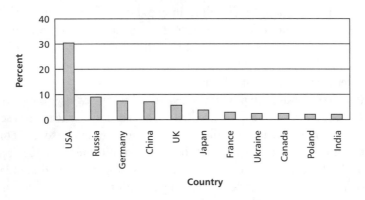

GRAPH 2

PER CAPITA CARBON EMISSIONS, 1999

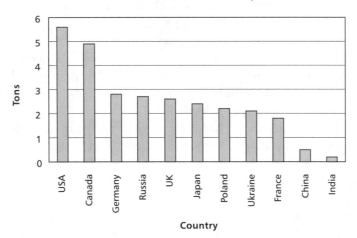

Source: World Resources Institute, "The U.S., Developing Countries, and Climate Protection: Leadership or Stalemate?" June 2001 <www.wri.org/wri/>.

CHAPTER 8

Political Economy of War and Imperialism

ARTICLE 37

Return of the Iron Triangle

The New Military Buildup

BY JAMES M. CYPHER

January/February 2002

The U.S. government's Commission on National Security/21st Century, convened in October 1998, was a who's who of industry, government, and military—that is, of the country's power elite. Former Senators Gary Hart and Warren Rudman chaired the Commission. Its commissioners included Martin Marietta CEO Norm Augustine and former House Speaker Newt Gingrich. Its 29 "study group members" came from top universities like MIT and Princeton, and think tanks including the RAND Corporation, the Cato Institute, and the Brookings Institution. The Commission also enjoyed the cooperation of the Departments of Defense and State, as well as top intelligence agencies like the CIA and the National Security Agency (NSA). In 1998, the Commission began a major review of U.S. military strategy. Its aim? To redesign the institutional structure of the military for the post-Cold War era.

The Commission's 1999 report *New World Coming: American Security in the 21st Century*, outlined a strategy for the United States to "remain the principal military power in the world." In the coming century, the report argued, the United States will become increasingly vulnerable to direct "nontraditional" attacks—against its information-technology infrastructure, for example. It will have to intervene abroad more frequently to deal with state fragmentation or to ensure an "uninterrupted" supply of oil from the Persian Gulf region or elsewhere. And it will face rivals in its drive to dominate space. The report concluded that to ensure continued U.S. dominance, U.S. military spending will have to rise dramatically.

BIG AND HEAVY, FAST AND LIGHT

The Clinton administration, which had overseen a dramatic decline in military spending over the course of the 1990s, basically ignored the Commission's conclusions. It now looks, however, like U.S. military doctrine will follow many of the recommendations in *New World Coming*.

The Department of Defense's latest big picture document, the October 2001 *Quadrennial Defense Review*, aims both to "restore the defense of the U.S. as the department's primary mission" and to build forces capable of moving rapidly overseas. Not to be outdone, the Army has produced two major documents outlining plans to retain the military's heavy aircraft and tank forces while developing lighter, faster units that it can deploy virtually anywhere in the world within 96 hours.

The post-September 11 era of military spending will allow the Pentagon to have its cake and eat it too—continuing major Cold War-era weapons systems and funding the cyber-age "Revolution in Military Affairs" (RMA). The RMA emphasizes high-tech warfare—communications networks, satellites, robot observation planes, smart bombs, night-vision instruments, highly mobile "light" armor, and global positioning system (GPS)-equipped soldiers—over old-fashioned heavy-weapons systems. Many Pentagon officials and major weapons contractors feared the RMA because it could disrupt the method of military contracting going back to the beginning of the Cold War—building a huge arsenal of ships, planes, tanks, and missiles to confront the Soviet "threat." Military officials had built their careers on that approach, and weapons contractors had made many fortunes from the resulting arms contracts. They feared that the RMA would marginalize them. The novelty of the Army's approach is to spend enough money to keep everyone happy, funding the "old military" and the "new military" alike.

BALANCING THE IRON TRIANGLE

The "Iron Triangle" forms the U.S. military establishment's decision-making structure and includes its major interest groups. One side of the triangle includes the "civilian" agencies that shape U.S. military policy—the Office of the President, the National Security Council, the Senate and House Armed Services Committees, and civilian intelligence agencies like the CIA and NSA. A second side includes the military institutions—the Joint Chiefs of Staff, the top brass of the Air Force, Army, Marines, and Navy, the powerful "proconsul" regional commands (known as "CINCs"), and, in a supporting role, veterans' organizations like the American Legion and the Veterans of Foreign Wars. At the *base* of the triangle are the 85,000 private firms that profit from the military contracting system, and that

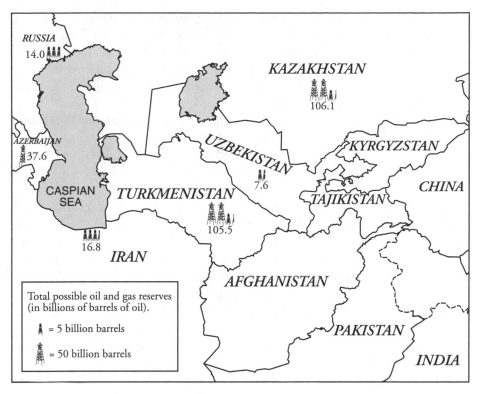

Source: U.S. Department of Energy, Energy Information Administration, "Caspian Sea Region," June 2000. Russia figure for area bordering Caspian Sea only.

use their sway over millions of defense workers to push for ever-higher military budgets.

Everyone in the Iron Triangle knew that the Bush Administration would increase military spending. The question was whether the increase would be vast enough to fund the old weapons systems, the "Star Wars" National Missile Defense scheme, and the RMA. And if not, who would pay the price? On February 13, 2001, President Bush announced that the United States would be moving beyond the Cold War model and into the RMA. In March 2001, he submitted a 2002 budget that upped military spending by only $14 billion over Clinton's 2001 budget. Many powerful members of the Iron Triangle, who had staked their careers on the old system, could now foresee their marginalization.

They were not about to go without a fight. Between March and August 2001, they struggled to save outmoded weapons systems like the F-22, the most expensive fighter plane in history, and the plan to build the unreliable V-22 Osprey aircraft, a project that then-Secretary of Defense Dick Cheney nearly killed eleven years before. It was, according to *The New York Times*, a battle "as intense and intemperate as any in recent memory" within the Iron Triangle.

Even before September 11, Secretary of Defense Donald Rumsfeld advocated a revised military budget with a total spending increase of $52 billion. He still favored, however, reconfiguring the military along RMA lines, reducing military units, cutting bases, and retiring unneeded weapons systems. Even while he proposed the larger spending increase, Rumsfeld's opponents in the Pentagon succeeded in portraying him as weak, unfocused, and "spiraling down." Legislators fought him on base closures, contractors resisted any reduction in lucrative weapons contracts, the Armed Services fought him on manpower reductions, and Democrats resisted the National Missile Defense program—which Rumsfeld had spearheaded. Post-September 11 emergency spending allocated an additional $25.5 billion to military objectives. In all, military spending will rise by at least $58.6 billion over 2001 levels, a 19% increase—just exceeding Rumsfeld's goal. ("Special Appropriations" will probably push the basic military budget even higher during the current fiscal year.) Now, Rumsfeld will be able to make a down payment on the RMA, while the vested interests will see plenty of funds for the old-style "legacy system" military.

Fighter-plane programs will get an incredible $400 billion in new multi-year contracts. Lockheed Martin will get $225 billion over 12 years to build nearly 3,000 Joint Strike Fighter planes for the Air Force, Marines, and Navy. According to *Business Week,* Lockheed also stands to make $175 billion in sales to foreign buyers over the next 25 years. Drowning in its record trade deficit, the United States desperately needs the boost to the trade balance provided by arms exports. The Joint Strike Fighter, if it brings in the expected $175 billion in export sales, may go down in history as the largest single boost to the balance of payments ever. Currently the United States controls 50% of the global arms market, with foreign military sales running at $16.5 billion in 1999. That figure will be on the rise as new weapons are delivered to Pakistan, Uzbekistan, Tajikistan, Oman, the United Arab Emirates, and Egypt.

Looking ahead, the RMA's fantastic weaponry—and its enormous costs—are only just beginning to emerge. Northrup Grumman, General Atomics, and Boeing are speeding robot airplanes into production. Other contractors are developing thermal imaging sensors to "see" targets through night, distance, fog, and even rock formations. The Navy is promoting a new destroyer-class warship, the DD-21, loaded with cruise missiles and guns capable of hitting targets 100 miles inland. Known as the "stealth bomber for the ocean," the DD-21 is estimated to cost $24 billion. Cost overruns of 300% are common, however, so there's no telling what taxpayers will ultimately pay.

THE ECONOMIC IMPACT

Bush justified his mammoth June 2001 tax cut partially as a measure to reverse the economic downturn that began the previous March. In October 2001, he proposed further tax cuts as an "economic stimulus" package. The two tax cuts combined, however, will likely provide less of a short-term boost than the nearly $60 billion increase in military spending. Most of the June tax cut will go to people with high incomes, who tend to spend a smaller proportion of the additional income they receive from a tax cut. And a large portion of what they do spend, they tend to spend on imported luxury goods, rather than domestic goods.

Most of the proposed "stimulus" program suffers from the same problems, plus a few more. The new proposal also includes a clause allowing businesses a bigger write-off for equipment as it decreases in value. But a corporation can take the write-off while spending on capital depreciation that they would have done anyway. The same is true of the elimination of the corporate "alternative minimum tax," which had set a tax "floor" for corporations no matter how many deductions they could claim. Corporations will use these windfalls to pay off debt or to invest outside of the United States.

Compare this to the $60 billion in new military outlays. Most of this money will go to civilian suppliers who will use it to pay for domestic labor, materials, and equipment. Only a modest portion, 5-10%, will leak out of the United States to military base operations. (Even that may not be as large a "leak" as it might seem, since base employees stationed overseas often buy U.S. exports.) Moreover, because of the new emphasis on the RMA, the military will be buying more newly designed weapons than it has in a long time, and this will have a strong impact on the economy (see box).

But will this counter the current recession? University of Texas economist James K. Galbraith has argued that the United States will need $600 billion in new spending in 2002 to pull out of the recession. However, only about $214 billion will come from increases in emergency and military spending plus the two tax cuts. Reduced interest rates will also stimulate new spending, but probably not on the scale required. If Galbraith is correct, even the massive outlays for the military will fall far short of the sum needed to turn the U.S. economy around.

What about its long-term effects? Some claim that increased military spending will drain U.S. productivity and slow long-term growth. But much of the United States' growth during the post-WWII period was stimulated by military spending. As *Business Week* noted in October 2001:

> Defense spending on research and development has sparked much innovation. Microchips, radar, lasers, satellite communications, cell phones, GPS, and the Internet all came out of Defense Dept. funding for basic research at the Massachusetts Institute of Technology, Stanford University and national laboratories. There were breakthroughs at IBM and Bell Laboratories, and all were commercialized by Intel Corp., Motorola Inc., and other corporations.

The same is true of artificial intelligence, supercomputers, high-speed fiber optics, and many other breakthroughs. The bulk of information technologies, in fact, were developed through massive R&D investments in military technology.

MILITARY PURCHASES AND LINKED INVESTMENT EFFECTS

To deliver the brand-new weapons the Pentagon wants, military contractors will have to either create or drastically alter their production systems. This means that in addition to the nearly $60 billion worth of goods and services bought, military contractors will have to invest in new capital goods needed for new production lines. Through these "linked investment" effects, the $60 billion could end up translating into nearly $132 in total spending (public and private).

How?

$24 billion (40% of the $60 billion) will likely be spent on research, development, testing, and production of new systems. But contractors will need new production lines to build these new systems. Economists estimate that the companies will have to invest three dollars in capital for each dollar of new output. So contractors will have to invest $72 billion (3 x $24 billion) in new structures, machines, and equipment. This means that current military orders could put into motion $96 billion ($24 billion + $72 billion) in new spending, plus the remaining 60% of the original $60 billion ($36 billion). The total impact, then, would be an economic stimulus of $132 billion ($96 billion + $36 billion).

This estimate is probably too high, because contractors will use some old capital to produce the new weapons and because some of the new military spending will be spent on imports. Still, much of the new spending will go to new technologies. The information technology sector will probably gain the most, since the RMA and the next "generation" of weapons will be loaded with far more information technology than hardware. Already in 2000, according to *Business Week*, electronics and communications components accounted for 40% of weapons purchases. So the jump in military spending will function as an industrial policy for the information technology and communications industries, boosting these hard-hit sectors of the U.S. economy.

The argument that military spending undercuts productivity must be seen in a broader context: Conservative economists have long argued that government spending does not increase investment because it causes an offsetting reduction in private investment—known as "crowding out." Some liberal economists have appropriated this argument to oppose military spending as a drain on the economy. That argument underestimates the structural importance of military spending and the arms industry to capitalism. The new military buildup is not likely to "crowd out" private investment, but to stimulate investment and technical innovation. The military buildup will definitely "crowd out," however, spending on public needs, such as a viable rapid rail system, public education, and a national health care system—all of which could greatly enhance productivity. More military spending will focus inordinately on information technology and other high-tech systems. More artificial intelligence technologies, global positioning systems, robot planes, and thermal imaging sensors, however, are not going to house, educate, or heal people who lack housing, education, or health care.

BIG VISIONS, BIG PLANS

The current military buildup is about much more than countering the slide in the high-tech sector, or countering the current economic recession. It is about consolidating the United States' position as the only superpower. Continued U.S. dominance requires continued control of the world's most important traded commodity—energy. The United States imports 52% of the oil, and a growing share of the natural gas, that it consumes. The profits of oil giants like Shell, Exxon/Mobil, and Chevron/Texaco come from their global control of oil and gas resources. Securing this control is one of the major functions of the U.S. military.

U.S. foreign policy will focus increasingly on securing global resources, longtime observer and critic of U.S. military affairs Michael Klare argues in his new book *Resource Wars*. (This stands in contrast to the Cold War era, when directly economic motives were less important to U.S. foreign policy than the superpower rivalry with the USSR.) The Pentagon and other centers of U.S. power clearly view Middle East energy resources as a "vital interest," warranting massive military outlays and the export of the top-level weapons to client regimes in the region. Between 1990 and 1997, the United States exported $42 billion in arms to the Persian Gulf states, of which $36 billion went to Saudi Arabia.

This focus on the oil-exporting regions will only rise under the Bush administration. Even though the Bushes never really established themselves in the oil industry, their tilt toward "big energy" is unmistakable. George W. Bush's number-one corporate donor was Houston's Enron Corporation, the ill-fated energy trader; Vice President Dick Cheney comes fresh from his job as CEO of Dallas' Halliburton Corporation, the world's largest oil-well service company; and Condoleezza Rice served as a director of the Chevron Corporation before becoming National Security Advisor.

"Oil runs the world and the Saudis are the linchpin of oil production," a unnamed senior administration official told the *New York Times* in October 2001. The United States has struggled in the past to reduce its reliance on Middle East oil supplies—pressuring Mexico and Venezuela to increase production, hoping for big increases from Colombia's rich oilfields, and so on. Since 1990, the United States has reduced OPEC oil from approximately 61% of its total oil imports to 52%—so only about 27% of the oil consumed in the United States now comes from OPEC (including Venezuela). But this is not the whole story: The United States has also assumed the role of military guarantor of oil stability for Europe and Japan. The growing instability of the Persian Gulf states, in spite of the huge sums that they and the United States have committed to military defense, portends even greater U.S. military involvement in the region for the foreseeable future.

Meanwhile, near the Gulf, two alternative sources of oil are becoming increasingly attractive—the Caspian Sea region and the rest of the former USSR. U.S. oil companies are now plunging into Russia. Halliburton has 300 specialists in Western Siberia struggling to revive the Samatlor oilfield, while Shell and Exxon/ Mobil are investing in a new field off Shakalin Island. Exxon has committed $5 billion to the effort over the next five years. Russia is now exporting about 3.3 million barrels a day, nearly half what Saudi Arabia exports. But if the oil giants invest in new pipelines, Russian exports could leap to 5.3 million barrels a day by 2004, according to *Business Week*. Much of this new oil, and huge quantities of natural gas—one third of the world's gas reserves are located in the former Soviet Union—would come from the Caspian Sea region of Central Asia, the biggest economic prize since the United States took effective control of Saudi oil in February 1945.

This makes Afghanistan, through which a major Caspian pipeline would likely run, a strategic linchpin of the global energy industry and the world economy. U.S., European, and Russian gas and oil firms have taken a major interest in the Caspian region's vast oil and gas reserves since the early 1990s. Major pipelines now carry these resources to Turkey, from which they can be shipped to Western Europe, the United States, and the rest of the world. Unocal, Pennzoil, British Petroleum, and Amoco were major participants in the Azerbaijan International Operating Company (AIOC), a large-scale project to build pipelines from the Caspian Basin to Turkey and the Black Sea. Unocal has also proposed a pipeline from Turkmenistan, Uzbekistan, and Kazakhstan through Afghanistan to India and Pakistan, and to the Pakistan coast for export to China—though the company now says it has shelved the project.

The U.S. military is now developing a long-term presence in Central Asia, which it will undoubtedly use to secure the rich supply of Caspian oil and gas. The Pentagon has been courting the government of Uzbekistan for years, giving its officers military training in the United States since 1995, and conducting military exercises in Uzbekistan since 1999. In November 2001, the U.S. military began negotiating with the government of Tajikistan to use former Soviet military bases there during the U.S. war in Afghanistan. Considering that a U.S. garrison has been permanently stationed in Saudi Arabia since the Gulf War, it seems unlikely that the U.S. military will leave either Uzbekistan or Tajikistan after the Afghanistan war.

The outcome of this high-stakes struggle remains to be seen. Russia and the Caspian region resemble the Persian Gulf region in their fragile social foundations. So shifting to the former for imported oil and gas will not eliminate the United States' reliance for energy on states with huge potential for instability. If an Afghanistan pipeline is ever built, however, it will help give U.S. and Russian oil interests leverage they have not had in decades over the Persian Gulf region, just by making the Gulf's oil supplies a much smaller part of global production. Moreover, with energy demand in developing Asia predicted to surpass that of North America by 2020, it will give the United States added leverage over these economies. The current U.S. power play in Central Asia, in short, dramatically increases the likelihood that the U.S. military will succeed in achieving the goals articulated by the Commission on National Security/21st Century— securing control of the global energy supply, and maintaining the United States' position as the world's only superpower.

RESOURCES U.S. Commission on National Security/21st Century, *New World Coming: American Security in the 21st Century*, 1999 <www.nssg.gov>. Michael Klare, *Resource Wars*, Metropolitan Books, 2001. James Galbraith, "The War Economy," Levy Economic Institute, 2001 <www.levy.org>.

ARTICLE 38

Ruling the Empire

BY ALEJANDRO REUSS

March/April 2003

Every few years, the President issues a document called the "National Security Strategy of the United States." Always eagerly awaited, the document is often described as the administration's "blueprint" for U.S. foreign policy. But it's really more like a press release, designed to give the U.S. government's global aims a noble-sounding spin.

The Bush administration's new "National Security Strategy," issued September 2002, abounds with pious lip service: On the subject of democracy, it applauds the "elected leaders replac[ing] generals in Latin America" without mentioning who put the generals in power in the first place. On the environment, it calls for "global efforts to stabilize greenhouse gas concentrations" without mentioning that the U.S. government had scuttled the Kyoto Protocol. On the global economy, it decries as "neither just nor stable" a state of affairs "where some live in comfort and plenty, while half of the human race lives on less than $2 a day," yet it offers no solution other than more "free markets and free trade."

The document's crowning hypocrisy, however, is its repeated use of the buzz-phrase "a balance of power that favors freedom," as if that were what the U.S. government was really after. You get the distinct feeling that the drafters don't believe in it for a minute. By its final and most important section, on the country's "National Security Institutions," the document abandons all pretext. The "unparalleled strength of the United States armed forces, and their forward presence, have maintained the peace," it declares. The United States must "reaffirm the essential role of American military strength" and "build and maintain our defenses beyond challenge." It must maintain forces "strong enough to dissuade potential adversaries" from the dream of ever "surpassing, or equaling, the power of the United States."

Well, if those are the real aims of U.S. ruling elites, they're off to a good start. In 2001, U.S. military spending—the highest, by far, of any country in the world—exceeded the combined spending of the next eight countries—Russia, France, Japan, the United Kingdom, Germany, China, Saudi Arabia, and Italy (see Graph 1). In fact, U.S. military spending represented over one third of the total of the *entire world*. This grotesquely overgrown war machine comes at no little cost. In 2001, total federal military spending (including interest payments on past military spending and benefits for former military personnel) devoured about one third of the federal funds portion of the budget (not including trust fund items like Social Security), as much as spending on health, income security, education, nutrition, and housing *combined* (see Graph 2).

In light of these realities, the "balance of power" rhetoric isn't really fooling anybody. Writing in the mainstream *Christian Science Monitor*, Gail Russell

GRAPH 1
2001 MILITARY SPENDING

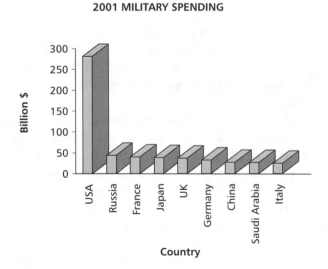

Source: Stockholm International Peace Research Institute, *SIPRI Yearbook 2002*.

GRAPH 2
2001 FEDERAL FUNDS BUDGET (EXCLUDES SOCIAL SECURITY)

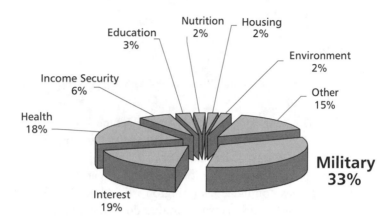

Source: National Priorities Project. Includes only the federal funds portion of the federal budget.
Military includes veterans' benefits and the military share of interest on the national debt.

Chaddock argues that the document "asserts American dominance as the lone superpower—a status no rival power will be allowed to challenge." It is a vision, she says, of a "Pax Americana" (the modern-day equivalent of Roman imperial power). Even the senior defense policy analyst at the right-wing Cato Institute, Charles V. Peña, writes that "although it's all dressed up with the rationale of extending liberty, democracy, and freedom around the globe (except, of course, in Saudi Arabia and Pakistan)" the document really envisions a "Pax Americana enforced by dominant military power and ... U.S. forces deployed around the globe."

None of this is exactly news. The United States, after all, has been a major imperial power in the Western Hemisphere for over a century. And it has been the single dominant capitalist power for more than half that period. The truth, however, should be clearer than ever. As the title of Peña's article puts it: "The New National Security Strategy Is American Empire."

ARTICLE 39

War on the Earth

BY BOB FELDMAN

March/April 2003

In this era of "permanent war," the U.S. war machine bombards civilians in places like Serbia, Afghanistan, and Iraq. It also makes "war on the earth," both at home and abroad. The U.S. Department of Defense is, in fact, the world's largest polluter, producing more hazardous waste per year than the five largest U.S. chemical companies combined. Washington's Fairchild Air Force Base, the number one *producer* of hazardous waste among domestic military bases, generated over 13 million pounds of waste in 1997 (more than the weight of the Eiffel Tower's iron structure). Oklahoma's Tinker Air Force Base, the top toxic waste *emitter*, released over 600,000 pounds in the same year (the same amount of water would cover an entire football field about two inches deep).

Just about every U.S. military base and nuclear arms facility emits toxics into the environment. At many U.S. military target ranges, petroleum products and heavy metals used in bombs and bullets contaminate the soil and groundwater. And since the Pentagon operates its bases as "federal reservations," they are usually beyond the reach of local and state environmental regulations. Local and state authorities often do not find out the extent of the toxic contamination until after a base is closed down.

Active and abandoned military bases have released toxic pollution from Cape Cod to San Diego, Alaska to Hawaii. In June 2001, the Military Toxics Project and the Environmental Health Coalition released the report "Defend Our Health: A People's Report to Congress," detailing the Pentagon's "war on the earth" in the United States and Puerto Rico. The contaminants emitted from military bases include pesticides, solvents, petroleum, lead, mercury, and uranium. The health effects for the surrounding communities are devastating: miscarriages, low birth weights, birth defects, kidney disease, and cancer.

Even the Defense Department itself now acknowledges some of the environmental destruction wrought by the U.S. military worldwide. The Pentagon's own Inspector General documented, in a 1999 report, pollution at U.S. bases in Canada, Germany, Great Britain, Greenland, Iceland, Italy, Panama, the Philippines, South Korea, Spain, and Turkey. Again, since even U.S. military bases abroad are treated as U.S. territory, the installations typically remain exempt from the environmental authority of the host country.

Activists worldwide have called attention to the scourge of toxic pollution, target-range bombardment, noise pollution, abandoned munitions, and radioactive waste unleashed by U.S. bases. The International Grassroots Summit on Military Bases Cleanup in 1999 brought together 70 representatives of citizen groups affected by U.S. military contamination. The gathering adopted an "Environmental Bill of Rights for Persons, Indigenous Peoples, Communities and Nations Hosting Foreign and Colonial Military Bases," declaring that past and present military bases "threaten health, welfare, and the environment, [as well as] future generations." The document emphasizes that the burden of environmental destruction has fallen disproportionately on "economically disadvantaged communities, women, children, people of color and indigenous people." And it demands that the "foreign and colonial" armed forces responsible for the contamination bear the costs the cleanup."

Yet until the era of "permanent war" and global U.S. militarism gives way to an era of world peace, the U.S. military machine will likely remain above the law. And the Pentagon will continue its "war on the earth."

MILITARY POLLUTION IN THE UNITED STATES

Alaska   U.S. military land fills, drum storage areas, fuel spill areas, and leaking underground storage tanks have polluted communities surrounding Cape Romanzof Long Range Radar station in Hooper Bay, Alaska. While fishing near Fort Greeley, Alaska, members of local indigenous tribes have found canisters of mustard gas left over from the 1950s and 1960s—when the U.S. military tested biological and chemical weapons at the site.

Lassen County, California   The Sierra Army Depot—where the military burns and detonates munitions—ranked as California's top source of air pollution in 1999, releasing 17% of all the toxic air emissions for the entire state. Increased cancer rates have been reported in both the surrounding county and the nearby Pyramid Lake Indian Reservation in Nevada.

San Diego, California   The largest polluter in San Diego is the U.S. Navy, which has created 100 toxic and radioactive waste sites in San Diego Bay over the last eighty years. The National Oceanic and Atmospheric Administration found that the bay had the country's second-most-toxic estuary sediments, with the pollution concentrated around Navy and Navy-contractor sites. Fish in San Diego Bay contain high levels of mercury and radioactive compounds. The Navy also spilled over 11,000 gallons of oil into the bay in 1998.

Makua Valley, Hawaii   In the Makua Valley, the U.S. Army's live-fire assault training has caused fires and erosion and introduced alien plants and animals. These activities have threatened over 40 endangered plant and animal species, including the elpano bird. Homes and churches have also been destroyed by the fires and erosion. In addition, heavy metals and other pollutants from the base have contaminated the soil and groundwater.

Cape Cod, Massachusetts Toxic pollution from the Massachusetts Military Reservation, former site of Otis Military Base, has contaminated drinking water in the nearby town of Falmouth. Over the years, the military "recycled" old ammunition and hazardous wastes at Otis by openly burning them. It also dumped 6 million gallons of aviation fuel directly on the ground. By 1986, Falmouth's cancer rate was 38% higher than the state average.

Concord, Massachusetts Starmet, a company that manufactured depleted uranium ammunition for the U.S. military, contaminated Concord's groundwater and soil with uranium. Local residents have contracted some cancers at rates up to twice those of other Massachusetts residents.

Colonie, New York A plant which manufactured 30mm depleted uranium rounds for the U.S. military contaminated a nearby residential community, where the soil was found to contain 500 times more uranium than normal.

Oklahoma City, Oklahoma The Agency for Toxic Substance and Disease Registry found the average birth weight in the Kimsey neighborhood near Tinker Air Force Base to be about two ounces lower than in other Oklahoma City neighborhoods. It attributed the low birth weights to Kimsey residents' greater exposure to chemicals released from the base.

Isla De Vieques, Puerto Rico After fifty years of U.S. Navy target practice, Isla de Vieques has more craters per square kilometer than the moon. The Navy's use of bombs, depleted uranium, and Agent Orange on Vieques has produced a cancer rate 26% higher than in the rest of Puerto Rico. Vieques's children also show high levels of mercury and lead. The Navy, which occupies 26,000 of the island's 33,000 acres, has also contaminated the soil, destroyed its coral reefs, and emitted toxic heavy metals into the marine environment.

Memphis, Tennessee The Pentagon's Defense Distribution Depot began operating as a chemical-weapons dump in the heart of Memphis' African-American community in 1942—and didn't warn residents of the danger. The depot contaminated the soil and groundwater. People who live nearby suffer a disproportionate number of miscarriages, birth defects, childhood cancers, and kidney ailments.

San Antonio, Texas Kelly Air Force Base ranked as the county's fifth-largest air polluter before its 2001 closing. Metals, solvents. and fuel from the base also contaminated the local groundwater. Over 70 former Kelly Air Force Base workers have developed Lou Gehrig's Disease in recent years. The U.S. Agency for Toxic Substance and Disease Registry found elevated levels of cancer, low birth weight, and birth defects in the San Antonio neighborhood closest to the base.

Washington State The U.S. Navy is the leading cause of oil spills off the Washington coast. The Navy spilled over 10,000 gallons of oil into Puget Sound in 1998. It also tests depleted uranium weapons in prime fishing waters nearby.

MILITARY POLLUTION WORLDWIDE

Afghanistan Following the Pentagon's 2001-2002 military campaign in Afghanistan, the Uranium Medical Research Center (UMRC) sent two scientific teams to Afghanistan to examine the effects of U.S. bombing on Kabul. Many residents, the UMRC teams found, had symptoms consistent with uranium exposure (joint pains, flu-like illnesses, bleeding mucous membranes, etc.). One fourth of the Kabul newborns examined had health problems consistent with uranium, including lethargy, skin rashes, and enlarged heads.

Canada The U.S. military built a network of radar sites in Northern Canada between 1953 and 1958. Cancer-causing agents were used in the construction and maintenance of the sites, which are now contaminated.

Colombia Large-scale herbicide spraying under the "Plan Colombia"—ostensibly for coca eradication—has caused "serious human health effects; large-scale destruction of food crops; and severe environmental impacts in sensitive tropical ecosystems," according to a 2002 report of the *Aerial Spraying Review*, an environmental publication. There is also evidence that the Pentagon-sponsored fumigation campaign has caused a "loss of agricultural resources, including fish kills and sickness and death of livestock." Border areas of Ecuador have also been contaminated.

Greenland In 1968, a B-52 carrying four nuclear bombs crashed near the Pentagon's Thule Air Force base in northern Greenland, causing severe plutonium contamination of the area.

Indochina Nearly thirty years after the end of the U.S. war in Southeast Asia, many of the affected ecosystems have still not recovered, according to the Environmental Conference on Cambodia, Laos and Vietnam (Stockholm, 2002). Ten percent of southern Vietnam's forests (including one-third of the coastal mangoes, which play a vital role in the coastal ecosystem and fish habitats) were destroyed by the 72 million liters of herbicide the U.S. military dropped during the Vietnam War era. Arsenic and dioxin in the herbicides are expected to pose a health threat long into the future. Since 1975, 50,000 civilians have been killed by the landmines and other weapons the U.S. military left behind. The U.S.'s vast bombing campaign also left millions of large bomb craters.

Iraq U.S. bombing of oil facilities in January 1991 caused spills of 6 to 8 million barrels of crude oil, killing about 30,000 marine birds. For nearly a year afterwards, oil well fires spewed toxic soot. The bombing also poisoned Iraqi water supplies. In addition, according to Iraq's Ministry of Health, depleted uranium from U.S. weapons has contaminated the soil and plants in southern Iraq, causing cancers and deformities associated with uranium exposure.

Okinawa U.S. military exercises with live artillery have caused forest fires, soil erosion, and earth tremors—leaving sections of Okinawa barren and shell-ridden. Toxins emitted by the U.S. military have infiltrated Okinawa's land, water and air, and have been linked to low birth weights and elevated rates of leukemia and other cancers. Noise pollution at Kadena Air Base may also be a cause of low birth weights.

Panama The U.S. military left firing ranges in the Panama Canal Zone littered with thousands of unexploded rounds. A July 1998 Pentagon report found that the U.S. Army Corps of Engineers dumped tons of soil from a project to widen the canal onto 92 acres in Panama's Empire Range, damaging the rainforest ecosystem. A 1997 study for the U.S. Army also discovered the carcinogen TCI in the ground water at Fort Koblhe—at twenty times the level acceptable under U.S. federal law.

Philippines The former site of Clark Air Base has contaminated the groundwater. The U.S. military also dumped hazardous waste in a municipal landfill in a residential area of Mabalacat. The power plant at the Subic Bay Naval Base emitted untreated pollutants directly into the air. Toxic waste from the destruction of excess bombs and ammunition were poured into local streams. In addition, most of the sewage generated at the Subic Bay base was discharged each day, untreated, directly into the bay.

Serbia After the U.S. military bombed a petrochemical complex in the suburbs of Belgrade in 1999, the destroyed plastics factory and ammonia production unit released toxins such as chlorine into the air.

South Korea Oil from the Yongsan 8th garrison's base has contaminated the soil and water. Asbestos has been found around the Camp Indian base. In May 1998, a ruptured pipeline at the Mt. Rackun military base polluted a large section of a South Korean forest conservancy area. U.S. military drills and maneuvers have also damaged farmlands and destroyed crops. Oil discharged by the U.S. Army has polluted the Sankogos River, contaminated farmland, and destroyed crops. Off the coast of South Korea, the U.S. military has used small islands as bombing ranges, creating noise pollution for nearby villages. The ammunition left behind has also injured residents.

RESOURCES Safety Forum Research/Safetyforum.com <www.safetyforum.com>; Military Toxics Project and Environmental Health Coalition, "Defend Our Health: A People's Report to Congress," (June 2001); Greenpeace <www.greenpeace.org>; East Asia/U.S. Women's Network Against Militarism <www.apcjp.org/womens_network/skorea.htm>; Okinawan Peace Network of Los Angeles <www.uchinanchu.org>; Organization for the Prohibition of Chemical Weapons Technical Assistance Visit, Final Report, 8/14/01; *Financial Times*, 9/7/01; Ecocompass/IslandPress; Fellowship of Reconciliation Panama Campaign <www. forusa.org/program/panama>; *Coastal Post* newsmonthly <www.coastalpost.com>

Dollars & Sense would like to acknowledge and thank the Military Toxics Project (MTP) for much of the information in this article. The MTP seeks to "unite activists, organizations, and communities in the struggle to clean up military pollution, safeguard the transportation of hazardous materials, and to advance the development and implementation of preventive solutions to the toxic and radioactive pollution caused by military activities." For more information readers can write to Military Toxics Project, P.O. Box 558, Lewiston, ME 04243, call 207-783-5091 or visit <www.miltoxproj.org>.

ARTICLE 40

Is It Oil?

BY ARTHUR MacEWAN

May/June 2003

efore U.S. forces invaded Iraq, the United Nations inspection team that had been searching the country for weapons of mass destruction was unable to find either such weapons or a capacity to produce them in the near future. As of mid-April, while the U.S. military is apparently wrapping up its invasion, it too has not found the alleged weapons. The U.S. government continues to claim that weapons of mass destruction exist in Iraq but provides scant evidence to substantiate its claim.

While weapons of mass destruction are hard to find in Iraq, there is one thing that is relatively easy to find: oil. Lots of oil. With 112.5 billion barrels of proven reserves, Iraq has greater stores of oil than any country except Saudi Arabia. This combination—lots of oil and no weapons of mass destruction—begs the question: *Is it oil* and not weapons of mass destruction that motivates the U.S. government's aggressive policy towards Iraq?

THE U.S. "NEED" FOR OIL?

Much of the discussion of the United States, oil, and Iraq focuses on the U.S. economy's overall dependence on oil. We are a country highly dependent on oil, consuming far more than we produce. We have a small share, about 3%, of the world's total proven oil reserves. By depleting our reserves at a much higher rate than most other countries, the United States accounts for about 10% of world production. But, by importing from the rest of the world, we can consume oil at a still higher rate: U.S. oil consumption is over 25% of the world's total. (See the accompanying figures for these and related data.) Thus, the United States relies on the rest of the world's oil in order to keep its economy running—or at least running in its present oil-dependent form. Moreover, for the United States to operate as it does and maintain current standards of living, we need access to oil at low prices. Otherwise we would have to turn over a large share of U.S. GDP as payment to those who supply us with oil.

Iraq could present the United States with supply problems. With a hostile government in Baghdad, the likelihood that the United States would be subject to some sort of boycott as in the early 1970s is greater than otherwise. Likewise, a government in Baghdad that does not cooperate with Washington could be a catalyst to a reinvigoration of the Organization of Petroleum Exporting Countries

YEARS OF RESERVES AT CURRENT ANNUAL PRODUCTION RATES*

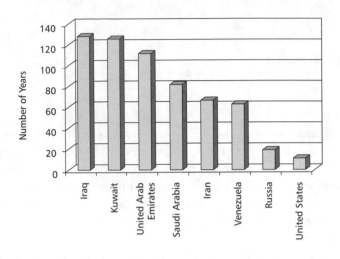

*The number of years it would take to use up existing reserves at current production rate.
Past experience, however, suggests that more reserves will be found. In the 1980s, the world's
proven reserves expanded by 47%, even as the consumption continued apace. With a more
rapid rate of economic growth in the 1990s, and thus with the more rapid rate of oil consumption, the world's reserves rose by almost 5%.

Source: BP Statistical Review of World Energy 2002 <www.bp.com/centres/energy2002>

(OPEC) and the result could be higher oil prices.

Such threats, however, while real, are not as great as they might first appear.
Boycotts are hard to maintain. The sellers of oil need to sell as much as the buyers need to buy; oil exporters depend on the U.S. market, just as U.S. consumers
depend on those exporters. (An illustration of this mutual dependence is provided
by the continuing oil trade between Iraq and the United States in recent years.
During 2001, while the two countries were in a virtual state of war, the United
States bought 284 million barrels of oil from Iraq, about 7% of U.S. imports and
almost a third of Iraq's exports.) Also, U.S. oil imports come from diverse sources,
with less than half from OPEC countries and less than one-quarter from Persian
Gulf nations.

Most important, ever since the initial surge of OPEC in the 1970s, the organization has followed a policy of price restraint. While price restraint may in part be
a strategy of political cooperation, resulting from the close U.S.-Saudi relationship
in particular, it is also a policy adopted because high prices are counter-produc-
tive for OPEC itself; high prices lead consumers to switch sources of supply and
conserve energy, undercutting the longer term profits for the oil suppliers. Fur-

thermore, a sudden rise in prices can lead to general economic disruption, which is no more desirable for the oil exporters than for the oil importers. To be sure, the United States would prefer to have cooperative governments in oil producing countries, but the specter of another boycott as in the 1970s or somewhat higher prices for oil hardly provides a rationale, let alone a justification, for war.

OIL CONSUMPTION 2001

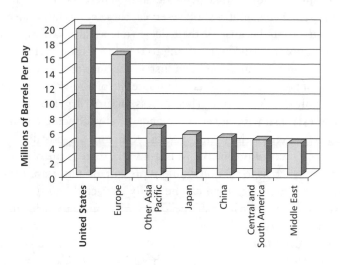

PROVEN OIL RESERVES 2001

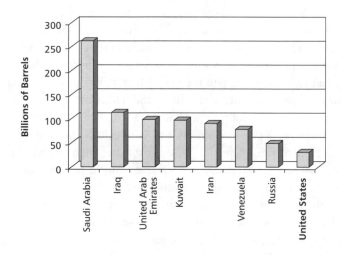

Source: BP Statistical Review of World Energy 2002 <www.bp.com/centres/energy2002>

THE PROFITS PROBLEM

There is, however, also the importance of oil in the profits of large U.S. firms: the oil companies themselves (with ExxonMobil at the head of the list) but also the numerous drilling, shipping, refining, and marketing firms that make up the rest of the oil industry. Perhaps the most famous of this latter group, because former CEO Dick Cheney is now vice president, is the Halliburton Company, which supplies a wide range of equipment and engineering services to the industry. Even while many governments—Saudi Arabia, Kuwait, and Venezuela, for example—have taken ownership of their countries' oil reserves, these companies have been able to maintain their profits because of their decisive roles at each stage in the long sequence from exploration through drilling to refining and marketing. Ultimately, however, as with any resource-based industry, the monopolistic position—and thus the large profits—of the firms that dominate the oil industry depends on their access to the supply of the resource. Their access, in turn, depends on the relations they are able to establish with the governments of oil-producing countries.

From the perspective of the major U.S. oil companies, a hostile Iraqi government presents a clear set of problems. To begin with, there is the obvious: because Iraq has a lot of oil, access to that oil would represent an important profit-making opportunity. What's more, Iraqi oil can be easily extracted and thus produced at very low cost. With all oil selling at the same price on the world market, Iraqi oil thus presents opportunities for especially large profits per unit of production. According to the *Guardian* newspaper (London), Iraqi oil could cost as little as 97 cents a barrel to produce, compared to the UK's North Sea oil produced at $3 to $4 per barrel. As one oil executive told the *Guardian* last November, "Ninety cents a barrel for oil that sells for $30—that's the kind of business anyone would want to be in. A 97% profit margin—you can live with that." The *Guardian* continues: "The stakes are high. Iraq could be producing 8 million barrels a day within the decade. The math is impressive—8 million times 365 at $30 per barrel or $87.5 billion a year. Any share would be worth fighting for." The question for the oil companies is: what share will they be able to claim and what share will be claimed by the Iraqi government? The split would undoubtedly be more favorable for the oil companies with a compliant U.S.-installed government in Baghdad.

Furthermore, the conflict is not simply one between the private oil companies and the government of Iraq. The U.S.-based firms and their British (and British-Dutch) allies are vying with French, Russian, and Chinese firms for access to Iraqi oil. During recent years, firms from these other nations signed oil exploration and development contracts with the Hussein government in Iraq, and, if there were no "regime change," they would preempt the operations of the U.S. and British firms in that country. If, however, the U.S. government succeeds in replacing the government of Saddam Hussein with its preferred allies in the Iraqi opposition, the outlook will change dramatically. According to Ahmed Chalabi, head of the Iraqi National Congress and a figure in the Iraqi opposition who seems to be currently favored by Washington, "The future democratic government in Iraq will be grateful to the United States for helping the Iraqi people liberate themselves and getting rid of Saddam.... American companies, we expect, will play an important and leading role in the future oil situation." (In recent years, U.S. firms have not been fully frozen out of the oil business in Iraq. For example, according to a June 2001 report in the *Washington Post*, while Vice President Cheney was CEO at Halliburton Company during the late 1990s, the firm operated through subsidiaries to sell some $73 million of oil production equipment and spare parts to Iraq.)

The rivalry with French, Russian and Chinese oil companies is in part driven by the direct prize of the profits to be obtained from Iraqi operations. In addition, in order to maintain their dominant positions in the world oil industry, it is important for the U.S. and British-based firms to deprive their rivals of the growth potential that access to Iraq would afford. In any monopolistic industry, leading firms need to deny their potential competitors market position and control of new sources of supply; otherwise, those competitors will be in a better position to challenge the leaders. The British *Guardian* reports that the Hussein government is "believed to have offered the French company TotalFinaElf exclusive rights to the largest of Iraq's oil fields, the Majoon, which would more than double the company's entire output at a single stroke." Such a development would catapult TotalFinaElf from the second ranks into the first ranks of the major oil firms. The basic structure of the world oil industry would not change, but the sharing of power and profits among the leaders would be altered. Thus for ExxonMobil, Chevron, Shell and the other traditional "majors" in the industry, access to Iraq is a defensive as well as an offensive goal. ("Regime change" in Iraq will not necessarily provide the legal basis for cancellation of contracts signed between the Hussein regime and various oil companies. International law would not allow a new regime simply to turn things over to the U.S. oil companies. "Should 'regime change' happen, one thing is guaranteed," according to the *Guardian*, "shortly afterwards there will be the mother of all legal battles.")

Oil companies are big and powerful. The biggest, ExxonMobil, had 2002 profits of $15 billion, more than any other corporation, in the United States or in the world. Chevron-Texaco came in with $3.3 billion in 2002 profits, and Phillips-Tosco garnered $1.7 billion. British Petroleum-Amoco-Arco pulled in $8 billion, while Royal Dutch/Shell Group registered almost $11 billion. Firms of this magnitude have a large role affecting the policies of their governments, and, for that matter, the governments of many other countries.

With the ascendancy of the Bush-Cheney team to the White House in 2000, perhaps the relationship between oil and the government became more personal, but it was not new. Big oil has been important in shaping U.S. foreign policy since the end of the 19th century (to say nothing of its role in shaping other policy realms, particularly environmental regulation). From 1914, when the Marines landed at Mexico's Tampico Bay to protect U.S. oil interests, to the CIA-engineered overthrow of the Mosadegh government in Iran in 1953, to the close relationship with the oppressive Saudi monarchy through the past 70 years, oil and the interests of the oil companies have been central factors in U.S. foreign policy. Iraq today is one more chapter in a long story.

THE LARGER ISSUE

Yet in Iraq today, as in many other instances of the U.S. government's international actions, oil is not the whole story. The international policies of the U.S. government are certainly shaped in significant part by the interests of U.S.-based firms, but not only the oil companies. ExxonMobil may have had the largest 2002 profits, but there are many additional large U.S. firms with international interests: Citbank and the other huge financial firms; IBM, Microsoft, and other information technology companies; General Motors and Ford; Merck, Pfizer and the other pharmaceutical corporations; large retailers like MacDonald's and Wal-Mart (and many more) depend on access to foreign markets and foreign sources of supply for large shares of their sales and profits.

The U.S. government (like other governments) has long defined its role in international affairs as protecting the interests of its nationals, and by far the largest interests of U.S. nationals abroad are the interests of these large U.S. companies. The day-to-day activities of U.S. embassies and consular offices around the world are dominated by efforts to further the interests of particular U.S. firms—for example, helping the firms establish local markets, negotiate a country's regulations, or develop relations with local businesses. When the issue is large, such as when governments in low-income countries have attempted to assure the availability of HIV-AIDS drugs in spite of patents held by U.S. firms, Washington steps directly into the fray. On the broadest level, the U.S. government tries to shape the rules and institutions of the world economy in ways that work well for U.S. firms. These rules are summed up under the heading of "free trade," which in practice means free access of U.S. firms to the markets and resources of the rest of the world.

In normal times, Washington uses diplomacy and institutions like the International Monetary Fund, the World Bank, and the World Trade Organization to shape the rules of the world economy. But times are not always "normal." When governments have attempted to remove their economies from the open system and break with the "rules of the game," the U.S. government has responded with overt or covert military interventions. Latin America has had a long history of such interventions, where Guatemala (1954), Cuba (1961), Chile (1973) and Nicaragua (1980s) provide fairly recent examples. The Middle East also provides several illustrations of this approach to foreign affairs, with U.S. interventions in Iran (1953), Lebanon (1958), Libya (1981), and now Iraq. These interventions are generally presented as efforts to preserve freedom and democracy, but, if freedom and democracy were actually the goals of U.S. interventions the record would be very different; both the Saudi monarchy and the Shah of Iran, in an earlier era, would then have been high on the U.S. hit list. (Also, as with maintaining the source of supply of oil, the U.S. government did not intervene in Guatemala in 1954 to maintain our supply of bananas; the profits of the United Fruit Company, however, did provide a powerful causal factor.)

The rhetorical rationale of U.S. foreign policy has seen many alterations and adjustments over the last century: at the end of the 19th century, U.S. officials spoke of the need to spread Christianity; Woodrow Wilson defined the mission as keeping the world safe for democracy; for most of the latter half of the 20th century, the fight against Communism was the paramount rationale; for a fleeting moment during the Carter administration, the protection of human rights entered the government's vocabulary; in recent years we have seen the war against drugs; and now we have the current administration's war against terrorism.

What distinguishes the current administration in Washington is neither its approach toward foreign affairs and U.S. business interests in general nor its policy in the Middle East and oil interests in particular. Even its rhetoric builds on well established traditions, albeit with new twists. What does distinguish the Bush administration is the clarity and aggressiveness with which it has put forth its goal of maintaining U.S. domination internationally. The "Bush Doctrine" that the administration has articulated claims legitimacy for pre-emptive action against those who might threaten U.S. interests, and it is clear from the statement of that doctrine in last September's issuance of *The National Security Strategy of the United States of America* that "U.S. interests" includes economic interests.

The economic story is never the whole story, and oil is never the whole economic story. In the particular application of U.S. power, numerous strategic and political considerations come into play. With the application of the Bush Doctrine in the case of Iraq, the especially heinous character of the Hussein regime is certainly a factor, as is the regime's history of conflict with other nations of the region (at times with U.S. support) and its apparent efforts at developing nuclear, chemical, and biological weapons; certainly the weakness of the Iraqi military also affects the U.S. government's willingness to go to war. Yet, as September's *Security Strategy* document makes clear, the U.S. government is concerned with domination and a major factor driving that goal of domination is economic. In the Middle East, Iraq and elsewhere, oil—or, more precisely, the profit from oil—looms large in the picture.

An earlier version of this article was prepared for the newsletter of the Joiner Center for War and Social Consequences at the University of Massachusetts-Boston. This article was largely prepared before the start of the war on Iraq.

ARTICLE 41

In Harm's Way

The Working Class on the
War Front and the Home Front

BY RODNEY WARD

May/June 2003

> "Old man Bush wasn't half the president his son is. When the father was president, I only took a 15% pay cut. Now that his idiot son is president, I get to take a 40% pay cut. Way to go, George!"
>
> *—a US Airways Fleet Services union activist*

> "I've had enough of being fired at from all directions. I just want to go home."
>
> *—a U.S. Marine, speaking to BBC News*

Irst, the obvious: In Iraq, a U.S. and allied military made up of working-class soldiers has fought against a working-class Iraqi military. But the war tears at the lives of working people in the United States as well. As Martin Luther King observed about an earlier war, the bombs raining down on the "enemy" also jeopardize the futures and livelihoods of people in poor and working-class communities in the United States.

On any number of dimensions, the war in Iraq is hurting working people back home. The U.S. soldiers who return will find their benefits slashed by Congress and their prospects limited by continuing economic stagnation. The massive cost of the war and occupation robs resources from those who can least afford it and exacerbates federal and state budget crises. In turn, the social safety net is unraveling further just as wartime anxiety pushes the economy back toward recession.

The Bush administration is using wartime insecurity as a pretext to strip union rights from many federal workers and to intensify the criminalization of immigrant communities. In the private sector, entire industries—most notably, the airlines—are using the moment as an opportunity to bludgeon unions and savagely restructure their workplaces. As the shooting in Iraq winds down, an unwelcome occupation begins that will drain more resources away from meeting urgent human needs; just as important, it will prolong an atmosphere of crisis that gives cover for those whose agenda is to weaken the union movement and workers' rights.

WORKING WARRIORS

The modern U.S. military is vaunted as an all-volunteer force, but the truth is more complex. Conscription was ended in 1973 as a result of antiwar protest at home and, more important, among soldiers. Since then, the Department of Defense has built a voluntary military, primarily on a system of economic incentives. The military targets communities that have been devastated by disinvestment for recruitment, and military service has become a primary economic opportunity structure for working-class communities, disproportionately so for people of color.

Oskar Castro of the Youth and Militarism Project of the American Friends Service Committee (AFSC) points out that "most people didn't sign up because they were gung-ho warriors. Most people signed up for the college money and wonderful career opportunities, leadership skills and respect" that military recruiters offer—attractive promises to a young person whose alternatives are a dead-end job or unemployment. Researchers at the Rand Corporation found that low personal or family income and unemployment (particularly long term) increase the chances that someone will enlist. Not surprisingly, the military "seems to resemble the makeup of a two-year commuter or trade school outside Birmingham or Biloxi," note *New York Times* reporters David Halbfinger and Steven Holmes. As a result, close observers of military enlistment like the Central Committee for Conscientious Objectors refer to today's recruitment strategy as a "poverty draft."

Half of the 3.2 million soldiers in the U.S. military are reservists. In addition to the emotional trauma soldiers and their loved ones experience during a wartime mobilization, reservists also endure significant economic hardships. As they are activated from civilian jobs, many face dramatic pay cuts and disruption of health benefits. Tod Ensign of Citizen Soldier, an advocacy group for soldiers, explains, "Take an EMT making $42K driving an ambulance, enough to support a wife and two or three kids in a working-class suburb of New York City. They will earn $18K-22K once activated. Setting aside the risk of war, these people are taking heavy hits, often 30% to 50% cuts in pay!" Though some unionized workers have contractual pay protections in the event of reserve call-up, most reservists are out of luck. Civilian bills at best stay the same; with one parent absent, child care costs may go up. One New York City reservist explained that activation would mean his family would lose their home.

And when the war is over, the GIs will return home to find that politicians—many of whom used privilege to avoid military service themselves—are mouthing support while actually pulling the rug out from under soldiers' futures. On March 20, the Congress overwhelmingly passed a resolution to "express the gratitude of the Nation to all members of the United States Armed Forces." Then, early the next morning, the House of Representatives voted to cut funding for veterans' health care and benefit programs by nearly $25 billion over the next ten years. The cuts are designed to accommodate the massive tax cuts the Bush administration has been pursuing—while the war diverts the public's attention.

The government track record on ignoring postwar problems like Agent Orange, post-traumatic stress disorder, and Gulf War Syndrome does not bode well for the soldiers fighting the current war. Says the AFSC's Castro, "Even the military doesn't support the troops. Families are not supported. When it comes to dollars and cents, the military doesn't put its money where its mouth is."

Speaking of money, Defense Secretary Donald Rumsfeld's strategy for the Iraq war was based on the cost-cutting lean, just-in-time production model favored by corporate restructuring consultants. Rumsfeld apparently quashed the logistics plans of experienced officers, pressuring them to stage far fewer personnel and much less hardware in the Gulf than they considered adequate. Observers of the impact of lean restructuring in the corporate world report that increased work-place injuries are a major result. One wonders what impact importing this model into the battlefield will have on soldiers and civilians.

UNION BUSTING AS HOMELAND SECURITY

Meanwhile, on the home front, both public- and private-sector workers are suffering a savage assault. The fiscal crisis brought about by war spending, recession, and tax cuts for the wealthy is squeezing public workers at all levels, resulting in wage freezes and elimination of entire departments. Thousands of public-sector workers are losing their jobs. Treasury Department worker Renee Toback reports that her department was told their budget would be "taxed" to pay for the war in Iraq.

At the same time, the Bush administration has stripped thousands of federal workers in the hastily cobbled-together Department of Homeland Security of union rights in the name of national security. The Department of Defense is developing plans to do the same. Are fearful employees with no voice on the job in the best position to protect national security? No. But it's no surprise that the administration's agenda prioritizes union busting over public safety. AFL-CIO Organizing Director Stewart Acuff says, "The most outrageous thing they [the Bush administration] said was that they had to remove union rights from the Department of Homeland Security when all of the people who answered the call on September 11, all of the firefighters and cops who died trying to save people, were union members! And 90% of the people who cleaned up in the aftermath were union members as well." Against this backdrop, the administration has also called for the privatization of as many as 800,000 non-postal federal jobs. If Bush succeeds, this move would replace large numbers of union jobs with non-union ones at lower pay and with less accountability; it would strike a huge blow at the strength of public-sector unions. (Naturally, Bush also plans to privatize Iraqi health care and education.)

Diane Witiak, an American Federation of Government Employees (AFGE) spokeswoman, describes the current atmosphere: "If you dare to oppose the administration, you're almost considered a traitor. We resent that the administration considers unionization and patriotism incompatible. In fact, [unionization is] essential. [The administration] will go back to the old cronyism and favoritism that the Civil Service Act corrected. It's only a matter of time before Bush starts with the private sector!"

Much as Witiak predicted, the administration is using the national-security pretext to erode the rights of some private-sector workers as well. Last year, Homeland Security director Tom Ridge called the president of the west coast longshore union. He claimed a strike would harm national security and threatened dockworkers with replacement by military personnel. Ultimately, it was management that locked out the dockworkers, but Bush invoked the Taft-Hartley Act and threatened to prosecute International Longshore and Warehouse Union members who engaged in any kind of work slowdown or other industrial action.

More broadly, efforts are under way in Congress to ban strikes by airline workers and to pass a number of other anti-worker measures. Among these are expansion of the restrictive Railway Labor Act's jurisdiction to include certain industries now under the umbrella of the National Labor Relations Act, making it harder for workers in these sectors to win union recognition and severely limiting their right to strike. Another legislative initiative would eliminate "card-check," the system of conducting a union recognition election once a certain number of representation petition cards have been signed by workers at a particular facility. In recent years, card-check has been the chief mechanism of successful union organizing drives. The AFL-CIO's Acuff points out that "the direction the government is moving in will indeed have a chilling effect on mobilizations, collective activity, demonstrations and direct action, all necessary parts of contract and bargaining campaigns and union strength. This administration, by law and by culture, is trying to stigmatize or make illegal the kinds of activity that are necessary to build union workplace strength."

WHAT DOES A TERRORIST LOOK LIKE?

Wartime is always dangerous for immigrant communities. When the towers collapsed on September 11, they crushed the movement to give undocumented immigrants amnesty. Since then, immigrants have been subject to a dramatically stepped-up campaign by the federal government to find and deport them. Rachael Kamel, AFSC education director, points to "growing attempts to criminalize immigrant workers—all now justified in the name of security." As the next episode in the now-permanent war on terror, the war in Iraq only serves to extend the period in which such policies appear legitimate.

For example, the Social Security Administration (SSA) sends so-called no-match letters to employers when it finds that a worker's Social Security number does not match SSA records. These letters serve to intimidate workers, since employers can threaten to turn them in to the Immigration and Naturalization Service (INS). The number of no-match letters has increased 800% since 9/11.

Similarly, special registration of immigrants from a select list of countries, mostly in the Middle East and Southern Asia, has snared thousands of people with minor visa infractions, many of whom face deportation. (Of bizarre note is the case of Iraqi exile Katrin Michael. She met with President Bush on March 14 to recount the gas attack she survived, and then found herself on the INS deportation list the next week, according to a *Washington Post* story.)

All of this has a powerful impact on worker organization because, for the past decade, immigrant workers have been the bedrock of aggressive labor organizing campaigns in economically strategic states like California, Texas and New York. Last year in Los Angeles, 60 workers active in organizing the Koreatown Assi Supermarket were placed on indefinite suspension after their names appeared on no-match letters. And the same Homeland Security rules that stripped newly-federalized airport screeners of union rights also banned immigrant workers in those positions. As a result, 7,000 immigrant airport security screeners—some of whom had just succeeded in winning union representation—have been fired. (See "Immigrant Workers in the Crosshairs," article 21.)

SHOCK AND AWE FOR AIRLINE WORKERS?

Amid official and unofficial repression against public sector workers and immigrant communities, the economy appears stalled and is likely heading for a double-dip recession. The World Bank is already estimating that the Iraq war will reduce worldwide economic growth by one-half of a percentage point during the first six months of this year.

When the economy is weak, the industries most affected make cuts wherever they can, and workers bear the brunt of industry restructuring. The airline industry continues to be the crucible of this restructuring; as such, it provides an instructive case study. Before the war, the industry's Air Transport Association predicted 70,000 layoffs (100,000 if a terrorist attack accompanied the war) in addition to the thousands already cut since September 11, as well as $4 billion in additional losses. Editorials intoned about "Airline Apocalypse."

True to their word, airlines began shedding employees by the thousands as soon as the bombs started to fall on Baghdad. Continental laid off 1,200, with more to come, Northwest, 4,900, while United and American (possibly in Chapter 11 bankruptcy reorganization by the time you read this) plan to get rid of thousands more. Jeff Matthews, the Aircraft Mechanics Fraternal Association's national contract coordinator at Northwest, told Reuters: "Northwest is using the Iraq conflict as an excuse to justify mass layoffs planned before the conflict started. The number of planned layoffs is far larger than would be justified based on the number of planes Northwest is removing from service." One United employee and Marines veteran describes wartime layoffs as United's own campaign of "shock and awe."

All of these airlines have succeeded in, or are in the process of, extracting concessions on levels unheard of in the history of the industry. Of particular importance has been US Airways' use of the war as leverage to terminate the defined-benefit pension plan for its pilots. At a time when defined-benefit plans are underfunded by about $300 billion in the United States, this is alarming. Representative Bernie Sanders (I-Vt.) warned in the *Wall Street Journal* that "this could set a horrible precedent by making it easier for companies to renege on the retirement promises they made to their workers." Nomi Prins, author of the forthcoming book *Money for Nothing*, points out, "The poor stock market is offering a convenient excuse for companies that already desired to reduce future plan benefits."

The airlines cite the war as a major reason for the concessions they demand. United mechanic Jennifer Salazar-Biddle remarked, "The crisis is real, but the graft is unbelievable." In fact, executive compensation in the midst of the industry's crisis has shocked and awed even Republicans. Responding to reports of the doubling of Delta CEO Leo Mullin's compensation package, Sen. John McCain (who champions eliminating airline workers' right to strike) exclaimed, "You ought to be ashamed of yourself." Nonetheless, a new bailout is in the works for the airline industry. The bailout bill does include a cap on executive compensation, but at 2002 levels—a good example of closing the barn doors after the escape. It also requires the airline companies to reduce operating costs, a provision that will primarily bleed workers. The only bone the bill offers airline workers is a meager extension of their unemployment benefits.

CHAIN OF CHANGE

Wars have always had a deep impact on working people. In addition to the slaughter of war, wars have often undermined the strength of working class organization. Government repression tied to World War I all but destroyed the Industrial Workers of the World and the Socialist Party. Workplace regimentation in World War II played an important role in the long-term bureaucratization of unions, replacing militant shop floor activity with safer routinized grievance and arbitration procedures.

On the other hand, soldiers returning from war have also played an important role in reviving struggles at home. At the end of World War II and during the Vietnam War, opposition to the war surfaced among GIs, along with discussions of soldiers' rights to free speech and even to unions. Soldiers returning from Vietnam played an important role in the antiwar movement as well as rebellions within a variety of unions, most notably the wave of auto-worker wildcat strikes from 1969 to 1972. African-American soldiers returning from both of these wars parlayed their wartime experiences into civil-rights activism.

There are some hopeful signs that workers will fight back against the current wave of assaults on their rights. Transportation Security Administration (TSA) employees are continuing to organize themselves with AFGE in spite of TSA director James Loy's directives to the contrary. AFGE succeeded in securing a one-year moratorium on the de-unionization of the Department of Homeland Security. Federal workers in Seattle and dozens of other localities have begun a campaign of public rallies to protest privatization.

Time will tell how working people in the military will respond to what they are enduring today. One thing is clear, though: The immediate impact of the war has been to strengthen the hands of corporations and weaken unions and other worker organizations while placing thousands of working people in harm's way. In the long term, whether grassroots activists can turn this tide will depend on how they understand and address the class dimensions of this and future wars.

RESOURCES *Soldiers & Veterans:* Citizen Soldier <www.citizen-soldier.org>; Military Families Speak Out <www.mfso.org>; Veterans for Common Sense <www.veteransforcommon sense.org>; National Gulf War Resource Center <www.ngwrc.org>; *Immigrant Rights:* National Network for Immigrant and Refugee Rights <www.nnirr.org>; *Labor:* US Labor Against War <www.uslaboraga instwar.org>; Dept. of Homeland Security Workers <www. dhsworkers.org>; Association of Flight Attendants <www.afanet.org>; Airline Mechanics Fraternal Association <www.amfanatl.org>; *See also:* David Cortright, *Soldiers in Revolt: The American Military Today* (Anchor Press/Doubleday, 1976); Kim Moody, *An Injury To All* (Routledge, 1997).

ARTICLE 42

The Emperor's New Clothes

BY NICK THORKELSON AND ALEJANDRO REUSS

March/April 2002

CORRUPTION OF LOCAL ELITES

THEN

NOW

YOU'VE GOTTA HAND IT TO THE WHITE MAN.

REMEMBER: YOU CAN'T MAKE AN OMELETTE WITHOUT BREAKING A FEW EGGS."

LONG AS THEY'RE NOT MY EGGS!

HARVARD KNOWS

A SMALL PART OF THE BOOTY FROM EUROPE'S EMPIRES IN ASIA & AFRICA WENT TO LOCAL LANDOWNERS & PRINCES WILLING TO ENFORCE IMPERIAL RULE. BRITAIN GAVE COMFORTABLE CIVIL SERVICE JOBS TO EDUCATED INDIANS TO SECURE THEIR LOYALTY.

FOR ADMINISTERING WHAT THEIR U.S. ADVISORS CALLED "SHOCK THERAPY"—THE OVERNIGHT PRIVATIZATION OF THE FORMER SOVIET ECONOMY—THE RUSSIAN ELITE (FORMER PARTY LEADERS) WAS REWARDED WITH GREAT WEALTH. MEANWHILE RUSSIA'S AVERAGE REAL INCOME FELL 40%.

CHANGING THE RULES IN MID-GAME

THEN

NOW

WE'RE GOOD AT MAKING CLOTH. YOU'RE GOOD AT GROWING STUFF.

TRYING TO ARTIFICIALLY BUILD UP YOUR INDUSTRY WITH TARIFFS WOULD IMPINGE ON MY FREEDOM — AND YOURS! DON'T YOU AGREE?

BRITAIN PROTECTED ITS INDUSTRY FROM CHEAPER AND BETTER IMPORTS UNTIL ABOUT 1830. ONLY THEN, WHEN BRITISH GOODS COULD SELL CHEAPLY AND ASIAN MANUFACTURING HAD BEEN LARGELY SUPPRESSED, DID BRITAIN DROP ITS PROTECTIONIST POLICIES.

TO LIVE LIKE US YOU MUST THINK LIKE US.

BEFORE WORLD WAR II YOU THOUGHT TARIFFS WERE A PRETTY GOOD IDEA.

THAT WAS THEN. THIS IS YOU.

WHEN MEXICO, ARGENTINA OR INDONESIA NEED LOANS, THEY ARE TOLD BY THE IMF TO GIVE UP CAPITAL CONTROLS AND STATE-GUIDED INDUSTRIALIZATION, EVEN THOUGH THESE POLICIES BROUGHT ABOUT THE DEVELOPMENT OF JAPAN & KOREA.

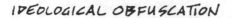

IDEOLOGICAL OBFUSCATION

THEN

"WHEN THE MISSIONARIES CAME, THEY HAD THE BIBLE & WE HAD THE LAND. THEY TAUGHT US TO CLOSE OUR EYES TO PRAY. AND WHEN WE OPENED THEM AGAIN, WE HAD THE BIBLE AND THEY HAD THE LAND."

—DESMOND TUTU

LORD HAVE MERCY.

OFFICE OF
CHRISTIANIZING THE HEATHEN
CIVILIZING BACKWARD PEOPLES
FIGHTING COMMUNISM
HUMANITARIAN INTERVENTION
UNITING AGAINST TERRORISM

NOW

THE "WAR ON TERRORISM" IS THE RATIONALE FOR RE-INTRODUCING U.S. TROOPS INTO THE PHILIPPINES, REVERSING A LONG-FOUGHT & HARD-WON STRUGGLE TO REMOVE THEM. IN FACT, U.S. MILITARY INTERVENTION IS LIKELY TO WORSEN THE UNDERLYING PROBLEM (THE MUSLIM MINORITY'S POWERLESSNES & POVERTY) BUT IT COULD SUCCEED IN NAILING DOWN U.S. CONTROL OF REGIONAL POLICY AND STRATEGIC WATERWAYS.

TRADE IN MISERY

THERE'S AT LEAST ONE SIGNIFICANT DIFFERENCE BETWEEN CLASSICAL IMPERIALISM & TODAY'S NEOLIBERAL REGIME:

THEN

"THE EMPIRE, AS I HAVE ALWAYS SAID, IS A BREAD AND BUTTER QUESTION...

HEAR HEAR   PIP PIP

...IF YOU WANT TO AVOID CIVIL WAR, YOU MUST BECOME IMPERIALISTS."

— CECIL RHODES, 1895

IMPERIALISM WAS SOLD AS A WAY OF REDUCING CLASS CONFLICT BY SHIFTING THE WORST BURDEN OF EXPLOITATION FROM EUROPEAN TO OVERSEAS WORKERS.

BUT TODAY...

LABOR FLEXIBILIZATION

NEOLIBERALISM DEMANDS DEVASTATING SACRIFICES FROM WORKERS IN RICH AND POOR COUNTRIES ALIKE.

GRR! FLEX!   GRR! FLEX!

THIS DIFFERENCE MAY BE THE NEOLIBERALS' UNDOING.

NICK THORKELSON & Alejandro Reuss

CHAPTER 9

Alternatives

"They Can Walk With Their Heads Up"

An Interview with Joao Pedro Stedile, National Board Member,
Movimento dos Trabalhadores Rurais Sem Terra

BY CYNTHIA PETERS AND JUSTIN PODUR

May/June 2002

I n Brazil, where there is fertile land, wealth and a tropical climate," said Jean
Ziegler, UN special rapporteur on the right to food, after a recent visit there,
"hunger is not a destiny." Rather, it is "the product of a totally unjust order.
Those who die of hunger in Brazil are assassinated."

Brazilian government officials were outraged by Ziegler's strong words, and
pointed to their recent successes in improving health care and education, and
in lifting millions out of extreme poverty. Still, the government does not dispute
the fact that 40,000 Brazilians die every year of hunger and malnutrition-related
diseases, and that more than 23 million of Brazil's 170 million people are malnourished.

How has Latin America's most resource-rich country ended up with such a
large part of its population struggling to survive? Brazil's recent decades of dictatorship and still powerful military, its high concentration of wealth and land-
ownership, and its struggle to develop under the weight of immense debt and
IMF-enforced neoliberal economic policies have contributed to a fractured and
impoverished society.

In the early 1960s, populist president Joao Goulart antagonized the U.S.-allied Brazilian military by instituting rent controls, seizing unused lands, nationalizing the petroleum industry, and restricting the repatriation of profits by foreign investors. Brazilian generals staged a coup in 1964, ushering in a 21-year military dictatorship that violently suppressed opposition political parties, independent labor unions, student movements, and landless workers' organizations. It also presided over the so-called Brazilian economic miracle—a dozen or so years of rapid growth financed by loans from foreign banks. This debt, incurred by the generals, helped enrich a few, but left to the general population a legacy of huge interest payments and punitive economic policies.

After a sustained economic crisis in the 1970s and early 1980s, brought on by skyrocketing oil prices and the generals' heavy borrowing, the military dictatorship signed an austerity agreement with the IMF in 1983. Being the world's largest debtor nation affected Brazil's poor in predictable ways. In order to generate cash to make interest payments on the debt, more and more land was put towards cash crops like coffee and soy, displacing hundreds of thousands of subsistence farmers. Many fled to the cities, where they settled in burgeoning shantytowns. Others were relocated to places such as the Amazonian Rondonia, where they cleared forests in an effort to farm the land. World Bank-sponsored programs, such as hydroelectric dams that flood vast tracts of rainforest and displace thousands of indigenous people, have contributed to the social and ecological disaster. Brazil suffers not just from its immense foreign debt, but also from the hidden costs of environmental destruction, many internally displaced people, and an impoverished rural population—what many Brazilians call the "social debt."

Even during the dictatorship, workers in Brazil's growing industrial sector organized powerful and combative unions. The unions and the fragments of the Brazilian left that had survived 15 years of dictatorship founded the left-wing Workers' Party (PT) in 1979. These developments helped spur the policy of *abertura*—or "opening"—which the Brazilian dictatorship implemented as a way to control the transition to civilian rule. The easing of repression, in turn, led to the growth of grassroots social change movements, such as the Landless Workers' Movement (Movimento dos Trabalhadores Rurais Sem Terra, or MST), and of opposition political parties such as the PT. Since the return to elections in 1988, the PT has won key state and local elections, and instituted important reforms. Perhaps its most groundbreaking reform is the participatory budget—a decision-making system that allows citizens a direct say over portions of their municipal budgets. The PT's best-known leader, the popular former auto worker Luis Inacio "Lula" da Silva, almost won the presidency in 1989 and won in 2002.

The MST, with support from the Catholic Church, began its struggle in 1985, taking over an unused plantation in the south of the country. The occupiers gained title to the land two years later. Since then, the MST has helped 300,000 families settle on previously idle land, while close to 100,000 other families are living on land they have occupied, waiting for government recognition. In May 2000, 30,000 MST members took over federal buildings across the country in a successful bid to persuade President Fernando Henrique Cardoso to address the country's extreme economic inequality. In response to pressure from the MST, Cardoso promised $1 billion in reforms. In addition to its successful resettlement program and considerable grassroots power, the MST boasts a sophisticated literacy program for adults and adolescents, as well as 1,000 primary schools, in which 2,000 teachers work with about 50,000 kids. According to Bill Hinchberger, writing for *The Nation* (March 2, 1998), "the MST represents Latin America's most dynamic popular movement south of Chiapas."

As such, it is not popular among certain segments of Brazilian society. The police and military, as well as landlords' private gunmen, still target activists. According to the Roman Catholic-run Pastoral Land Commission, over 1,100 people were killed in land disputes between 1985 and 1999. And only 47 cases have gone to trial, leading to just 18 convictions. In 2001, 16 MST activists were murdered, and few of the cases were properly investigated or brought to trial. "At least ten landowners are threatening me, saying that I will be next," José Brito, president of the Agricultural Workers Union of Rondon in the state of Para, has told the press. "Even thought I have registered complaints to the police station, I have never been called to give a deposition. Whoever fights for life here will have his own life threatened."

In addition to violent repression, the MST faces other challenges. According to Global Exchange, "landowners and some elected officials are trying to repeal the clause of the Brazilian constitution that says land should be used for social purposes—and can be redistributed if it is not. That provision has formed the legal foundation of the MST's occupations of unused lands." Furthermore, the World Bank's $2 billion "land bank" program, which offers loans to small farmers to purchase land, is transparently designed to undermine the grassroots-based MST. The MST must also contend with "free trade" agreements that knock down trade barriers, allowing cheap food to be imported from abroad, and undercutting domestic markets. The struggle ahead remains enormous. Today, 3% of Brazil's population still owns two-thirds of the country's arable land, much of which lies idle. Meanwhile, millions of peasants struggle to survive by working in temporary agricultural jobs.

At an MST cooperative in Herval, in the southern state of Rio Grande do Sul, which I visited in February 2002, I saw productive farms, well-built homes with electricity and running water, schools, and cultural activities. If the 40,000 who die from hunger each year in Brazil are the victims of "class warfare," as the UN's Ziegler argues, the MST is on the front line—fighting back, not with bullets, but with mass organizing and grassroots pressure to meet basic human needs.

While in Herval, Canadian activist and writer Justin Podur and I had the opportunity to talk with Joao Pedro Stedile, a member of the MST's national board.   —*Cynthia Peters*

*   *   *   *   *

D&S: What are the MST's main achievements?

JPS: Our most important success of all has been to build an organization and a social movement. We've won back the worth and dignity of the peasant. That has immeasurable value. It doesn't show up in statistics. But when a person stops being humiliated, stops being a slave, and they can walk with their head up, master of their own future, that's the most important thing we're building.

Beyond that, over the last 18 years, we've gotten land for 300,000 families, and though many of them remain poor, nobody in our settlements goes hungry. Everybody has work all year around. There are schools in all the settlements. All the children go to school. Everyone can build their own home. The houses may be humble, but nobody has to pay rent to anyone. At the very least, the people enjoy the basic rights of all people. That's what retaking the land means.

We're not satisfied with these modest achievements. Because in Brazil there are four million landless families. Our struggle is to broaden the movement, open up more battles, mobilize more people, because it's not just a matter of allowing a few people to solve their problems. This is important, of course. It offers an example. It's a form of mass education. But the fundamental thing is to change society, and solve the problems of all Brazilians, of all the poor.

D&S: You spoke of changing society. What are the next steps for the MST?

JPS: The challenges are huge. It's not going to be an easy struggle, nor a quick one. The road ahead will be rocky, not smooth. But there are both long-range struggles and more immediate ones.

In the long term, we're doing battle over what may decide the future of our country. I'm talking about the U.S. offensive to impose the Free Trade Area of the Americas (FTAA) on the Americas as a whole. The FTAA is more than a trade agreement. It is the U.S. government's plan to control our land, our wealth, our development, our technology, our currency, and our language. It would mean our submission to the interests of U.S. capital—to the less than 500 corporations at the top. And if that happens, we're back to being a colony, this time under the rule of the United States. So we have to fight to keep the FTAA from being imposed on Brazil. And not just on Brazil, but on the whole of Latin America. What we're going to do over the course of the coming months and years is help inform the people, organize them, raise their consciousness. In addition to fighting for land, health, and shelter, we have to stop the FTAA. That's going to mean demonstrations, mass meetings, lots and lots of different initiatives to inform and politicize people. Beyond that, every social movement has to continue its own specific work—we in the landless movement have to keep on occupying more and more landed estates. Our compatriots who have been displaced by dam construction will keep on fighting against the dams. The unemployed movements in the city will broaden their struggles for employment. The workers who are threatened will keep organizing, like for the general strike this March.

We're going to try and promote all these struggles in hopes of reawakening the people and reviving the mass movement here in Brazil. Because right now it's receding. With a revival of the mass movement, we can hope to change the government, and the reigning economic model.

D&S: What do you think of the Workers' Party's participatory budget process?

JPS: Well, there are some positive things about it, but also some criticisms to make.

D&S: What are the criticisms?

JPS: That, in the end, the people really only have a say over 5%—or, at the most, 10%—of the budget. Because the rest—including salaries, foreign debt payments, etc.—is fixed by law. All public budgets in Brazil have 13% of the total tied up by the IMF. They're required to deposit this in the bank to pay the debt. So, for example, in this state, which is governed by a people's government, by the left, education gets 11% of the budget, while the IMF gets 13%. That means the power of the people to change things through the participatory budget process is very limited.

D&S: So, what's the positive side?

JPS: It's that the participatory budget creates an opportunity for the people to voice their opinions. For the people to have a say about the overall problems of their society. It's like an exercise that points toward creating a general assembly of the society as a whole. Here in Rio Grande do Sul, we have a population of 12 million. You can't fit 12 million people into a single room. But the idea of the participatory budget process is that everyone can take part and have a say. So the main value of the process is not how much of the budget people have a say over, but as a democratic exercise that teaches people that they have a right to a say.

D&S: What would you say to activists and social movements in North America?

JPS: We're very interested in U.S. social movements. The landless movement enjoys the support of solidarity committees in many U.S. cities, which help us and help publicize our efforts. But what gratifies us the most is hearing about the people in the United States, even if they're not a majority yet, who are mobilizing as well, and fighting against their government. We understand that the people of the United States don't know the real impact of the actions of their government.

We hope that, slowly, they will begin to realize that, as peoples, we're the same. It's like an old U.S. journalist put it. He was a "cousin" or an "ancestor" of you who have come here from the United States. And he really said it in your honor. Because he was a social activist, and he went to cover the Spanish Civil War, like you have come here to Porto Alegre. When he came back, he wrote a book, which was called *No Man is a Foreigner*—meaning "man" in the general sense. What does that mean? That all peoples are alike. It's governments and capital, which enriches itself from the labor of others, that are bad. So we have to build a great, international alliance, which is what this forum is for. And we hope and expect that U.S. activists, fighting in the dragon's own gut, will help us kill this monster.

Translated from Spanish by Alejandro Reuss.

ARTICLE 44

Local Democracy and Development
The Kerala People's Campaign for Decentralized Planning

BY T. M. THOMAS ISAAC AND RICHARD W. FRANKE

The state of Kerala is well known for its history of social mobilization for better education, healthcare, public distribution of food, and fundamental structural changes such as land reforms. From 1996 to 2001 it witnessed another mass movement, this time for realizing the ideals of democratic decentralization. The Left Democratic Front (LDF) government that came to power in 1996 decided to devolve 35-40% of its Ninth Plan outlay for projects and programs to be formulated and implemented by local governments. A mass movement—popularly known as the People's Campaign for Decentralized Planning—was then launched to empower local governments to prepare plans in a transparent and participatory manner.

DEMOCRATIC PLANNING AND DEVELOPMENT

Thankamma looked out across the table. "We'll be getting four million and six thousand rupees." It was a hot, humid May evening in 1997. She scanned the faces of the other nine *panchayat* (village council) members. "Shall we proceed to a vote on our spending priorities?" she asked. The council members nodded their assent. In a formal motion a few moments later, they would approve a budget 51 times greater than any amount the village had ever spent in a single year.

Thankamma was nervous. Could they handle such responsibility with their limited education and experience? Could they carry out such vast projects as had been proposed and approved? On public land next to the panchayat office they were going to build a two-room veterinary hospital. A few hundred meters east of the village office they had decided to construct nine new classrooms for the government high school—classrooms that the villagers had been demanding for years from the state government. They would add toilets at the school and at local market centers, including separate facilities for women who often faced humili- ation and even physical threats while searching for a place to relieve themselves when working in public places. And the village would hire a full-time doctor for the health clinic and fix so many roads, build so many bridges and start up local industries and bring safe drinking water to all households and construct sanitary latrines everywhere and open a historical museum to attract tourists. They were even thinking about the environment: how could they protect their few remaining patches of forest?

In October and November of 1996 they had organized ten *grama sabhas* or ward assemblies. Each assembly required massive publicity, training of local discussion leaders, finding a location and time, and actually running a four-hour meeting with plenary sessions and small group discussions. Across Kerala, nearly three million had participated. In Panjal, attendance had averaged 180 per as- sembly, 13% above the statewide average of 159, but the council members and the local activists were disappointed at the turnout. They continued to think of their village as relatively backward and noticed that Thiruvilwamala, a nearby panchayat, had achieved 600-800 at some of its grama sabhas.

GLOSSARY

Eighth and Ninth Plans: Two of the central Indian government's five-year eco- nomic plans. The Eighth Plan spanned the years 1991-1996 and the Ninth Plan spanned the years 1996-2001. As part of each plan, states received outlays from the central government; the state of Kerala chose to devolve 35%-40% of its Ninth Plan outlay to local governments within the state.

Scheduled Caste (SC): The "untouchable" groups within the hereditary Indian caste system. SC members have historically been poor, subject to social exclusion, and responsible for society's most undesirable work.

Scheduled Tribe (ST): Indigenous groups outside the caste system which have also experienced social exclusion and discrimination. Nearly 600 individual tribal groups exist throughout India, mostly in small, physically remote communities with limited access to roads, electricity, schools, and medical facilities.

TABLE 1

MAJOR PHASES OF THE KERALA PEOPLE'S CAMPAIGN FOR DEMOCRATIC DECENTRALIZATION, FIRST YEAR OF THE CAMPAIGN: 1996-97 FOR NINTH PLAN FIRST YEAR 1997-98

Phase	Dates	Objective	Activities
1. Grama Sabhas	August 17 to November 1996	Identify felt needs of the people; generate participation and interest in the campaign	Meet at local school or other location; plenary sessions and small group discussions
2. Development Seminars	October 21 to December 1996 (in North) and to March 1997 (in South)	Assess resources and problems; list ideas for eventual formal projects	Collect data at local offices; carry out transect walks; write local development reports; conduct development seminar
3. Task Forces	January to July 1997	Turn proposals from Development Seminars into formal projects	Meet, discuss, and draft project proposals
4. Village and Municipal Councils	March 16, 1997 to March 1998	Finalize local plan	Prioritize projects; draft and approve local plan
5. Block and District Councils	April to November 1997	Finalize block and district plans	Analyze local plans; develop appropriate complementary projects
6. Volunteer Technical Corps–Expert Committees	March to December 1997	Appraisal and technical corrections to projects	Read, evaluate, suggest improvements to projects
7. Release of Funds and Project Implementation	June 5, 1997 to June 30, 1998	Implement and monitor the projects in the local plan	Open accounts, draw checks from treasury, set up beneficiary committees, hire contractors, activate monitoring committees

Source: Campaign documents.

Still, Panjal had managed to fulfill the formal requirements of the campaign for democratic decentralization that had been sweeping across Kerala since September 1996. After the grama sabhas, they had gathered data from the village offices, carried out one of the best transect walks in the area producing a fine diagram of the ecological zones, organized a development seminar, set up task forces, drafted project proposals, and were about to submit a formal plan to the State Planning Board for the projects the council had just voted to approve. Then would come the difficulties of implementation, monitoring, and trying to control corruption.

Three years and four plans later in June 2000 they looked back with both satisfaction and frustration. The panchayat plan for 2000-2001 was more detailed, more reflective, and better written than the first three; and now there were accomplishments to record as well as needs to respond to. The new school buildings were nearing completion, several new drinking water taps had been installed, many wells were cleaned or dug new, the veterinary hospital was finished and in operation, and plans were being laid for a new panchayat office complex with a community meeting hall. Volunteer labor had greatly lowered the cost of a tarred road across a paddy field opening a low-caste artisan community to modern transport for the first time.

Despite the many achievements, both representatives and activists in 2000 were more self-critical than congratulatory. They had failed in one of their most coveted goals—the Primary Health Center (PHC) still did not have 24-hour physician services or permanent beds and the nearest hospital was four kilometers distant. Agricultural production had been boosted slightly, but the outlook for generating income from farming was dimmed by the effects of national government price adjustments in conforming to international trade agreements over which villagers had no say.

Thankamma, the council, the local activists, and the 1,800 ordinary people who attended the Panjal grama sabhas in 1996 were concerned with the problems of their local community. Yet, they were part of the most radical and far-reaching experiment in democracy anywhere in the world in recent decades. It was an experiment in extending democracy from its representative form to one of participation. It was an experiment in using democracy as a major vehicle for economic growth and development. It was an experiment in creating alternatives to the neoliberal, corporate-dominated, "free trade" models of the economy. It is an experiment the whole world can learn from.

OVERVIEW OF THE PEOPLE'S CAMPAIGN

On Table 1 we give an outline of the phases of the campaign in its first year. All the phases were repeated in subsequent years, but the timing later on became more condensed as people learned how to organize, deliberate, plan, propose, revise, implement, monitor, and evaluate.

During its first three years, for which the data have been compiled, the campaign has yielded striking physical achievements. Across Kerala, local communities like Panjal together:

- Built 306,288 houses, compared with 269,988 built in the entire five-year span of the Eighth Plan of 1991-96.
- Built 117,173 of the new houses—38%—for SC (Scheduled or former untouchable caste) and ST (Scheduled or former untouchable tribal) households, compared with only 18,023—7%—during the Eighth Plan. Since about 12% of Kerala's people belong to SC/ST households, the figures suggest that under the Eighth plan housing inequality actually increased while the People's Campaign has made serious inroads to reduce it.
- Constructed 413,174 sanitary latrines, covering about 10% of all households. This compares with 125,000 during the entire Eighth Plan.

Universal preschool, improvement in the quality of education and in healthcare centers, and completion of rural electrification are also on the immediate agenda. Such targets would have appeared preposterous a few years ago. Total housing programs were taken up in all of Kerala's fourteen districts in the 2000-01 annual plans.

Kerala's critics often cite the state's lack of agricultural and industrial growth. The People's Campaign managed in its first three years:

- to bring 315,881 acres into additional food production activity, an increase of 5.6% over the cultivated area in 1992-93. This includes reclamation of wastelands—often via small-scale irrigation that the campaign has emphasized—and planting second and third crops;
- to increase the agricultural growth rate in 1998-99 to 3.82%, compared with an average of 1.3% in the previous three years;
- to increase milk production by 31% between 1998-99 and 1999-2000. In early 2000, the stocks increased by an additional 18%;
- to increase industrial growth in Kerala in 1998-99 to 7.2%
- to provide 84,917 persons with job training. If all the trainees got jobs, Kerala's high unemployment rate would have been reduced by 2.26%, but additional jobs in construction activities related to the campaign probably brought the unemployment rate down by another 3%, so that about 5% of joblessness was overcome;
- to create 3,804 new cooperatives; and
- to bring thousands of women into new job areas outside the home as autorickshaw drivers or in more traditional women's work in small-scale industries manufacturing soap, umbrellas, emergency lanterns, and ready-made clothing.

DECENTRALIZATION: NEOLIBERAL OR DEMOCRATIC?

Decentralization has been a frequent development prescription from first world to third world countries since the broad wave of independence movements came to

THE GREAT LABORATORY

From 1996 to 2001, Kerala became a vast laboratory with 1,214 local governments producing 1,214 local experiments each year for five years. Did ordinary people have any ideas? Could the local activists come up with solutions to problems that the experts had failed to imagine?

Better Grameen Banks?

One of the most important developments in the People's Campaign was the rise of new forms of microcredit at the village and neighborhood levels. Microcredit originated with the creation of the famous "Grameen Bank" in Bangladesh in 1976 by economics professor Muhammed Yunus. The Grameen Bank lends small amounts to mostly women borrowers who form borrowing cells of five individuals. They pledge together to repay their loans, creating a social pressure base to ensure higher payback rates.

Most microcredit projects including the Grameen Bank seem to be evaluated primarily in terms of payback rates. In a detailed anthropological village study, Aminur Rahman discovered that the emphasis on high payback rates was linked to a number of possibly negative features on the loans. Bank employees were evolving into an oppressive bureaucracy intent on loan recovery regardless of the effects on the households, group pressure tactics within the cells were leading to social strife, and women were often verbally or physically assaulted by husbands or other male family members to seek and then to pay back loans. He also found that 70% of the loans were not used for the purpose for which they were requested. Many loans came to be used to pay back other loans so that local economic development was not likely to result from the bank's activities.

In Kerala, self-help groups (SHGs) and neighborhood groups (NHGs) were encouraged to develop rotating credit associations that would match their own savings with supplementary credit from local cooperative banks. An SHG or NHG would put forth a production project such as a cooperative to manufacture umbrellas, soap, sandals, incense, tailored clothing, or electrical equipment, or to set up a cooperative store or tea shop. The village council would consider the project within the context of the local plan with the idea of distributing investment projects to maximize interconnections and to avoid overinvestment in any particular activity.

On approval of the project, financing sources would be patched together: the participants might raise 25% of the funds through a rotating credit association in which each household deposits Rs 10 per week for a year. This money is then matched with a low-interest loan from a bank. Local planning funds can be used to make up shortfalls, to guarantee the loans, or as startup funds to stimulate the project in the first place.

Why are the Kerala microcredit projects better than the existing Grameen Bank counterparts? The Kerala projects emphasize the solidarity of the SHGs to undertake production together rather than simply using social pressure to compel individuals to repay loans. The Kerala projects encourage local empowerment and do not pit poor households directly against a professional bank bureaucracy that has a set of interests potentially in conflict with the borrowers. Finally, the Kerala projects are—in theory at least—connected to an overall village development plan in which the outcomes of the loans in terms of products have an immediate local impact.

power in the mid-twentieth century. The same five decades since 1950 have seen a push by the rich countries—the North—to open up the economies of the South to trade and private investment. It would not be surprising if many in the South suspected decentralization of being part of a grander scheme to weaken third world states in order to gain greater access to cheap labor and raw materials.

As early as 1989, the World Bank began to assert that "evaluating governance within debtor countries is within its jurisdiction." Through Structural Adjustment Programs (SAPs), third world states were ordered to diminish their protections of their poorest citizens. Richard Falk notes that "'predatory globalization' has eroded, if not altogether broken, the former social contract that was forged between state and society during the last century or so."

Since 1995, shrinking the third world state has been furthered by the creation of the World Trade Organization (WTO), described by Philip McMichael as a body of "global managers [who] assume extraordinary powers to manage the web of global economic relations lying across nation-states, often at the expense of national and/or democratic process.... Their proceedings are secret, denying citizen participation." WTO bureaucrats can overrule national attempts to use tariffs, taxes, or other government devices to protect workers or businesses.

What does decentralization have to do with SAPs and the WTO? All three have been introduced at the same time and emanate from the same first world agencies. A USAID consultant, Riita-Liisa Kolehmainen-Aitken, noted that decentralization is occurring "in countries under structural adjustment, where funding agencies such as the World Bank are important partners in the process of reform and, in many instances, its driving force." SAPs and free trade rules from the WTO essentially take over from the third world state at the top. International agencies centralize and dominate at the global level what had been at least partially the independent prerogatives of nation-states. This centralization of international economic power in the hands of the first world-appointed bureaucrats is the essence of what today is referred to as "globalization." Decentralization weakens third world states by erosion from the bottom. One element of this erosion is privatization. In Mexico, a World Bank/IMF model, more than 80% of the 1,555 government-owned companies were sold or dissolved during 1980s SAPs. Tens of thousands of jobs were eliminated. Throughout the third world, governments have been ordered to sell off thousands of state-owned or operated companies, often at rock-bottom prices for which they are scooped up by the rich.

Decentralization plays a further role in the SAP/WTO scenario by transferring state responsibilities to lower levels of government. This is supposed to reduce government expenses, a key element of SAPs. It may also be intended to deflect some of the dangers to the central government by making lower administrative levels the targets of popular protest and thereby weakening the ability of opposition movements to forge national campaigns.

THE KERALA EXPERIMENT: DEMOCRATIC DECENTRALIZATION
AS A MECHANISM FOR RESISTANCE?

If decentralization can be part of the neoliberal strategy to weaken third world states and assist in selling off the people's assets through privatization, can it also be an alternative mechanism of development and therefore a means of resistance to first world-dominated globalization? We believe progressive and hopeful elements of decentralization can be seen in the Kerala experiment. The emphasis must be placed on the *democratic* element—democratic because it is buttressed by powerful and active civil society organizations, democratic because it is sustained by a state-level ministry genuinely committed to its success, and democratic because it draws upon the skills and idealism of thousands of ordinary people who come to play active roles in its implementation.

In Kerala, democratic decentralization draws its inspiration not from first world advisors but from the Gandhian tradition and the twentieth-century Indian independence movement. The Indian nationalist perspective on decentralization differs from that of the international aid agencies and the World Bank. Village self-rule (*grama swaraj*) was a powerful ideal that mobilized the masses to struggle for independence. This nationalist vision of decentralization acquires renewed significance in the present era of globalization. It challenges imperialist global domination.

In Kerala it was a state government under the control of the Left that took the decision to launch a campaign to decentralize. Because the Kerala experiment is part of a political project of the Left parties, and because those parties hold to a program of ending inequalities to the greatest extent possible, we see in the Kerala experiment a far larger set of goals than to develop a mere administrative design. And because the Kerala Left parties see themselves as among the inheritors of the Gandhian ideals of national independence and self-reliant communities, decentralization in Kerala is seen consciously as a tool for resisting predatory globalization, no matter from what source it emanates. We believe seven elements of the Kerala experiment can be identified that illustrate these Left ideals in practice. Left-led decentralization is for those who would put up sustained resistance to the IMF, World Bank, and U.S. government—and in many cases, their own local or national elites that cooperate with predatory globalization.

1. Planning—Not Unregulated Market Growth or Mere Cuts in Expenditures. Kerala's decentralization project recognizes a role for market forces and private entrepreneurs. It included an attempt to make government spending more efficient. But the People's Campaign aimed at fostering a planned form of development, not simple unregulated market expansion.

2. Active and Informed Citizens, Who Further Strengthen Civil Society. While depending on an extensive civil society base for its initial thrust, the People's Campaign attempted to create new civil society organizations and to invigorate those already functioning.

3. Egalitarian-Oriented Redistribution: Caste, Class, and Gender Struggles. The Kerala campaign set aside a subplan for SC and a separate subplan for the ST population, the two traditionally most oppressed groups. The campaign further attempted to jump-start a process of women's empowerment, through the many projects and training programs. Women got access to more plan funds, jobs, services, and political power than ever before in Kerala.

4. Planning from Below and Above: Functional Diversification of Tasks. The Kerala experiment involved a range of planning activities at four levels: grama (rural) panchayat or urban neighborhood, block, district, and state. Different levels of government undertook different planning tasks according to what is appropriate. The goal was to implement as many projects as possible at the lowest levels. Each higher level was charged with filling the gaps and with planning what it could do more effectively than other levels.

5. Cooperatives Not Corporations. Kerala's decentralization recognizes the role of private initiative and is not automatically hostile to privatization of government enterprises. But the emphasis on private development initiatives is for worker ownership. Small-scale cooperatives were encouraged to provide more jobs, especially to low-caste workers and to women, supported by local credit and subsidized by the plan funds to get them started.

6. Local Production for Local Markets. Local cooperatives were encouraged to produce for local markets. Umbrellas, soap and detergents, school uniforms, certain electrical products, traditional medicines, and agricultural products lend themselves to such a strategy and all were experimented with in the campaign. Kerala's planners and activists realize they cannot completely insulate their communities from international trade and the consequences of decisions made by the

WTO, IMF, World Bank, or central Indian government in New Delhi. The lesson is that the greater the number of jobs that are linked to local community or regional markets, the more protected they can be against economic catastrophes resulting from outside forces they do not control.

7. Environmental Sustainability. Like many third world areas, Kerala faces an acute environmental crisis: ravaged high mountain forests, polluted rivers, waterlogged lowlands, salinization of coastal marshes, and many others. Kerala's environmental crisis clearly leads toward a loss of productive resources, and the People's Campaign planted certain elements of environmental awareness and the concept of watershed planning. A few panchayats have set up environmental protection or rehabilitation projects such as a drainage canal, a bird sanctuary and biodiversity park, non-toxic mosquito control, and massive efforts at reclamation of mangrove marshes in some areas. These experiments were shared with communities across the state because of the role of the State Planning Board in organizing seminars.

WHAT KERALA MEANS

We recognize both the arrogance and the futility of telling activists in other places to "organize and struggle as people have done in Kerala." Nevertheless, Kerala's achievements in decentralization, however fragile and incomplete, provide a sense of what is possible, an indication of how difficult true democratic decentralization will be, and an inspiration for those in other places who strive to bring meaningful people's empowerment and democracy to their portion of our highly unequal world.

Excerpted from the authors' book Local Democracy and Development: The Kerala People's Campaign for Decentralized Planning *(Lanham: Rowman & Littlefield, 2002).*

ARTICLE 45

The Middle Way

Swedish Social Democracy

BY CHARLES SACKREY AND GEOFFREY SCHNEIDER

At the turn of the 20th century Mark Twain coined the phrase, the "Gilded Age," to describe the excesses and decadence of wealthy American society. This was when the most powerful people in the American economy, appropriately termed the "robber barons," controlled the direction of our country. It was the economic climax of the Industrial Revolution in the U.S., and the U.S. was an exceedingly wealthy nation—or at least a few people were wealthy. The Gettys, Rockefellers, Vanderbilts, Goulds, et al., held virtual monopolies on our natural resources, banks and railroads, and did business without any significant government intervention. There were few corporate taxes or regulations and no laws to protect labor.

At the same time that the United States became increasingly mired in inequality at every level of society, Sweden took steps toward the development of a more humane, egalitarian system. The Liberal Party government passed the National Pension Act in 1913 to provide security for the aged, more than twenty years before the United States implemented its own social security system. In 1918 a Liberal Party-Social Democratic Labor Party coalition government passed a new poor law, turning the responsibility of assisting anyone in need over to local governments, while the central government contributed administrative support. This law was to remain the cornerstone of Sweden's assistance programs for the next 40 years.

THE SAP'S FUNCTIONAL SOCIALISM: 1932-1968

Sweden's Social Democratic Labor Party (SAP) was founded in 1889, and began to influence economic policy immediately after its formation. At that point, it stated its guiding principles as follows:

1. Legislation to guarantee to every Swedish citizen a simple and decent standard of living...[Social Democrats] hold that it is the duty of society to provide for the needs of the aged, invalids, widows, and those who have lost their income through no fault of their own.
2. Housing and child benefits for needy families so that they should not be forced to lower their standard of living because they have children to raise. [The] idea is to distribute the expense over the entire population as a collective responsibility.

3. Social welfare to be ... the inherent right of every citizen irrespective of his financial status.

In order to implement its philosophy, the SAP was forced to compromise with employers and political opponents. Compromise was possible because although the philosophy behind the SAP's ideas was socialist in nature, the SAP was not dogmatic or rigid. The Social Democrats pursued the goal of a better life for all Swedes, and allowed the economy to operate within a capitalist system as long as it could achieve this goal.

The Social Democrats saw the problems associated with free-market as well as with state-controlled systems. From 1920 to 1932, recessions plagued Sweden's free-market economy as a succession of governments, some including the SAP, failed to stabilize the economy adequately. There was also an unequal distribution of income and wealth, and a significant percentage of the population lived in poverty. But the SAP did not adhere to the idea of state-controlled production in response to these problems, fearing the inefficiency that could come from a command-style economy.

Instead, once the SAP was firmly entrenched as Sweden's ruling party in 1932, it allowed the capitalist norm of private ownership to continue, intervening in the economy whenever the needs of labor were not met. As in the U.S. capitalist system, there were wealthy entrepreneurs who owned and controlled much of Swedish industry, but the SAP limited their power and influence. The SAP devised taxes on income and profits so that it was profitable for business owners to reinvest in productive activities and to create jobs. Entrepreneurs were allowed to make a fortune in Sweden, but only if they expanded employment, produced socially useful products, and limited the destruction of the environment. Thus the SAP permitted the private sector to pursue profits as long as firms achieved social goals.

De-Commodification

One of the primary (socialist) goals of the SAP was the de-commodification of the Swedish people. "De-commodification" meant taking people, and what they needed to live decent lives, out of the marketplace as mere commodities to be bought and sold. In the SAP principles mentioned above, for example, childcare is treated as a fundamental need because, as is stated, "[Swedish citizens] should not be forced to lower their standard of living because they have children to raise." In many market systems, families that have children must lower their standard of living because, in paying for the costs associated with caring for and raising children, they have less money to spend on other goods. In the United States, child-care is sold as a commodity only to families that can afford the service. When examined objectively, privatizing childcare is an exploitative practice that impacts the lower wage earners most dramatically. The same can be said for housing, medical care, dental care, and services for the disabled.

After the Social Democrats were voted into power in 1932, they introduced legislation that began to fulfill the principles of de-commodification embedded in their social philosophy. The SAP instituted housing subsidies and a national pension scheme in 1935, and in 1938 added socialized dental care. By the 1950s, the SAP had installed a national health plan and laid the foundation for a comprehensive network of de-commodified rights for all Swedish citizens.

Economic Stabilization and Full Employment

When an economy enters a recession, tax revenues decrease as businesses downsize and workers lose jobs. In such circumstances, many governments decrease spending to counter the reduction in tax revenues, thereby keeping the budget balanced. But cuts in government spending during a recession put even more people out of work, making the recession even worse. Instead, starting in the 1930s, Sweden *increased* spending in recessions by borrowing money to invest in public works projects, to train workers and to create jobs. This way, the flow of production and income was stabilized, spending didn't decrease dramatically in recessions, industry was encouraged to invest, and the economy was bolstered until industry's investments brought employment back to normal levels.

In addition to using government spending to stave off recessions, the Swedish government instituted a counter-cyclical investment tax credit system called the Investment Reserve in 1938. Firms were allowed to deposit funds with the government which could be invested tax free if invested *in Sweden at specified times*—during a recession. If invested at another time, the firm would have to pay taxes on the funds. Thus the government encouraged the private sector to invest counter-cyclically, stabilizing the economy even further.

With cooperation between unions, employers' associations, and the government, unemployment in Sweden exceeded 3% only *three times* from 1951 to 1991, without causing significant inflation. The agreement was that real wages were increased annually at the rate of one-half percent below the national average rate of labor productivity growth. This meant that if workers increased their productivity by 3%, they would receive a raise of 2.5%, and employers would keep the rest. This formula insured that workers benefited from increases in productivity but also guaranteed that wages did not increase too quickly, thus keeping inflation in check. The key point here is that if workers increase their productivity by 3%, this lowers firms' costs by 3%, since the same work force is now producing 3% more than before. Because firms' costs have decreased by 3%, firms can increase wages by as much as 3% without having to increase prices at all. Ultimately, wage increases only cause inflation if wages increase *faster* than productivity increases.

Sweden offers a striking contrast to the U.S. system where productivity increases by laborers often do *not* result in higher wages. From 1973 to 1997, the average productivity of a U.S. worker increased by 34%, but average wages for workers actually *declined* by 14%. U.S. workers actually lost ground when they increased productivity!

Solidaristic Wage Policy

Another key economic policy was Sweden's *solidaristic wage policy*. This meant equal pay for equal work: all workers at all firms doing the same type of work would be paid the wages that workers in the most efficient, internationally competitive firms were paid. Wages were set nationally in a centralized bargaining process that included employers, labor unions, and the government. The equalization of wages reduced competition between workers, creating a more cooperative environment for labor and removing the inequality of less pay for comparable work. An important byproduct of this policy was that women began receiving pay equal to men. All workers then received the same annual wage increases, based on productivity growth. A provision was later added to the solidaristic wage policy to increase the wages of low-wage workers faster than the rest, to make Sweden even more equal.

Another consequence of the solidaristic wage policy was that firms experiencing rapid growth did not have to raise wages faster than other firms did. Typically, firms in growing industries (such as 1990s high-tech firms in the United States) have to pay laborers a premium in order to keep them. But because of the solidarity wage policy in Sweden, the best, most competitive firms did not have to grant additional wage increases when they were doing well, allowing them to make large profits. Meanwhile, firms experiencing hard times were not able to reduce wages. Thus the solidaristic wage policy caused expanding industries to do better, and contracting industries to struggle even more. The result was a reallocation of capital to profitable, expanding industries from contracting industries.

Active Labor Market Policies

Another way of maintaining full employment was via *active labor market policies*. For those who became unemployed, there were generous unemployment benefits with a time limit, training and education with a stipend, and money for relocation costs if needed. If a worker was still unemployed when the benefits ended, there was employment available in short term public works projects (the Swedish government established itself as the "employer of last resort" for those workers who could not find work after a certain period of time). Unemployed Swedish workers were given money, time, training, and moving assistance to make sure they could find a good job to replace the one they lost. And if they could not find a job, they were put to work in community projects that needed attention.

Full employment is beneficial to any economic system: all workers remain productive, the stream of income and spending supports the economy, industry profits and invests, tax revenues support the government, which in turn supports the full employment system, resulting in a self-sustaining economy in which everyone benefits. This helps to explain the widespread support in Sweden for a socialist model of development that is almost inconceivable in the United States. By 1968, Sweden's system was the envy of much of the world. Swedish firms were internationally competitive, Swedish workers were among the best paid in the world, and poverty and homelessness were eliminated. But labor leaders still thought Sweden could be improved.

SWEDEN BECOMES MORE SOCIALIST: THE LABOR OFFENSIVE, 1968-1976

Despite the relative generosity of the Swedish welfare state, labor leaders were dismayed at the vast profits being earned by Sweden's huge transnational corporations that in part resulted from the solidarity wage policy that controlled wage increases at the most profitable firms. The SAP believed that the vast wealth being generated for a few individuals was unfair and threatened the integrity of the system. Labor wanted to negotiate a fairer distribution of the excess profits that firms were receiving because of union wage restraint.

The SAP also began to move more explicitly towards traditional socialism during this period through the institution of *wage earner funds*: employee investment funds that were to be funded by taxes on corporate profits. The SAP intended the funds to be used to buy up shares of companies, so workers could gradually gain a voice in all business decisions. Once labor leaders became owners, they would sit on corporate boards and directly influence corporate decision making. Laborers could then keep firms from moving overseas, or downsizing workers unnecessarily. The funds would also inject Swedish firms with new capital for investment, and gradually generate a more equitable distribution of ownership and wealth as workers became part owners, and eventually majority owners, in all large Swedish firms.

Unfortunately, these demands by labor and concessions by employers came at a time when the world was facing a global recession. The oil crisis of 1973 began a period of worldwide economic instability that would change the economic landscape of many industrialized nations. Sweden in particular suffered, because it was totally dependent on imported oil as its energy source. Inflation reached 10% in 1974, unemployment increased, and capital experienced rapidly rising costs in a highly regulated system that limited the ability of a firm to escape these high costs. This is when profound economic, political and welfare changes began to take place, resulting in what some have termed "the decline of the Swedish model."

CAPITAL'S OFFENSIVE, 1976-1999

The economic difficulties of the early 1970s caused Swedish voters to oust the SAP and elect a center-right government that was more conservative, and more sympathetic to industry. This ushered in an era in which big corporations successfully fought to roll back taxes and the welfare state. The erosion of the Swedish system began when employers abandoned the practice of centralized bargaining with labor that had been in existence since 1938. Instead, they turned to bargaining individually with their labor unions, undermining the solidaristic wage policy that had been a cornerstone of Swedish social democracy. The "divide and conquer" strategy was somewhat successful. With such a vital element of the system disempowered, corporations excluded workers more and more from the decision-making process, and increasingly moved operations overseas.

Along with the center-right government, employers worked to cut taxes and decrease government spending and government control over the economy. For example, the investment tax credit system, which gave businesses incentives to invest during recessions, was abolished. Corporations were now free to invest whenever they wished without tax penalties. But an even more significant change was the deregulation of capital markets in the 1980s, as Swedish firms were allowed to invest abroad instead of just at home, and funds could be moved freely internationally for the first time in many years.

The result of the newfound ability of capital to invest wherever it wanted, and tax cuts that increased the amount of money at capital's disposal, was a boom in asset markets. Money flowed rapidly into real estate, art, and other speculative, non-productive assets, resulting in huge price increases for these assets—a speculative boom. Unfortunately, as spending increased but productivity did not, an overheated economy resulted, generating inflation as high as 10.5% in 1990. Sweden's central bank responded to the overheated economy with tight money policies, generating huge increases in interest rates to rein in inflation. Real interest rates reached an incredible 14% in 1992, leading to significantly higher unemployment, as consumer spending dropped and business investment collapsed.

The Swedish Welfare State Since 1976

A major goal of the conservatives who ruled Sweden from 1976-1982 and 1991-1994 was to reduce the size of the Swedish welfare state, by reducing taxes and cutting government spending on social programs. They reduced the top tax rate from 85% to 50%, extended sales taxes to make up revenue, and reduced but did not eliminate benefits for parental leave, health and dental care, housing, unemployment, retirement and sick leave. These policy changes helped to produce a doubling of the poverty rate in Sweden from 1978 to 1992, although the Swedish poverty rate nonetheless remains the lowest in the world. Sweden also experienced the inevitable decrease in equality in all areas—the rich grew richer while the poor grew poorer, wage inequality between men and women increased, and opportunities were no longer as equal.

Even more drastic changes in the welfare state were enacted during the 1991-1993 recession. A new center-right government, elected in 1991, instituted corporate welfare programs (subsidies and tax breaks for corporations), and privatized education, child-care, and health care in some cases. Prior to this time, Swedes had widely accepted the idea that benefits should be universal, and not subject to the inequities of the market (i.e., de-commodified), so these changes marked a significant departure in philosophy.

The Results of Capital's Offensive

Since capital's offensive began in the 1970s, all Swedish governments have pursued a less regulated form of capitalism. Even when the SAP has been in power recently (the SAP governed from 1982 to 1991 and from 1994 to 1999), it, too, largely pursued a market-based agenda. The pursuit of these policies on the part of all political parties in Sweden is strikingly similar to political developments in England and the United States, where conservative groups pushed the economy in a free-market direction, formerly liberal groups (Democrats in the U.S., the Labor Party in England, the SAP in Sweden) turned to a moderate market-based approach, and organized labor ceased to be as powerful a voice in national politics.

As in the United States, Sweden is now dominated by huge transnational corporations (TNCs). Industrial concentration in Sweden is extremely high (a small number of large firms dominate the economy), in part because of the solidaristic wage policy which made it more profitable for large, efficient, export-oriented companies. As these companies increased in size and power, they pushed for a deregulated market approach to the economy, along with membership in the European Union so that they would have even more mobility and more markets in which to operate. Swedish TNCs now attack any form of government regulation in the popular press, criticizing the "public sector," the "welfare state," and "collectivism," while supporting the market economy, which supposedly generates a "free and good society." Sweden's CEOs now regularly threaten to relocate outside of Sweden unless the government creates a more business-friendly environment for them. And many businesses are carrying out these threats. Despite being profitable, Volvo closed its taxpayer-financed plants that experimented with worker autonomy and a more humane work place, moved some operations overseas, and sold out to Ford.

Cuts in government spending and the high interest rates necessary to fight inflation resulted in chronically high levels of unemployment in the 1990s. But it is important to remember that being unemployed in Sweden does not have the devastating consequences that it can have in the United States, because of the generous welfare system and the potential for retraining for a new job. And Sweden remains committed to equality and to collective decision-making, with the participation of labor, capital and the government. With the SAP continuing to enjoy broad-based support and with labor unions still relatively powerful, the "Swedish model" will be in place for the foreseeable future, albeit in a somewhat less progressive form than its 1970s incarnation.

THE CASE FOR SWEDISH SOCIAL DEMOCRACY

The experiences of Sweden demonstrate the possibility of a "Middle Way" between unregulated capitalism and command communism: social democracy. In Sweden, social democracy has resulted in an economy that is remarkably prosperous, and one that has the least poverty, the most equitable income distribution, and the highest levels of spending on health and education in the developed world. Sweden may not be paradise on Earth, but it has proved that a country can maintain full employment, be efficient and productive, and give every citizen the right to decent levels of food, clothing, health care, to a job, and to some control over their lives. In the United States, most things are allocated based on how much money a person has, which gives unprecedented levels of freedom and choice to the very wealthy, but leaves much of the population without the basic necessities of life. Perhaps the United States is the land of the free—if you're very rich. But for everyone else, social democracy seems to provide more freedom and better opportunities.

Excerpted from Chapter 8 of the authors' book Introduction to Political Economy, *3rd ed. (Economic Affairs Bureau, Inc., Cambridge, MA).*

ARTICLE 46

Factory Takeovers in Argentina

BY ANDRÉS GAUDIN

October 2003

It started timidly at first, in the mid-1990s, with workers occupying factories abandoned by their owners and getting them up and running again. But the phenomenon took off in December 2001, when the Argentinean economic crisis hit and massive street protests forced the country's president, Fernando de la Rua, from office. Four years of recession had capped off a decade of neoliberal policies, leaving thousands of domestically owned small and medium-sized businesses struggling or abandoned. Since 2001, in the face of growing unemployment and the state's failure to foresee or address the crisis, thousands of workers have restarted abandoned factories themselves. By taking over factory plant and equipment, these workers have put the right to work above employers' property rights, and have made some think that Argentina is at the beginning of a revolutionary process.

"We're a new social actor; we're creating a new consensus," reads the constitution of the National Movement of Recovered Enterprises (known by its Spanish initials, MNER). "In the face of the failure of company management, we felt we had to replace individual effort with collective effort, as the crisis demanded. By raising the flag of self-management, we were able to go from a situation of social conflict to a productive consensus. In 1955, we [workers] had a 51% share of the national income; now we get just 17%. We're using democratic organization like workers' cooperatives to fight for a more just distribution." With this declaration, the workers have given a preliminary answer to the big questions about the country's economic future: How should income and wealth be distributed? How should workers organize themselves at the worksite and in the larger society? And how should industry itself be organized?

Although Argentina's occupied or "recovered" factories constitute a small world, there still aren't reliable statistics on them. An academic study done by the University of Buenos Aires (UBA), however, reports that about 140 factories have been or are being "recovered," and about 12,000 workers have used this strategy to keep their jobs.

THE SHAPE OF THE CRISIS

Argentina's factory recoveries are taking place amid a catastrophe of unemployment, poverty, off-the-books work, and wage cuts. Workers at companies abandoned by their owners see factory occupations and self-management as the only way to avoid unemployment, exclusion, and marginalization.

- In Argentina, employment is measured twice a year, in May and October. Before a slight improvement in May 2003, official figures showed 17.8% unemployed in an "economically active" population of 13.8 million people. In truth, about 21.4% are unemployed, since in the official figures, people receiving $50 a month from the government (about $1.70 a day to cover basic necessities for a four-person family) count as employed.

- Almost 4 million people (45.1% of the employed population) work off the books; they are workers without being officially declared as such. This means they don't have any rights as workers or any social insurance. They do not get paid vacations, retirement pensions, or disability benefits. They have no unemployment insurance, worker's compensation, or health coverage. Off-the-books work has been on the rise in Argentina since the so-called "tequila crisis," Mexico's devaluation of its currency in 1995. At the time, off-the-books workers formed about 35% of the labor force. By 1998, the figure had already reached 38%. And in May 2003, after the Argentinean financial crisis of 2001-2002, it stood at 45.1%. As shocking as this national average is, in nine of the country's 23 provinces, off-the-books work exceeds 50% of total employment, topping out at 58.5% in the northeastern province of Corrientes.

- According to the International Labor Organization, the Argentinean working day is one of the longest in the Western world, and wages are much lower than those in other Western countries. While workers in the global North work between 1,300 hours per year (in Norway) and 1,800 hours per year (in the United States), Argentinean workers average about 2,000 hours per year. The average wage of an Argentinean worker, however, is just 10%-20% that of a European or North American worker, and has about 30% the purchasing power.
- Measured in terms of income, 54.7% of Argentina's population falls below the poverty line, and over a quarter of those below the poverty line are considered "indigent." With a population of 36.2 million people, this means 17.8 million people are poor, and 4.7 million are indigent. The number of indigent people reaches 5.5 million—14.3% of the country's households—when measured in terms of housing quality, access to utilities, sanitation, and school attendance. Among Argentinean households, 17.6% lack bathing or shower facilities, 50.8% do not have running water, 60.2% have no access to medicine, and 71% lack phone service.

This is the context in which Argentinean workers have occupied factories. The workers involved, it should be clear, have not done so from ideological motives, but as a way out of even more severe poverty. But their strategy differs from traditional union struggles, and has put workers in new and unfamiliar situations for which few have sufficient training: they are self-managing bankrupt enterprises, trying to overcome shortages of working capital and other necessities, and confronting a poor economic climate and unfavorable legal norms. Workers who have taken over factories have done so knowing that they would face tremendous obstacles.

COOPERATIVE ECONOMICS

The recovery process usually begins when an enterprise is sued by its creditors, when the Department of Justice declares it bankrupt, or when its owners, unable to pay their debts, simply abandon the firm. Then the workers take over the plant, put up the wages or severance pay owed them, and, with the agreement of the authorities or the owners themselves, rent the premises and machinery.

In most cases, the workers are given two years to pay back creditors. "For us, those two years are fundamental, because they allow us to keep working—to avoid unemployment—and study the viability and profitability of the enterprise," explains attorney Luis Caro, an advisor to the recovered firms. "It's a reasonable time frame for figuring out at what point and in what form it may be possible to make an offer of repayment to creditors." That there is a legal process for factory recoveries is significant. As Caro notes, "We have been able to get many judges to agree that when the destiny of the society is in the balance, private property should come after the right to work."

During the first two years, recovered factories face a series of difficulties. First, workers need to recover the confidence of suppliers and customers swindled by the old owners. They also need to acquire managerial and marketing expertise, since in many cases, managers leave along with the owners. Gabriela Dorrego, a management consultant, observes that recovered enterprises often lack accounting, legal, and marketing skills, and have to contract with outside agents to put their products on the market. To help workers gain administrative skills, the MNER has signed an agreement for free advice with the Assembly of Small and Medium Businesses (APYME). The public National Institute of Social Economics (INES) also offers training. Besides needing administrative expertise, many factories lack working capital, forcing them to sell their services to customers which supply raw materials and which then market the finished product. Finally, according to Dorrego, recovered enterprises have trouble investing enough to develop and compete. Together, these challenges prevent the factories from being as productive as they could be. Osvaldo Porro, manager of the recovered meatpacking plant Yaguane, says that it took two years for his factory to break even on a contract.

The recovered sector, although socially significant, also represents a tiny portion of the Argentinean economy. More than 12,000 workers are employed in the recovered sector, but measured in relation to an economically active population of 13.7 million, recovered enterprises employ scarcely 0.08% of the labor force. To take another measure of these enterprises' economic weight, 32% are located in factory complexes over 30 years old, using obsolete technology and equipment.

The factories vary widely in size: 13% of recovered enterprises surveyed in the UBA study employ 10 or fewer workers; 23% employ between 11 and 20; 40% , between 21 and 50; and 24%, more than 50 workers. Of the roughly 140 enterprises under workers' self-management, about half are in the metalworking sector, followed by the printing and food industries. During 2003, some service enterprises—cleaning services, hotels, and schools—have also joined the ranks.

From their first discussions, managers of recovered enterprises understood the need for their factories to complement each other—whether by jointly purchasing raw materials and other inputs to secure better prices, or by producing inputs for one another to increase production and ensure lower prices. Today, economic relations among recovered enterprises still do not exist for reasons that the workers themselves are unable to explain. But 55% of recovered enterprises' output is used as inputs by other businesses (41% is destined for consumers), which has led to some research on the ways that recovered enterprises might complement each other and increase the overall size of the sector.

Despite the obstacles they face, almost all recovered factories have now stabilized. None of them is working at full capacity, and their development is limited by a lack of capital, by an inability to make technological changes, and by legal difficulties in accessing export markets. Nonetheless, the recovered enterprises are not in danger of failing; and if any of them do fail, it will not be for the workers' lack of ability, but because of potential legal decisions that could hand the factories and machinery back to the failed owners.

Dorrego maintains that the recovered factories have done more than preserve jobs—itself an accomplishment. They create the possibility for workers to learn about the production process in sectors currently growing due to import substitution or competitiveness on the world market. They also break down hierarchical labor relations and establish "horizontal" decision-making structures: recovered factories hold assemblies where all workers can contribute to decisions. Most importantly, argues Dorrego, they have gradually involved state, provincial, and national governments in the "recovery" project, and have promoted collaboration among different people and organizations—both within the enterprises themselves, and with professionals, universities, civil society organizations, and state institutions.

COOPERATION, WORKERS' CONTROL, AND CLASS STRUGGLE

Knowing that workers do not mean to bring about revolutionary change, but simply aim to ensure steady employment for themselves, the state (ambiguously) and employers' organizations (with perfect clarity) have made their own proposals for the recovered factories. Their idea is to limit the workers' claim to one of establishing cooperatives to maintain employment. A claim of this scope does not challenge the private property system or employers' power in the economy; it assimilates factory recoveries into capitalism. As part of their effort to defuse the threat of recovery initiatives, employers and the state want to see that the factories—if they must stay in the hands of workers—exist in forms similar to regular commercial enterprises, whether as nationalized firms controlled by bureaucrats, or as cooperatives that reproduce traditional distributions of knowledge and power. The state has also tried to present recovered enterprises as part of its own labor policy, and to show off the peacefulness and legality of the recoveries.

These strategies aim to prevent the factory recoveries from rekindling a debate that surged in Argentina during the 1970s about the best strategy for working-class organization and resistance under capitalism. On one side were the promoters of a politics of workers' control, and on the other side were the defenders of cooperativism. Each proposed a different way of dealing with the fact that under capitalism, workers are formally deprived of understanding and control of the production process, the product of labor, and the proceeds from the sale of this product. Today, Argentinean workers' autonomous action of resisting, occupying, producing, and marketing has challenged capital's monopoly over knowledge and authority, and the debate has reemerged, though more among advanced sectors of the workers' movement than among workers in recovered factories.

For Marxist economist Eduardo Lucita, "Underlying the debate between cooperativism and workers' control is the opposition between a rupture with the logic of capital and a reintegration with it." Under the cooperative form of organization, which supposes voluntary association and self-management, the workers gain a source of work, a more egalitarian distribution of income, and productive gains that come from a different rationality of management. According to Lucita, it is clear that these conditions are infinitely better than the current ones. Nonetheless, cooperatives cannot escape the logic of market competition, which puts wage levels, conditions of work, and productivity in play. Pay, work time, and the pace of work all impact the final cost of the product, and this is fundamental to capitalist competition.

Supporters of cooperativism typically point to two models to emulate: the Argentinean factory Zanello and the Spanish town of Mondragon. Zanello, which manufactures tractors, is a unique case. When the factory's Italian owners—attracted to the country in the 1990s by the neoliberal promise of low wages and labor "flexibility"—decided to abandon it, the workers were able to come to an agreement with several interested parties. They formed a corporation in which 33% of the factory remained in the hands of the workers, 33% of the power went to the firms that market the tractors and provide the capital, 33% went to the top technical personnel of the factory, and the remaining 1% went to the City of Villa Maria (in the province of Cordoba), where Zanello is headquartered. The organizational model chosen, the corporation, is one of the principal forms of the capitalist firm. The Mondragon Corporation is a utopian example taken as a model by the MNER, and workers at recovered factories often refer hopefully to it. Almost fifty years old, Mondragon is now the largest business group in the Basque region and the seventh largest in all of Spain. It includes more than 150 cooperative enterprises and 60,000 workers, and has a working capital of over 8 billion euros. Mondragon may be the most successful example of cooperative enterprise within a capitalist economy.

On the other hand, workers' control, which also assumes voluntary association and autonomy, allows the enterprise to remain under capitalist ownership (private or state), while the workers, through organized struggle against the capitalists, assume control of the enterprise's production process and financial accounting. Lucita notes that the Argentinean situation has some unusual features: given the employers' abandonment of factories and the state's failure to assume responsibility for them, there are enterprises now functioning under a system of workers' control where there is no capitalist for workers to assert control over.

CRISIS AND CONSCIOUSNESS

From its beginnings, the MNER borrowed the slogan "To occupy, to resist, to produce" from Brazil's Landless Workers' Movement. This slogan, the MNER says, summarizes the stages that the workers pass through: not only maintaining their source of employment, but also creating an enriching experience of self-management and cooperation, and ultimately assuming an active role in the reconstruction of a country and a society razed by neoliberalism.

Workers in recovered factories speak proudly of having been able to restart their factories and keep their jobs after the flight of the owners. Says Alicia Esquivel, an administrative worker at CIS, a bus body shop: "When we occupied the plant, there wasn't much to think about: either we acted to run things for ourselves, without an employer to solve all the problems, or we became unemployed for good, in a country where once you have lost your job you don't get it back. Thank God that we didn't make a mistake." Her description, full of emotion and lacking in ideological definition, is common among workers in recovered factories.

The UBA study confirms that the take-overs have not produced political or ideological changes among participants. The psychologists and sociologists who took part observed a notable increase in workers' self-esteem and a broad development of solidarity, but have found that these changes did not move workers toward a larger anticapitalist vision. "In general, these workers do not seem to be conscious that they have broken with one of the basic premises of capitalism," say the UBA academics, "so they do not move beyond the restarting of the factory, do not stop to consider what would be the best organizational form to guarantee the survival of the enterprise or for this experience to embrace new groups of workers."

The directors of some of the recovered enterprises have tried to tie their destiny to that of the workers' movement as a whole, but so far this has not borne fruit. In September 2002, when the Central Union of Argentinean Workers held its congress, a group from the MNER presented a document linking the recovered enterprises and the workers' movement, but the idea was not supported by the mass of workers in recovered enterprises. Likewise, the MNER has kept itself at the margins of the movement against the Free Trade Area of the Americas (FTAA), so it has not developed a relationship with what might be called the "anticapitalist" movement in Argentina.

For now, workers are winning the first battles in the "war" for their jobs. But in making the workers take the capitalist models of Zanello and Mondragon as their paradigms, the employers are winning the ideological battle. What predominates today in the recovered sector is workers' direct management. This development reflects the nature of the crisis in Argentina: it is not a revolutionary crisis, but it is one where the high level of concentration of capital does not leave room of a reformist way out of the impasse.

But even if the workers do not consciously embrace the larger implications of their struggle, their autonomous action—"occupying, resisting, producing"—calls into question the capitalist monopoly of authority and knowledge. In embryonic form, a new power is beginning to confront the powers that be.

Translated from Spanish by Alejandro Reuss.

ARTICLE 47

Wages For Housework

The Movement and the Numbers

BY LENA GRABER AND JOHN MILLER

September/October 2002

The International Wages for Housework Campaign (WFH), a network of women in Third World and industrialized countries, began organizing in the early 1970s. WFH's demands are ambitious—"for the unwaged work that women do to be recognized as work in official government statistics, and for this work to be paid."

Housewives paid wages? By the government? That may seem outlandish to some, but consider the staggering amount of unpaid work carried out by women. In 1990, the International Labor Organization (ILO) estimated that women do two-thirds of the world's work for 5% of the income. In 1995, the UN Development Programme's (UNDP) Human Development Report announced that women's unpaid and underpaid labor was worth $11 trillion worldwide, and $1.4 trillion in the United States alone. Paying women the wages they "are owed" for unwaged work, as WFH puts it, would go a long way toward undoing these inequities and reducing women's economic dependence on men.

Publicizing information like this, WFH—whose International Women Count Network now includes more than 2,000 non-governmental organizations (NGOs) from the North and South—and other groups have been remarkably successful in persuading governments to count unwaged work. In 1995, the UN Fourth World Conference on Women, held in Beijing, developed a Platform for Action that called on governments to calculate the value of women's unpaid work and include it in conventional measures of national output, such as Gross Domestic Product (GDP).

So far, only Trinidad & Tobago and Spain have passed legislation mandating the new accounting, but other countries—including numerous European countries, Australia, Canada, Japan, and New Zealand in the industrialized world, and Bangladesh, the Dominican Republic, India, Nepal, Tanzania, and Venezuela in the developing world—have undertaken extensive surveys to determine how much time is spent on unpaid household work.

THE VALUE OF HOUSEWORK

Producing credible numbers for the value of women's work in the home is no easy task. Calculating how many hours women spend performing housework—from cleaning to childcare to cooking to shopping—is just the first step. The hours are considerable in both developing and industrialized economies. (See Table 1.)

What value to place on that work, and what would constitute fair remuneration—or wages for housework—is even more difficult to assess. Feminist economists dedicated to making the value of housework visible have taken different approaches to answering the question. One approach, favored by the UN's International Research and Training Institute for the Advancement of Women (INSTRAW), bases the market value of work done at home on the price of market goods and services that are similar to those produced in the home (such as meals served in restaurants or cleaning done by professional firms). These output-based evaluations estimate that counting unpaid household production would add 30-60% to the GDP of industrialized countries, and far more for developing countries. (See Table 2.)

A second approach evaluates the inputs of household production—principally the labor that goes into cooking, cleaning, childcare, and other services performed in the home, overwhelmingly by women. Advocates of this approach use one of three methods. Some base their calculations on what economists call opportunity cost—the wages women might have earned if they had worked a similar number of hours in the market economy. Others ask what it would cost to hire someone to do the work—either a general laborer such as a domestic servant (the generalist-replacement method) or a specialist such as a chef (the specialist-replacement

TABLE 1

**WOMEN'S TIME SPENT PER DAY PERFORMING HOUSEHOLD LABOR,
BY ACTIVITY, IN HOURS:MINUTES**

Country	Childcare Time	Cleaning Time	Food Prep Time	Shopping Time	Water/Fuel Collection	Total Housework Time[a]
Australia (1997[b])	2:27	1:17	1:29	0:58	n.a.	3:39
Japan (1999)	0:24	2:37	n.a.	0:33	n.a.	3:34
Norway (2000)	0:42	1:16	0:49	0:26	0:01	3:56
United Kingdom (2000)	1:26	1:35	1:08	0:33	n.a.	4:55
Nepal (1996)	1:28	2:00	5:30	0:13	1:10	11:58

Note: Some activities, especially childcare, may overlap with other tasks.

[a] Totals may include activities other than those listed.

[b] Only some percentage of the population recorded doing these activities. Averages are for that portion of the population. Generally, figures represent a greater number of women than men involved.

Sources: Australia: <www.abs.gov.au/ausstats>; Japan: <www.unescap.org/stat>; Norway: <www.ssb.no/tidsbruk_en>; United Kingdom: <www.statistics.gov.uk/themes/social_finances/TimeUseSurvey>; Nepal: INSTRAW, *Valuation of Household Production and the Satellite Accounts* (Santo Domingo: 1996), 34-35; <www.cbs.nl/isi/iass>.

TABLE 2

VALUE OF UNPAID HOUSEHOLD LABOR AS % OF GDP,
USING OUTPUT-BASED EVALUATION METHOD

Country	% of GDP
Canada (1992)	47.4%
Finland (1990)	49.1%
Nepal (1991)	170.7%

TABLE 3

VALUE OF UNPAID HOUSEHOLD LABOR
IN CANADA AS % OF GDP, 1992

Evaluation Method	% of GDP
Opportunity Cost (before taxes)	54.2%
Specialist-Replacement	43.0%
Generalist-Replacement	34.0%
Output-Based	47.4%

Source: INSTRAW, *Valuation of Household Production and the Satellite Accounts* (Santo Domingo: 1996), 229.

method)—and then assign those wages to household labor. Ann Chadeau, a researcher with the Organization for Economic Cooperation and Development, has found the specialist-replacement method to be "the most plausible and at the same time feasible approach" for valuing unpaid household labor.

These techniques produce quite different results, all of which are substantial in relation to GDP. With that in mind, let's look at how some countries calculated the monetary value of unpaid work.

UNPAID WORK IN CANADA, GREAT BRITAIN, AND JAPAN

In Canada, a government survey documented the time men and women spent on unpaid work in 1992. Canadian women performed 65% of all unpaid work, shouldering an especially large share of household labor devoted to preparing meals, maintaining clothing, and caring for children. (Men's unpaid hours exceeded women's only for outdoor cleaning.)

The value of unpaid labor varied substantially, depending on the method used to estimate its appropriate wage. (See Table 3.) The opportunity-cost method, which uses the average market wage (weighted for the greater proportion of unpaid work done by women), assigned the highest value to unpaid labor, 54.2% of Canadian GDP. The two replacement methods produced lower estimates, because the wages they assigned fell below those of other jobs. The specialist-replacement method, which paired unpaid activities with the average wages of corresponding occupations—such as cooking with junior chefs, and childcare with kindergarten teachers—put the value of Canadian unpaid labor at 43% of GDP. The generalist-replacement method, by assigning the wages of household servants to unpaid labor, produced the lowest estimate of the value of unpaid work: 34% of Canadian GDP. INSTRAW's output-based measure, which matched hours of unpaid labor to a household's average expenditures on the same activities, calculated the value of Canada's unpaid work as 47.4% of GDP.

In Great Britain, where unpaid labor hours are high for an industrialized country (see Table 1), the value of unpaid labor was far greater relative to GDP. The British Office for National Statistics found that, when valued using the opportunity cost method, unpaid work was 112% of Britain's GDP in 1995! With the specialist-replacement method, British unpaid labor was still 56% of GDP—greater than the output of the United Kingdom's entire manufacturing sector for the year.

In Japan—where unpaid labor hours are more limited (see Table 1), paid workers put in longer hours, and women perform over 80% of unpaid work—the value of unpaid labor is significantly smaller relative to GDP. The Japanese Economic Planning Agency calculated that counting unpaid work in 1996 would add between 15.2% (generalist-replacement method) and 23% (opportunity-cost method) to GDP. Even at those levels, the value of unpaid labor still equaled at least half of Japanese women's market wages.

HOUSEWORK NOT BOMBS

While estimates vary by country and evaluation method, all of these calculations make clear that recognizing the value of unpaid household labor profoundly alters our perception of economic activity and women's contributions to production. "Had household production been included in the system of macro-economic accounts," notes Ann Chadeau, "governments may well have implemented quite different economic and social policies."

For example, according to the UNDP, "The inescapable implication [of recognizing women's unpaid labor] is that the fruits of society's total labor should be shared more equally." For the UNDP, this would mean radically altering property and inheritance rights; access to credit; entitlement to social security benefits, tax incentives, and child care; and terms of divorce settlements.

For WFH advocates, the implications are inescapable as well: women's unpaid labor should be paid—and "the money," WFH insists, "must come first of all from military spending."

Here in the United States, an unneeded and dangerous military buildup begun last year has already pushed up military spending from 3% to 4% of GDP. Devoting just the additional 1% of GDP gobbled up by the military budget to wages for housework—far from being outlandish—would be an important first step toward fairly remunerating women who perform much-needed and life-sustaining household work.

RESOURCES Ann Chadeau, "What is Households' Non-Market Production Worth?" *OECD Economic Studies* No. 18 (Spring 1992); Economic Planning Unit, Department of National Accounts, Japan, "Monetary Valuation of Unpaid Work in 1996" <unstats.un.org/unsd/methods/timeuse/tusresource_papers/japanunpaid.htm>; INSTRAW, *Measurement and Valuation of Unpaid Contribution: Accounting Through Time and Output* (Santo Domingo: 1995); INSTRAW, *Valuation of Household Production and the Satellite Accounts* (Santo Domingo: 1996); Office of National Statistics, United Kingdom, "A Household Satellite Account for the UK," by Linda Murgatroyd and Henry Neuberger, *Economic Trends* (October 1997) <www.statistics.gov.uk/hhsa/hhsa/Index.html>; Hilkka Pietilä, "The Triangle of the Human Ecology: Household-Cultivation-Industrial Production," *Ecological Economics Journal* 20 (1997); UN Development Programme, Human Development Report (New York: Oxford University Press, 1995); Wages For Housework <ourworld.compuserve.com/homepages/crossroadswomenscentre/WFH.html>

ARTICLE 48

The Washington Consensus and the Kerala Alternative

BY NICK THORKELSON

WHY IS DEMOCRACY INCOMPATIBLE WITH DEVELOPMENT? BECAUSE, AS ANY LEADING PUNDIT WILL TELL YOU:

So WHAT IF THE ONES DOING THE GROWING AREN'T THE SAME AS THE ONES DOING THE SACRIFICING? NEVER MIND, IT'S FOR THE (AGGREGATE) GOOD OF ALL!

ACTUALLY THERE **IS** ANOTHER WAY TO GO. WITHIN INDIA'S BORDERS, IN THE SOUTHERN STATE OF **KERALA** POPULAR ORGANIZATIONS HAVE REVERSED ALL THE INDICATORS. TRADE UNIONS, SMALL FARMERS' ASSOCIATIONS, WOMEN'S GROUPS, CULTURAL PROJECTS, CREDIT & CONSUMER COOPS, AND RADICAL PARTIES CREATE A SITUATION WHERE THE NEEDS OF THE MAJORITY COME FIRST.

THE DOWNSIDE IS **DISINVESTMENT:** BUSINESSMEN WOULD RATHER NOT DEAL WITH SECURE & INDEPENDENT WORKING PEOPLE.

STAGNANCY STATISTICS CAN BE MISLEADING THOUGH. CREDIT UNIONS ALLOW KERALA FARMERS TO SWITCH FROM RICE, WHICH PAYS OFF QUICKLY, TO CROPS LIKE COCONUTS & RUBBER THAT TAKE YEARS TO YIELD A RETURN. ON PAPER IT LOOKS LIKE AGRICULTURAL OUTPUT IS DECLINING.

> YOU MAY SAY I'M A DREAMER

THEY CALL IT THE **KERALA MODEL** BUT FAR FROM BEING A "MODEL"—

A PRESCRIPTION THAT CAN BE IMPOSED AT WILL ON A NATION OR REGION, KERALA REPRESENTS A LONG HISTORY OF PEOPLE PRESSING THEIR DEMANDS, LEARNING FROM THEIR MISTAKES, & EVENTUALLY BECOMING AN INTEGRAL PART OF DAY-TO-DAY ECONOMIC & POLITICAL DECISION-MAKING.

TIMELINE OF DEMOCRACY:

1920s: LOW-CASTE FARMWORKERS (ESHEVAS) & MUSLIM TENANT FARMERS (MUPLAHS) REBEL AGAINST HINDU LANDOWNERS ALLIED WITH BRITISH.

> I SAY
> BIT MUCH
> QUITE

1930s: ESHEVAS, FORCED OFF LAND BY BRITISH TAXATION & PRIVATIZATION, MOVE TO CITIES WHERE THEY STRIKE AGAINST BRITISH RULE.

40   STOP

1940s: MILITANTS RETURN TO COUNTRYSIDE, ORGANIZE FARM-WORKERS' STRIKES CULMINATING IN BLOODY 1946 PUNNAPRA-VAYALAR UPRISING.

SUBSEQUENT REPRESSION DRIVES LEFT UNDERGROUND.

1946: INDEPENDENCE BRINGS LITTLE CHANGE FOR RURAL POOR BUT IT DOES PROVIDE PUBLIC SPACE TO RESUME ORGANIZING.

1950s: TENANT FARMERS ORGANIZED BY CPI (COMMUNIST PARTY OF INDIA), WIN RENT & EVICTION CONTROLS.

I THINK YOU'D BETTER GO

WE THINK WE'LL STAY

1957: CPI WINS KERALA STATE ELECTION. LANDLORD MILITIAS RESPOND WITH "LIBERATION STRUGGLE" (DEATH SQUADS).

1959: CPI ATTEMPTS LAND REDISTRIBUTION; FIGHTING INTENSIFIES. INDIA PRESIDENT DISSOLVES CPI GOVT, REPEALS ITS PROGRAM.

1967: 2nd LEFT GOVT.: COALITION OF CPI & LEFT SPLITOFF CPI-MARXIST (CPI-M) ENACTS AGRARIAN REFORM. TENANTS BECOME LANDOWNERS.

THIS CHANGES EVERYTHING AS IT DESTROYS SOCIAL BASIS FOR LANDLORD MILITIAS.

AGRARIAN REFORM MEANS WORKERS & FARMERS BECOME LEADING FORCE IN KERALA. BUT IN 1980, FRUSTRATED BY DISINVESTMENT, CPI-M EMBRACES "CLASS COMPROMISE": MORE INCENTIVES & AUTONOMY FOR MANAGEMENT (BUT WITHOUT "LOW ROAD" OUTCOMES LIKE SWEATSHOPS & CHILD LABOR THAT ARE SEEN ELSEWHERE IN INDIA).

HERE & THERE

"IN THE NORTH [OF INDIA],... WHEN THERE IS A PROBLEM WITH UNIONS THEY JUST FIRE OR BUY OFF THE LEADER. SUCH PRACTICES ARE IMPOSSIBLE IN KERALA."

INDIAN MANUFACTURER

THEN & NOW

"IN THE PAST, WE WOULD HAVE TO GO TO THE LANDLORDS' HOUSE TO GET OUR PAY. WE WOULD STAND WITH OUR HEADS BOWED & OUR HANDS OUT. NOW HE MUST COME TO THE FIELD TO PAY US. IF HE DOESN'T HAVE EXACT CHANGE, WE SEND HIM OFF TO GET IT."

DALIT ("UNTOUCHABLE") FARM WORKER

ON & ON

NO, KERALA IS NOT PERFECT. BUT IT **IS** DEMOCRATIC.

WHICH MAKES IT AN ENDANGERED SPECIES. WITH INDIA UNDER THE THUMB OF THE TRANSNATIONALS, KERALA'S POPULAR FORCES ARE EPICENTERS OF RESISTANCE AND, THEREFORE, TARGETS OF REPRESSION. THE STRUGGLE CONTINUES.

NICK THORKELSON

THIS ACCOUNT IS HIGHLY INDEBTED TO PATRICK HELLER'S THE LABOR OF DEVELOPMENT.

Contributors

Frank Ackerman, a founder of *Dollars & Sense*, is Director of Research and Policy at the Global Development and Environment Institute at Tufts University.

Aziza Agia is a doctoral student in urban studies at the Massachusetts Institute of Technology and a *Dollars & Sense* associate.

Sarah Anderson is the Director of the Global Economy Program of the Institute for Policy Studies in Washington, D.C., and the co-author (with John Cavanagh and Thea Lee) of Field Guide to the Global Economy.

David Bacon is a journalist and photographer covering labor, immigration, and the impact of the global economy on workers.

Dean Baker and **Mark Weisbrot** are co-directors of the Center for Economic and Policy Research (www.cepr.net) in Washington, D.C.

Franco Barchiesi is a lecturer in the Department of Sociology, University of the Witwatersrand (Johannesburg, South Africa), and a member of the editorial collective of the magazine *Debate: Voices from the South African Left*.

Ben Boothby is a former *Dollars & Sense* intern and collective member.

Jessica Collins is a former *Dollars & Sense* intern.

James Crotty teaches economics at the University of Massachusetts, Amherst.

James M. Cypher teaches economics at California State University, Fresno.

Bob Feldman is an anti-war and anti-corporate writer-activist based in the Boston area.

Ellen Frank teaches at Emmanuel College in Boston and is a member of the *Dollars & Sense* collective.

Richard W. Franke is professor of anthropology at Montclair State University in New Jersey.

James K. Galbraith is professor at the Lyndon B. Johnson School of Public Affairs, University of Texas at Austin, and Senior Scholar of the Levy Economics Institute.

Andrés Gaudin is a Uruguayan journalist who went into exile in Argentina in 1972. He lives in Buenos Aires.

Susan George, the author of nine books, is President of the Observatoire de la Mondialisation [Globalization Observatory] in Paris and Vice-President of ATTAC France [Association for Taxation of Financial Transactions to Aid Citizens].

Lena Graber is a former *Dollars & Sense* intern.

Alex Hogan helped coordinate the Detroit stop of the Palestinian labor delegation to North America in 2002.

T. M. Thomas Isaac is the elected Member of the Legislative (state) Assembly from the Mararikkulam constituency in central Kerala and was until recently a professor at the Centre for Development Studies, Thiruvananthapuram, Kerala.

Gawain Kripke is a senior policy advisor at Oxfam America.

Kang-Kook Lee is a graduate student in economics at the University of Massachusetts, Amherst.

David L. Levy, a *Dollars & Sense* associate, teaches management at the University of Massachusetts, Boston.

Arthur MacEwan, a founder of *Dollars & Sense*, teaches economics at the University of Massachusetts at Boston.

John Miller, a member of the *Dollars & Sense* collective, teaches economics at Wheaton College.

Anuradha Mittal and **Peter Rosset** are co-directors of Food First/The Institute for Food and Development Policy, in Oakland, California.

Dena Montague and **Frida Berrigan** are Senior Research Associates at the Arms Trade Resource Center of the World Policy Institute, located in New York City.

Amy Offner is a *Dollars & Sense* co-editor.

Dara O'Rourke is an assistant professor of Urban Studies and Planning at the Massachusetts Institute of Technology.

Cynthia Peters is a freelance editor and writer, and political activist.

James Petras is an advisor and teacher for the Rural Landless Workers Movement in Brazil and an activist-scholar working with socio-political movements in Latin America, Europe, and Asia.

Karen Pfeifer is a professor of economics at Smith College.

Alejandro Reuss is a *Dollars & Sense* collective member, a historian of modern Latin America, and a doctoral student in economics at the University of Massachusetts, Amherst.

Robert J.S. Ross is a Professor of Sociology and Director of the International Studies Stream at Clark University.

Charles Sackrey is a retired professor of economics at Bucknell University.

Geoffrey Schneider is a professor of economics at Bucknell University.

Chris Sturr, a member of the *Dollars & Sense* collective, has a Ph.D. in philosophy and teaches Social Studies at Harvard University.

Todd Tavares is a former *Dollars & Sense* intern.

Nick Thorkelson is a cartoonist, painter and graphic designer whose drawings have appeared in *Dollars & Sense, The Boston Globe, The Progressive, The Free Comix, The Somerville Community News,* and publications of Fantagraphics, Greenpeace USA, the World Health Organization, and Work Rights Press. Examples of his work are on the web at www.nickthorkelson.com.

Heidi Vogt is a former *Dollars & Sense* intern.

Rodney Ward is a longtime labor and peace activist, laid-off flight attendant, and staff member at *Dollars & Sense*.

Timothy A. Wise, a former staff editor at *Dollars & Sense*, is deputy director of the Global Development and Environment Institute at Tufts University and the co-author of *Confronting Globalization: Economic Integration and Popular Resistance in Mexico* (Kumarian Press, 2003) <www.kpbooks.com>.

University of
Massachusetts
UMASS. Lowell

DEPARTMENT OF REGIONAL ECONOMIC
AND SOCIAL DEVELOPMENT

- Interdisciplinary curriculum focusing on how the interactions of business, policy makers, community groups, and professionals affect community development

- Focus on understanding that healthy and sustained economic development rests not only with business, but on community social structures

- Students and faculty involved with community partnerships and research

- Graduates prepared for professional roles involving research, consulting, and strategic planning in business, in local, state, and national development and planning agencies, and in nonprofit organizations working on economic and social development

- We offer a two-year Master of Arts and a Certificate Program

For more information, please visit our web site
<www.uml.edu/Dept/RESD>
or call 978-934-2900